Milk in Spain and the History of Diet Change

Food in Modern History: Traditions and Innovations

Series Editors:
Peter Scholliers
Amy Bentley

This new monograph series pays serious attention to food as a focal point in historical events from the late 18th century to present day.

Employing the lens of technology broadly construed, the series highlights the nutritional, social, political, cultural, and economic transformations of food around the globe. It features new scholarship that considers ever-intensifying and accelerating tensions between tradition and innovation that characterize the modern era. The editors are particularly committed to publishing manuscripts featuring geographical areas currently underrepresented in English-language academic publications, including the Global South, particularly Africa and Asia, as well as monographs featuring Indigenous and underrepresented groups, and non-western societies.

Published:

Food and Aviation in the Twentieth Century: The Pan American Ideal
Bryce Evans (2021)

Feeding the People in Wartime Britain
Bryce Evans (2022)

Rebellious Cooks and Recipe Writing in Communist Bulgaria
Albena Shkodrova (2022)

Globalization in a Glass: The Rise of Pilsner Beer through Technology, Taste and Empire
Malcolm Purinton (2023)

Apples and Orchards since the Eighteenth Century: Material Innovation and Cultural Tradition
Joanna Crosby (2023)

A History of Bread: Consumers, Bakers and Public Authorities since the 18th Century
Peter Scholliers (2024)

The Moral and Market Economies of Bread: Regulation and Reform in Vienna, 1775–1885
Jonas M. Albrecht (2024)

Gastrofascism and Empire: Food in Italian East Africa, 1935–1941
Simone Cinotto (2024)

Milk in Spain and the History of Diet Change

The Political Economy of Dairy Consumption since 1950

Fernando Collantes

BLOOMSBURY ACADEMIC
LONDON • NEW YORK • OXFORD • NEW DELHI • SYDNEY

BLOOMSBURY ACADEMIC
Bloomsbury Publishing Plc
50 Bedford Square, London, WC1B 3DP, UK
1385 Broadway, New York, NY 10018, USA
29 Earlsfort Terrace, Dublin 2, Ireland

BLOOMSBURY, BLOOMSBURY ACADEMIC and the Diana logo are trademarks of Bloomsbury Publishing Plc

First published in Great Britain 2025

A catalogue record for this book is available from the British Library.

A catalog record for this book is available from the Library of Congress.

ISBN: HB: 978-1-3504-0154-9
ePDF: 978-1-3504-0155-6
eBook: 978-1-3504-0156-3

Series: Food in Modern History: Traditions and Innovations

Typeset by Newgen KnowledgeWorks Pvt. Ltd., Chennai, India

To find out more about our authors and books visit www.bloomsbury.com and sign up for our newsletters.

For Maite, who left us too soon,
and Ernesto, who walks on accompanied by her memory.

Contents

Figures

Note to the reader: Information in *italics* refers to the Appendix

Tables

Introduction

The idea of investigating dairy consumption originated at Magda Quiñonero's apartment in Valencia around the year 2007. Magda's flatmate, Maria, an Englishwoman who had been residing in Spain for a few months, revealed during a snack time that she had encountered significant difficulties in finding milk that suited her taste in the country. Almost all brands had failed, one after another, as substitutes for the milk she used to consume in York. But now apparently, she had found the right brand. Beneath the obligatory facade of courtesy, I found it challenging to empathize. British exceptionalism had brought us Shakespeare, but also Benny Hill. Moreover, in places like the Valencian Community, a dark legend thrived regarding the perceived lack of interest among British expatriate communities in integrating into local life. Weren't these, after all, the individuals who had transformed entire neighbourhoods of Benidorm into a sort of New Liverpool, transplanting pubs, pints of Guinness, and the proverbial Premier League televised match on Saturday afternoons? So, there we were, facing the glass of milk that Maria had just served us, which had all the makings of being the penultimate triumph of British expatriates over the forces of cultural immersion.

But … Maria's milk had an exquisite flavour. It was a different kind of milk from what we were accustomed to, and, it had to be admitted, much better. Intrigued by what I presumed to be some kind of imported, delicatessen milk purchased from a specialized store, I saw Maria triumphantly present her discovery: a plastic bottle of pasteurized milk from the Spanish brand Clesa. This was a shock. It was one thing to discover that my usual milk was not the best in the world, and another to find out that the miracle Maria was seeking had been achieved by a type of milk that, despite being perfectly common during my childhood, had gradually disappeared from commercial establishments as ultra-high temperature (UHT) milk cartons gained popularity.

Had we regressed? This was a disconcerting thought for an economic historian because the dominant narrative in our field revolved around the epic transition of Spain and other societies from poverty to prosperity. The upward trend in our consumption of various goods and services, conveniently aggregated through market prices, was supposed to capture that progress. And yet, there we were in Magda's living room, at the peak of the consumption expenditure curves in the entire history of Spain, experiencing the limitations that this metric imposed on our understanding of reality. The idea of investigating the transformation of our diets from a perspective that linked the resolution of problems in poor societies to the emergence of new problems in wealthier societies began to take shape.

The book and its messages

A socio-economic study of dairy consumption in Spain over the last seventy years allows us to approach the way our diet has transformed, the reasons for these changes, and the consequences from the perspective of our well-being. The book is divided into four parts. Part I introduces the problem and consists of three chapters. Chapter 1 presents our understanding of the history of dietary changes in Spain and the Western world in general. Our emphasis is particularly on the period from 1950 to the present, during which we transitioned almost imperceptibly from combating hunger and deprivation to heading towards a different type of malnutrition. This is the rise and fall of good diets that the title of Part I refers to. After presenting various research programmes that have contributed to understanding these dietary changes, we identify the blind spots in the current state of the art, which are not only empirical but also theoretical.

In Chapter 2, we outline the theoretical framework that will be used throughout the rest of the book: an approach framed within the socio-economic thought of Joseph Schumpeter and his followers, with connections to the intellectual tradition linking the Annales historical school of Fernand Braudel's era and the agri-food economics of Louis Malassis. We define 'long waves' of dietary change in terms of Malassis's concept of 'food consumption model'. We evaluate these successive consumption models not only from the usual perspective of nutritional health but also from a broader socio-economic perspective. Finally, we favour a multicausal explanation of the long waves of dietary change, where the rise and fall of consumption models result from the convergence of parallel changes in relatively autonomous spheres, especially macroeconomics, the microeconomics of the food chain, and consumer culture.

Part I of the book concludes with Chapter 3, which delves into the case that will be the focus for the rest of the book. Here, we identify the two dairy consumption models that have prevailed in Spain over the last seventy years. The reconstruction of long-term statistical series of dairy consumption, appropriately disaggregated by product types and consumer profiles, reveals two distinct models: the first unfolded approximately between 1950 and 1990, focusing on the mass consumption of processed milk; the second took shape from 1990 onwards and was driven by dairy products. We find reasons to evaluate the second model more critically than the first.

These two consumption models, rather than any individual consumer or other individual actor in the food system, are the main protagonists of the book. The second and third parts are dedicated to their detailed analysis, each beginning with a chapter that exploits quantitative evidence to provide a structural perspective on the forces that led to the rise and fall of these consumption models. This initial chapter is followed by two more that, incorporating qualitative evidence, analyse in greater detail the internal dynamics of each consumption model.

Thus, Chapter 4 explores the wave of milk consumption growth that occurred between 1950 and 1990. The economic basis of this wave was the persistent strengthening of consumers' purchasing power. This, in turn, was made possible by changing combinations of improvements in their income levels and reductions in the relative price of milk. However, our statistical analysis finds that consumers were not always equally willing to channel their purchasing power gains into buying more milk. It was mainly from the mid-1960s onwards that consumer orientations became more favourable, and this window began to close as early as the 1980s.

Chapters 5 and 6 analyse the two major conjunctures of this dairy consumption model: before and after approximately 1965. In Chapter 5, we explain why, in the terms of Mussolinian echoes chosen by one of Francisco Franco's dictatorship ministers, Spain did not manage to win the 'battle for milk' in the 1950s and early years of the next decade. We show that, in a backward economy and an unequal society, incorporating milk into the diet required an excessively burdensome economic effort for numerous households. Additionally, although an increasing number of consumers were exposed to scientific and political messages favourable to milk consumption, they were not enthusiastic about the type of milk available in the market: raw, unprocessed milk, often subject to adulteration and fraud.

As analysed in Chapter 6, the victory in the 'battle for milk' occurred from the mid-1960s, when a favourable macroeconomic environment coincided with complementary changes in the food chain and consumer culture. The budget constraint facing households softened significantly due to economic growth, the benefits of which were distributed across the social pyramid, and to the cheapening of milk as a processing industry developed. Consumers, on the other hand, became more interested in directing these economic gains towards the purchase of milk because they now had access to processed milk, perceived as a quality upgrade compared to traditional raw milk. By 1990, most Spaniards had adopted a milk consumption pattern that, without imposing significant strains on their household economy, aligned with nutritional recommendations.

However, this was an unstable situation, and the protagonist of Part III of the book is precisely the very different consumption model that began to take shape in the late twentieth century and continues today. It is a model less aligned with nutritional recommendations: dairy consumption has become too low and has tended to increasingly rely on ultra-processed foods. It is also problematic from a socio-economic perspective: consumers mobilize economic resources beyond what is necessary to ensure an adequate basket, and most of that extra spending is poorly aligned with relevant social challenges or the promotion of a good life. Chapter 7 provides a structural overview of the rise of this new model. The expansion of consumers' choice space, made possible by vibrant innovation strategies of dairy companies, played a crucial role by presenting consumers with a new set of possible goals: a kind of second 'battle for dairy'. Faced with generally soft budget constraints, consumers showed diverse orientations, from disinterest in milk to enthusiasm for an entire new generation of highly processed dairy desserts.

We find a significant dividing line in the unfolding of this consumption model: the Great Recession that began to manifest in Spain in 2008. Chapter 8 analyses the rise of the new consumption model before that date. These were years of macroeconomic prosperity that opened numerous possibilities for consumers on various fronts. In the specific case of dairy, these possibilities were reinforced by consumer price reductions resulting from technological changes and efficiency gains in the production chain. Consumers began to lose interest in using these economic possibilities for the purchase of milk, a food about which a less positive discourse than in the past began to circulate. However, they were more than interested in fighting the second 'battle for dairy' proposed by industries through the launch of milk-based products appealing to health, convenience, or simply consumer gratification.

Chapter 9 explains why the Great Recession interrupted these trends. These were undoubtedly tougher times for households severely affected by macroeconomic turbulence and rising inequality. Nevertheless, the rationalizing pressure in the production chain continued to produce relative price reductions that quickly more than compensated, at least in the dairy world, for the deterioration in consumers' real income. However, the recession caused cracks in the type of dairy consumerism that had prevailed before 2008. Neither did industries continue launching new products at the same rate nor were consumers as interested in fighting the second 'battle for dairy'. Nor did a supposed return to the simpler dairy consumption pattern that had prevailed around 1990 occur. At the time of writing these lines, it is not obvious that a correction of the nutritional and socio-economic problems associated with this consumption model is underway.

Once the immersion in our case study is concluded, in Part IV of the book, we return to the surface to present its implications. We do so through two chapters, one oriented towards the academic perspective and the other towards the political perspective. Chapter 10 asks what we can learn from the milk battles for a more general analysis of dietary changes in Spain and the West from the Second World War to the present. The development of both battles strongly suggests that we cannot collapse the analysis of dietary change into narratives focused on macroeconomic development or the political economy of the food system. Instead, we have explained the creative destruction embodied by successive food consumption models through a combination of developments in different social subsystems. The power of combination must be taken seriously, so that macroeconomic history, business history, and cultural history (among others) are studied in parallel. These subsystems are interconnected, but they also retain a remarkable degree of autonomy, and thus the transformation of diets is a punctuated dynamic in which relatively stable paths of change alternate with periods of turbulence and transition.

Chapter 11 concludes the book with the political implications of our study. We cannot assume that capitalism or economic growth alone leads to good or bad diets. Capitalism has historically been necessary to improve the diet but not sufficient. Furthermore, over time it has become a factor capable of destabilizing adequate diets and promoting poor eating instead. The key is the extent to which economic and business dynamics are or are not accompanied by parallel dynamics in the social, political, and cultural spheres that put them at the service of good diets. History shows us that such a combination of factors is possible but by no means natural, spontaneous, or, for that matter, stable. Active policies are necessary to favour such a combination. This brings us to the main political message of the book: we must move beyond the ideology of the sovereign consumer and open a democratic conversation about the politics of consumption in affluent societies.

Acknowledgements

It has been such a lengthy journey, thirteen years since the commencement of this research with several interruptions caused by parallel projects, that expressions of gratitude abound. As is customary in such cases, there is a special fondness for those individuals who were generous and attentive in the uncertain beginnings. When I first delved into the field of nutrition, Xavier Cussó, from the economic history domain, and Cecilia Díaz Méndez, from sociology, opened the doors to their world and graciously welcomed me into it. When I wrote my initial work on the history of dairy consumption, Domingo Gallego and Alicia Langreo read it with great attention, providing detailed and relevant comments.

Over the years, I have undoubtedly benefited from the comments and suggestions of many other colleagues with whom I have had the fortune to collaborate in seminars and conferences. These include Ángel Luis González Esteban, Shane Hamilton, Juan Infante, Laurent Herment, Ernst Langthaler, Carin Martiin, Roser Nicolau, Noelia Parajuá, the late Josep Pujol, and Kendra Smith-Howard. Special thanks are owed to José Miguel Martínez Carrión for the support and interest shown in inviting me to conduct monographic seminars on dairy consumption, both in his department at the University of Murcia and later in the NISALDes network for the study of living standards. Santiago López invited me to deliver a seminar at the University of Salamanca for an audience comprising economic historians and economists, whose comments were very helpful, as were those of my colleagues in the Department of Economics at the University of Oviedo in another seminar held shortly before submitting this book to the press. Various facets of my research were presented at conferences organized by the European Rural History Organization, the Spanish Association of Economic History, the Spain-based Society for Agrarian History Studies (SEHA), the Agricultural History Society, the European Business History Association, the European Sociological Association, and the European Social Science History network. Additionally, presentations were made at the Ibero-American Colloquium on Rural Studies and the Uppsala conference titled 'Animal Husbandry in 20th Century Europe'. It may sound somewhat unusual, but I would also like to acknowledge the work of reviewer number 3 of the article that I published in the *Rural History* journal in 2015: whoever you are, you not only identified relevant problems in my initial text but also inspired me to unfold a conceptual framework that redirected (I believe, for the better) the course of my project.

Most of this research was done while I was employed at the University of Zaragoza, and it was funded entirely by successive projects granted by the Ministry of Science and Innovation and the Government of Aragón. In Zaragoza, there was an exceptionally conducive working atmosphere, receptive to the research orientations of each individual while simultaneously fostering integration into networks and teams. In my case, I have much to be thankful for regarding the facilities I always found to reconcile my professional obligations with family life, which transpired hundreds of kilometres away. Special thanks go to Luis Germán, Iñaki Iriarte and Vicente Pinilla, who were the principal investigators of these successive projects, and to Ernesto Clar for his constant comments and suggestions over the years. I also want to fondly remember Javier Puche, a great companion for many years who passed away during the final stages of writing this book.

The Centre for Agricultural Research and Training (CIFA: Centro de Investigación y Formación Agrarias) of the Government of Cantabria proved to be a welcoming place, custodian of a valuable documentary archive that I could consult thanks to the facilities granted by Manuel Mora and successive directors of the Centre. There, I had the fortune to get in touch with Ana Villar and her enthusiastic promotion of alternative dairy circuits, including (yes!) pasteurized milk. I am indebted to Javier Mata, head of the Law and Economics division of the library at the University of Cantabria, and Albert Herreria, who worked on my English at an early stage of this book project.

That this project crossed paths with the Bloomsbury publishing house has been a stroke of luck for which I owe thanks to Peter Scholliers. When we met at a conference in Brighton in 2016, where Peter's generosity and affability shone brightly, he genuinely expressed interest in my research. Despite collaborative projects seeming to be thwarted time and again by circumstances (from a parental leave to a global pandemic), he always seemed to be confident that the next time would be different. Once at Bloomsbury, I was fortunate to rely on the diligence and kindness of Maddie Holder and Megan Harris.

My mother, María Ángeles Gutiérrez, unknowingly played an important role in shaping this project. From a certain moment (not particularly late), when she realized that her son was still researching dairy, she could not resist making the same comment time and again. Not without some malice, she would say: 'Well, there certainly seems to be a lot to learn on the topic!'. Rather than moving me to tell her about the slowness inherent in any research, this recurring comment became an incentive to work harder and, why not, aspire to make that the last time I had to hear it!

My wife Elena, who was present at the revelation that took place in Magda Quiñorero's living room in Valencia, and my children Diego, Ana, and Álvaro, who arrived some years later, faithfully made their usual contribution: they left no room for the possibility that family life could get overshadowed by the comings and goings of the process of elaborating this book, much less revolve around its author's ego. You never want to waste your time, but this 'no committee' with which I live makes such a thing joyfully impossible.

Part I

The Rise and Fall of Good Diets

1

Something is rotten

Something is rotten in the state of our diet. Across the Global North, and increasingly in more countries in the Global South, consumers are engaging in high energy intake, consuming generous doses of fats and sugars, and becoming increasingly dependent on highly processed foods. But, as journalist Michael Pollan (2008: 10) notes in perhaps the bestselling book of our time on food-related issues, 'such a diet makes people sick and fat is something we have known for a long time'. For Pollan (2008: 11), if anything is demonstrated by the variety of 'traditional diets' now displaced by the 'Western diet', it is that 'the human animal adapts well to a lot of different diets. The Western diet, however, is not one of them.' In combination with lifestyle changes such as sedentary behaviour, food consumption has become the primary global source of disease, contributing to the increased prevalence of cardiovascular diseases, diabetes, and various types of cancer. Sociologists explain to us that nutrition has been 'problematized', but how can this have happened? For most of our history, the reason why most people could find their nutrition problematic was that they lacked access to a diet sufficient in quantity and quality. Hence, our collective history of widespread improvement in diets is one of the most undeniable success stories of the contemporary age. How is it possible that now, instead, we have slipped into a historical stage in which the transformation of diets has ceased to improve the well-being of people (Díaz Méndez and Gómez Benito, 2021; Flandrin, 2004; Fogel, 2004; Oddy and Atkins, 2009; Teuteberg and Flandrin, 2004)?

The Spanish paradox

Few countries illustrate as dramatically as Spain the sequence connecting classical malnutrition, involving some kind of food under-consumption, with

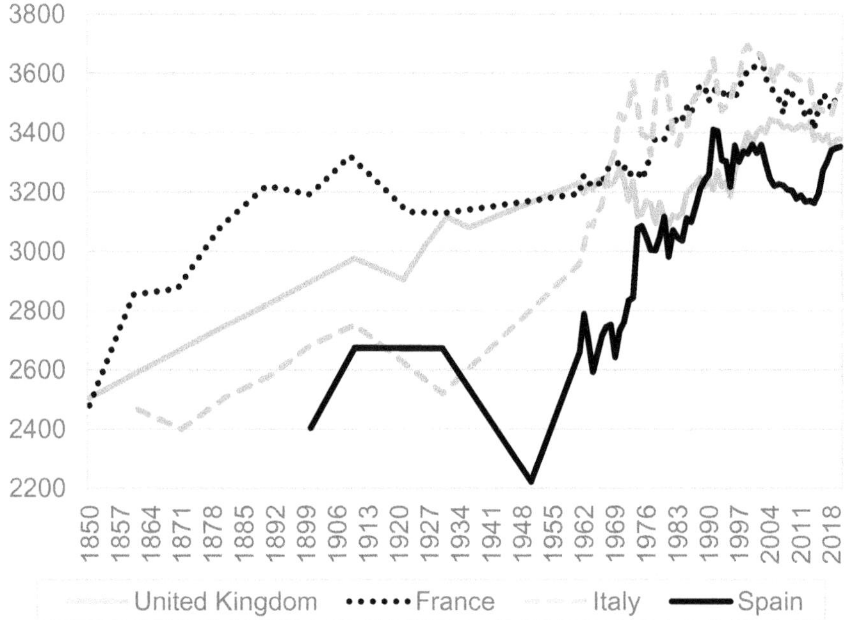

Figure 1.1 Apparent dietary energy supply in four Western European countries (kilocalories per person and day), 1850–2020.
Sources: 1850–1960: Cussó and Garrabou (2007: 75), Harris et al. (2014: 49), Oddy (2003: 114), Toutain (1971: 1977), Vecchi and Coppola (2006), Cussó et al. (2023: 82); 1960–2020: FAO (2023). See Appendix Table A1.

the more recent type of malnutrition that is common in affluent societies. Still around 1950, the starting point of our study, the spectre of classical malnutrition remained very present in the daily lives of most Spaniards. The caloric intake of the average consumer was still well below the level that had allowed the middle-class family in the UK or France to comfortably meet its needs since at least the beginning of the twentieth century (Figure 1.1). As Spain was also a highly unequal society, marked by the economic gap between a small elite of landowners and entrepreneurs on the one hand and a large mass of peasants, workers, and labourers on the other, the situation for most households was even worse. Just eight years earlier, in 1942, a famine had cruelly highlighted to what extent the energy availability for a significant portion of households was dangerously close to subsistence levels. Beyond energy, the Spanish diet suffered severe deficiencies in terms of proteins, minerals, and vitamins. It was an imbalanced diet: heavily reliant on cereals, legumes, and potatoes, and too poor in meat, fish, dairy, fruits, and vegetables (Cussó, 2005; del Arco, 2021).

The mediocrity of the Spanish diet around 1950 was partly a consequence of the disastrous circumstances the country had experienced during the 1930s and 1940s. Most families were still trying to rebuild their standard of living after the double impact of the Civil War of 1936–9 and the failure of the fascist-inspired economic policy implemented by dictator Francisco Franco during the post-war period. However, it is essential to appreciate that this conjuncture simply exacerbated structural problems that the Spanish diet had been facing for a long time.

Contrary to the cliché that presents the Mediterranean diet as a healthy pattern of consumption with very deep historical roots, the truth is that the nutritional status of Spaniards had been mediocre during the early modern period and had not improved clearly until the late nineteenth century. Still in the mid-nineteenth century, we find recurrent subsistence crises and significant periods of stagnation and even decrease in people's heights. It is true that, in the half-century before the Civil War, the diet had improved and seemed to be heading towards a horizon perhaps not very different from what the American physician Ancel Keys, a great popularizer of the virtues of the Mediterranean diet among the Anglo-Saxon public, would find in Italy or Greece shortly after the Second World War. Caloric intakes were still lower than in other more advanced Western countries, but they had started to be biologically sufficient for a vast majority of the population. The key improvement had been a strengthening of the consumption of staple grains, especially cereals, as well as an improvement in the regularity of such consumption. There were even slight signs of a diversification of the diet towards foods richer in proteins, vitamins, and minerals, including fruits, vegetables, and milk. However, by the time the Civil War broke out, and these slowly accumulated nutritional improvements vanished, it is evident that the spectre of classical malnutrition was still very present in Spain. In a society marked by a notable level of inequality, access to a sufficiently energy-rich food basket was still not fully guaranteed for the lower classes. Moreover, only the upper classes and a fraction of the urban middle class had managed to significantly diversify their diet, so most households continued to suffer from significant deficiencies when it came to proteins, vitamins, and minerals. It was this society modestly involved in the beginning of a nutritional transition, and not a society that had definitively overcome its classical malnutrition problems, that was harshly affected by the Civil War and the Francoist post-war period (Cussó and Garrabou, 2009; Martínez-Carrión, 2016; Medina-Albaladejo and Calatayud, 2020; Simpson, 1989).

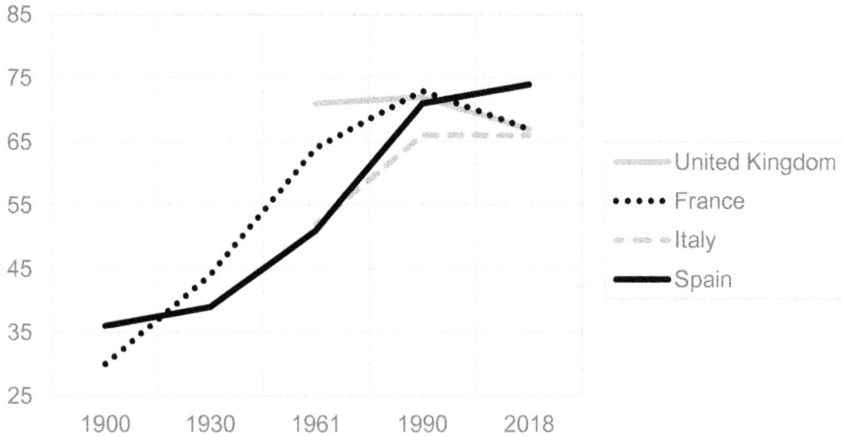

Figure 1.2 Share of dietary energy derived from foods other than cereals, roots, and tubers (%), 1900–2018.
Sources: 1900–90: Cussó and Garrabou (2007: 79, 85, 93–4); 2018: FAO (2023). See Appendix Table A2.

The speed with which this society left behind what in collective memory were marked as 'years of hunger' was impressive and has few parallels in the history of the Global North. In just over a generation, caloric intake converged with that of advanced countries, and the spectre of hunger gradually disappeared even for the lowest social strata. Furthermore, and remarkably, there was a drastic restructuring of the diet. Households reduced their consumption of those plant-based foods that had been the backbone of their diet until then, such as cereals, legumes, and potatoes. Instead, they increased their consumption of animal-based foods, such as meat, dairy, eggs, and fish, as well as fruits and vegetables. Like in other parts of Mediterranean Europe, a 'Westernization' of the diet was occurring (Figure 1.2). For a time, this undoubtedly improved the nutritional health of Spaniards. The diet began to align more closely with nutritional recommendations than had been the case before, and this was reflected in the notable improvements in biological indicators of well-being such as height. Some have suggested that an adequate diet was reached in the late 1960s, while others have delayed it to a date like the 1980s (Angulo et al., 1996; Clar, 2006; Contreras, 1997; Cussó and Garrabou, 2007, 2009; Cussó et al., 2018, 2023; Delgado, 2023a; Martínez Carrión, 2016; Trescastro-López et al., 2016).

However, the same excesses, imbalances, and problems that occurred in other Western countries would eventually begin to surface. One of Spain's most renowned nutritionists, Gregorio Varela (1992: 35), clearly perceived this at the beginning of the 1990s: '[Europeanization] has been for better and for worse, that is, many people have improved their diet, although there are also inconveniences from the diets of developed countries.' Indeed, caloric intake became as excessive as in those advanced countries that had long been seen as a reference for progress by generations of Spaniards. Although olive oil continued to dominate as the main fat in cooking, the sharp increase in the consumption of meat and other animal-based foods ended up introducing significant doses of saturated fats into the bodies of Spaniards. What initially was a certain recourse to a few processed foods turned increasingly into a diet intensive in ultra-processed foods with generous added doses of sugar, saturated fats, and salt. Although Spain continued to be closer than other countries to the ideal of the Mediterranean diet (and to correlates like commensality), the extent to which it had deviated from this diet was notable. Meanwhile, markers of nutritional health were deteriorating. Like in other parts of the Global North, the prevalence of various degenerative diseases and obesity increased rapidly (Cerrillo et al., 2023; Cussó et al., 2018, 2023; Díaz Méndez and Cardon, 2022; Díaz Méndez and Gómez Benito, 2008; Trescastro-López et al., 2016).

These developments contained a tremendous historical irony. The international reputation of the Mediterranean diet had only grown since Keys began to praise it after the Second World War. Based on a comparison between a few countries, especially Italy and Greece versus the United States and Finland, Keys had claimed that the Mediterranean diet was better for health than the 'Western diet'. The Mediterranean diet, with its moderate energy intake and lower dependence on animal-based foods, allowed the circumvention of the nutritional health problems that were beginning to be experienced in affluent countries, especially the growing prevalence of cardiovascular diseases. The message resonated, elevating the Mediterranean diet to a sort of real-world example of what a healthy diet could be. When Pollan (2008) tried to summarize to global readers what proper nutrition might consist of at the beginning of the twenty-first century, he essentially listed the three traits that would define the Mediterranean diet: eat real food, not too much, and mostly plants. However, as the Mediterranean diet was increasingly recognized internationally, to the point that it was even considered UNESCO heritage in 2013, consumers in countries like Italy and Spain seemed to distance themselves more from it, enthusiastically embracing the excesses and imbalances typical of the diet in other parts of the Global North. The rise of the Mediterranean diet as a global concept coincided with its decline as an empirical reality in Southern Europe. The paradox was striking (Frohlich, 2022; Medina, 2022; Smil, 2001, 2016). Among many others, Gregorio Varela's son, who had become an important nutritionist like his father before him, emphasized it: 'in Northern Europe, they are improving their eating patterns, moving towards the Mediterranean diet, the opposite is happening in Southern Europe, where there is rapid deterioration' ('Jornada ACES', 2015: 33).

Narratives

The initial analyses of dietary changes in Spain unequivocally centred around the country's progress along a path of economic modernization. Already in the early twentieth century, when signs of a certain quantitative and qualitative improvement in the diet became evident, economist Antonio Flores de Lemus (1914, 1926) established an explanatory framework that would significantly influence subsequent generations of economists and economic historians. Flores de Lemus observed that high-income households not only had a higher food intake than low-income households but also had a more diversified diet, where cereals, potatoes, and legumes gave way to meat, dairy, fruits, and vegetables. Consequently, the argument continued, it was to be expected that as household income levels increased over time, the diet of Spaniards would evolve in that direction. From this, Flores de Lemus concluded that it was important for the Spanish agricultural sector to prepare for a reorientation consistent with such trends.

When half a century later, economist José Manuel Naredo (1971) offered his influential interpretation of the evolution of Spanish agriculture, the facts seemed to vindicate Flores de Lemus. Indeed, at a time when Spain was immersed in its greatest wave of economic growth ever, the increase in households' disposable income was allowing them, according to Naredo, to diversify their traditional, predominantly plant-based diet and incorporate larger quantities of meat, milk, eggs, or fish. Other economists specializing in the food system, such as María Luisa Peinado (1985), adhered to this narrative, as did the entire first generation of Spanish economic historians who emerged in the 1970s and 1980s. For them, the message has been clear since then: some foods, especially those of animal origin, have elastic demands in response to changes in income, so the country's economic growth has led to a transformation of diets. Said transformation tended to be portrayed as a move away from malnutrition and, therefore, as positive for well-being. One of the country's most illustrious economists, Juan Velarde (2005: 12–13), thus underscores the decisive conceptual role of the notion of demand elasticity within the enduring narrative initiated by Flores de Lemus:

> What economists since Hicks have referred to as the income effect shines in this study. As income increases, Spaniards enhance their diet in meat, milk, and eggs, i.e., in rich proteins, while reducing the intake of carbohydrates and proteins from salted fish. This is a static approach, but Flores de Lemus … transforms the static into dynamic. Since production and income are functions of time, which can even be accurately formalized as linear functions, it is possible to replace income levels with time and ensure that, as the years pass, Spaniards will consume more meat, dairy products, eggs, and fruits and vegetables, and increasingly less salted fish, carbohydrates, and common wine.

Even though this developmental narrative has remained firmly entrenched in Spanish economic history (see, for instance, Maluquer de Motes, 2014), subsequent generations of researchers have redirected the explanation of dietary change towards the history of the food system. Ramon Garrabou and his disciple Xavier Cussó were the first to reconstruct the long series of food consumption in Spain, from the mid-nineteenth century to the late twentieth century, and conceptualized their results in terms of what economist Barry Popkin had then begun to call the 'nutritional transition'. This process entails a long-term change in diets consisting of a first phase of stabilization and increase in intakes and a second phase of diversification from the traditional plant-based foundation towards a greater presence of animal-origin foods. Soon, these pioneering efforts inspired other research, to which contributors such as Josep Pujol and Roser Nicolau added, aimed at studying in greater empirical detail the trajectories of key products within the Spanish nutritional transition, from basic grains to meat or milk, as well as a diversity of territorial patterns in dietary change within the country. The result was the identification of a Mediterranean variant of nutritional transition that, between approximately the late nineteenth century and 1960, had a horizon somewhat similar to what would eventually be praised internationally as the Mediterranean diet: a diet sufficient from a nutritional standpoint but lacking the dangerous trend of the 'Western' diet towards excessive consumption of animal and processed foods. However, this horizon would have shifted after 1960 as dietary changes aligned with the Western path of nutritional transition and its associated excesses (Cussó, 2005; Cussó and Garrabou, 2007, 2009; Cussó et al., 2018; Nicolau and Pujol, 2005, 2007; Pujol and Cussó, 2014; Pujol et al., 2007).

The narrative of these researchers, mostly affiliated with the Autonomous University of Barcelona, is not a story of the country's success in improving its diet. Instead, it is a narrative of the rise and fall of good diets. Through a systematic comparison between historical food consumption data and current recommendations from nutritional science, the Barcelona group concludes that, except for the disastrous circumstances of the Civil War and its aftermath in the 1940s, the nutritional health of Spaniards tended to improve until around 1980, after which it began to deteriorate. This evaluative dimension of the analysis has been complemented by biometric studies led by José Miguel Martínez Carrión, which found that the stature of Spaniards followed a pattern of change like the nutritional transition of the Barcelona group: an increase in the early twentieth century, interrupted by the Civil War and its aftermath, and resumed with great intensity from 1960 onwards. The subsequent stagnation of heights and an excessive increase in body mass index in the early twenty-first century also align well with the problems the Barcelona group finds in recent trends in food consumption (Candela-Martínez et al., 2022; Cussó, 2005; Cussó et al., 2018, 2023; Martínez Carrión, 2016).

To explain these dietary changes and their implications, the Barcelona group and other socio-economic historians (Clar, 2006; Gallego, 2016; Langreo and Germán, 2018) primarily turn to the dynamics of the food chain. In the words of Josep Pujol and Xavier Cussó (2014: 136), Spain's convergence towards the kind of dietary change taking place in other parts of Western Europe

> was not only a consequence of the intense and widespread rise in income levels during those years. It was also a result of the swift convergence observed in the production and commercialization conditions of food, arising from a novel set of biological, chemical, and mechanical innovations in the agri-food sector.

According to this narrative, Spain started from a relatively unfavourable structure of relative prices for the nutritional transition. Environmental conditions, particularly the aridity of the Mediterranean climate, had long limited the ability of farmers to adopt more intensive practices, as well as the capacity of the food system to shift towards livestock production. As a result, foods such as meat or milk traditionally had relatively higher prices than in other parts of Europe. The industrialization of agriculture and the food system, a process that began in the late nineteenth century but gained definitive momentum from 1960 onwards, would have decisively transformed this price structure. The so-called 'green revolution' spread in agriculture, leading to an intensive production system based on machinery, chemical fertilizers, and high-yield seeds and livestock breeds. Farmers incorporated into a food chain led by the processing industry, with its highly efficient systems of mass production. As a result, food became cheaper. This price effect would have been particularly striking for some of the careers of the nutritional transition. Meat, for instance, would have become affordable for all social classes, not just the affluent ones. The door was open for Spanish consumers to eventually emulate other consumers in the Global North in adopting an excessive and 'animalized' diet that would ultimately harm their health.

At this point, the narrative of these socio-economic historians converges with that constructed by a group of environmental historians and ecological economists led by Manuel González de Molina. These researchers have reconstructed a wide array of biophysical indicators to measure the enormous environmental impact caused by the technological modernization of Spanish agriculture and its incorporation into a highly industrialized and globalized food chain, processes that would have exceeded a dangerous threshold during the second half of the twentieth century. Although their interest has been on the supply side, they have frequently incorporated the demand side. At times, they have done so to explain the abandonment of the Mediterranean diet and the deterioration of the nutritional health of the Spanish because of this 'socio-metabolic transition' in the food chain. In other instances, they have reversed the terms and, by arguing that this transition has been induced by consumers' desire to transition to a diet with higher caloric intakes and a greater emphasis on animal-origin foods, they have presented environmental degradation as a new reason, added to health, to view recent changes in the Spanish diet pessimistically (González de Molina et al., 2020).

But what are the desires of these consumers dependent on? While the clash between the traditional macroeconomic narrative and a more microeconomic narrative was unfolding, other research delved into consumer culture and how various social and political influences may have shaped consumers' orientations and preferences. The two most dynamic groups in this regard have been historians of science and medicine, on the one hand, and food sociologists, on the other. The former, including prominent figures like Josep Bernabeu and Eva María Trescastro, have studied the dietary education programmes implemented by the Francoist dictatorship and how these may have sought to reform consumers' habits and, to some extent, grease the wheels of the nutritional transition. This connects with the research that the Barcelona group itself conducted on the first third of the twentieth century, leading them to question the premise, fundamental to the developmental narrative, that the income elasticity of demand was something like an inherent attribute of each food. Instead, there were social processes of constructing elastic demands: some key foods in the nutritional transition, such as milk, had originally very inelastic demands, and only the combined action of scientists, doctors, and public administrations had convinced the population that it was worth allocating their increased purchasing power to incorporate them more into their diet (Bernabeu and Barona, 2011; Pujol et al., 2007; Trescastro-López et al., 2016).

On the other hand, sociologists, originally led by Cecilia Díaz Méndez and Cristóbal Gómez Benito, have studied the dietary recommendations of Spanish public institutions from the 1960s to the present, finding an evolution from recommendations aligned with the nutritional transition towards others that emphasize the role of individual responsibility in avoiding the health dangers of an excessive and unbalanced diet. Nevertheless, from the voluminous research conducted by food sociologists in the last two decades, the image that emerges is that of a complex consumer. There is a concern for health and slimness that, in the words of Díaz Méndez and Gómez Benito (2004: 412),

> comes associated with a set of attributes that consumers correlate with 'healthy eating' and a particular physical appearance. The standards of good, healthy, adequate, rational nutrition, linked to a prudent diet, where the medical properties of food intertwine with the increasing importance of slimness, are distinctive of good health. Staying slim is a concern for the Spanish population.

However, consumers also show a keen interest in sensory pleasure, food innovations, and time-saving convenience foods. There is also a notable variety of consumer profiles, with oscillating and sometimes contradictory orientations, although almost all of them are absorbable within a food culture widely shared by different social strata. Finally, the Great Recession that began in 2008 emerges as a critical event that would have redirected preferences and buying habits, prompting many consumers to pay more attention than in the years before to the relative prices of different foods and, along the way, correcting some of the less healthy aspects of their pre-crisis diet (Contreras and Gracia, 2008; Díaz Méndez and Cardon, 2022; Díaz Méndez and Gómez Benito, 2010; Díaz Méndez et al., 2013).

Gaps

Although we have learned a great deal about the transformation of the Spanish diet from 1950 to the present, the state of the art is not without some weaknesses. Perhaps the most evident is related to the articulation of the different variables proposed by macroeconomic and microeconomic narratives. Although much of the history of the diet has been constructed as a microeconomic alternative to macroeconomic developmentalism, both perspectives ultimately converge on common ground: the increase in consumers' purchasing power to buy certain foods. The clash is ultimately a dispute about the proximate cause of such an increase: the rise in income levels (as in the developmentalist argument) or the reduction of relative prices (as in the argument about food chains). It is necessary to clarify which of these two forces, operating on the same empirical scale (consumers' purchasing power), is more powerful. Although the conversation has shifted towards food chains and relative prices, there have been few long-term measurements of the latter. Furthermore, despite the shift from a macro to a micro perspective, new generations of agricultural economists quickly revived Flores de Lemus's income effects, this time to explain the growing consumption of processed foods and time-saving convenience foods in households from the late twentieth century onwards (Angulo et al., 1996; Langreo and García-Azcárate, 2021; Rama, 1997). It is necessary to reintegrate the 'income effect' and avoid turning what was initially a healthy questioning of macroeconomic monism into a microeconomic monism focused on price effects.

It is also necessary to integrate these quantitative economic effects with qualitative variables regarding consumer orientations, tastes, and values. The latter have been convincingly brought to the forefront by historians of medicine and sociologists, but to be effectively integrated into a comprehensive explanation, they need to be articulated with the quantitative framework that has presided over the debate. In the context of a growing separation between quantitative and qualitative research, the challenge of creating some kind of empirical bridge that links both worlds remains pending. For example, we lack measurements of the extent to which consumer decisions were sensitive to changes in their much-referenced purchasing power.

These empirical challenges are compounded by another weakness in the state of the art: its focus on the average consumer. Although there have been significant advances in describing changes in diets for different consumer profiles (Medina-Albaladejo et al., 2023), these descriptions have not been triangulated with income or relative price data reflecting the specific circumstances of different social classes, regions of the country, or demographic groups. Consequently, available explanations for changes in diets continue to be largely based on statistical averages related to the average consumer, with little understanding of the way in which differentiated dynamics among different consumer profiles constructed those averages.

This lack of disaggregation even affects the description of changes in diets. The dominant narrative is increasingly one of 'great acceleration', in which, from around 1960, Spain leaves behind classical malnutrition and ends up succumbing to the hypercaloric and excessively 'animalized' diets of the rest of the West. However, the data presented in some of the most representative works of this narrative show a deceleration of such changes in the final years of the twentieth century and the beginning of the twenty-first (González de Molina et al., 2020; Pujol and Cussó, 2014). It is necessary to read the available evidence more nuancedly, but above all, it is necessary to accompany it with more disaggregated evidence according to the characteristics of the foods. The conversation has revolved around the plant or animal base of foods but has paid little attention to the natural or processed character of foods (Germán, 2009). This is understandable given the late development of a processing industry in Spain and the fact that the construction of long series of food consumption has had no choice but to rely on indirect estimation methods whose starting point is agricultural production. However, as we get closer to the present, it is doubtful that we can continue to approach food consumption from a perspective more focused on the raw materials sold by farmers than on the foods that consumers actually buy. When figures are presented today on the extent to which the Spanish diet depends on ultra-processed foods (Sánchez Perona, 2022), we lack historical references with which to relate them.

These empirical issues are closely related to the available sources and the priorities of different researchers, but they also reveal a fundamental theoretical problem. Just as the traditional developmentalist view was strongly anchored in neoclassical economic theory, the new narratives have a less clear theoretical framework. The income effect of developmentalists was basically an outwards shift of the negatively sloped demand curve inherent in neoclassical thought. In contrast, the subsequent reorientation of research towards food chains and consumer orientations has not been linked to any general theory of consumption. Although by default some of these contributions could be read in terms of neoclassical price effects and 'endogenous preferences', their original theoretical framework has rather been that of political economy, understood as a broader research field than economics alone and more attentive to the social positioning of individuals within structures and organizations (Martins, 2014; Stilwell, 2019). However, it cannot be said that this research has been clearly framed in a theory of consumption developed under these premises. In fact, in recent times, this is causing a certain dilution of the diet as an object of study and its subsumption into academic agendas that, as in the case of food sovereignty and socio-metabolic transition, are fundamentally oriented towards supply issues dealing with agricultural production models and their implications for social and environmental sustainability (González de Molina et al., 2020; Rivas and Cussó, 2023). Regarding the study of diets, the danger of microeconomic monism is then exacerbated.

The absence of a more explicit theoretical framework may also be affecting the evaluation of food consumption trends. The research reviewed in the previous section anchored its assessment of dietary change on nutritional criteria. This is of course a very relevant dimension, certainly the first one to consider, but is it enough? Already in the early 1980s, when the memory of malnutrition was still fresh in Spanish society, the great nutritionist Gregorio Varela outlined a problematic horizon not only because Spaniards were heading towards excessive calorie consumption but also because 'we spend too much money on food' ('El sector lácteo', 1983: 19). What Varela was intuiting is something that the neoclassical economist George Stigler (1945) had tried to quantify in the final years of Second World War: there may be substantial cost differences between those multiple combinations of foods that can be accepted as a healthy diet. How efficient are consumers in transforming their monetary expenditure into nutritional values? And, if they are apparently inefficient and (as Varela understood that was beginning to happen in Spain in the 1980s) are spending more than necessary to obtain a healthy food basket, maybe they are doing so because they are pursuing other values? If so, what are they? And what does all this mean in terms of the contribution that food consumption makes to well-being in general? These questions are absent from the Spanish academic conversation, but they are necessary to connect the debate about diets to the broader discussion about consumer society and its ambiguous relationship with what post-Keynesian researchers like Robert and Edward Skidelsky (2012) call the 'good life'.

The bigger picture

The purpose of this book is not only to clarify the Spanish case but to contribute to the international debate on the rise and fall of good diets. After all, the history of the rise and fall of good diets is common to all Western countries. For much of the modern era, especially from the mid-nineteenth century, the population of several countries was able to abandon what Fernand Braudel (1979: 100) calls the 'monotonous and difficult dietary regime' of the pre-industrial era. First in advanced countries and later in others, first among the upper classes and later among the rest, the 'nutritional transition' as described by Popkin unfolded: an increase and regularization of intakes and a diversification of the diet towards animal-origin foods. The result, at least for a time, was positive for nutritional health, as an increasing number of consumers achieved caloric, protein, vitamin, and mineral intakes in line with the recommendations that nutritional scientists had been producing since the early twentieth century. However, at some point in the second half of the twentieth century, first in the most advanced countries and later in others, a turning point began to be reached. In societies where degenerative diseases had replaced respiratory and digestive diseases as the main causes of death, continuing along the path of nutritional transition began to pose a threat to well-being. This threat was exacerbated by the growing share of ultra-processed foods in diets from the late twentieth century onwards (Buss, 1993; Floud et al., 2011; Fogel, 2004; Levenstein, 2003; Montanari, 1993; Oddy, 2003).

Spain's participation in a more general international dynamic does not end with these real-world events but also extends to the state of the art at the academic level. We find three distinctive, not very integrated narratives about the causes of the rise and fall of good diets in the West. The first is the developmental narrative that emphasizes the role of consumer income and, by extension, macroeconomic change. This has been formulated and reformulated at various times with various labels, the most influential of which has probably been Popkin's (1993) theory of nutritional transition, according to which the increase in income allows societies to transform their diet and make it more abundant and diversified. By 1960 in the most advanced countries and by 1980 in the rest, a diet more than abundant from a caloric perspective would have been achieved, and the weight of animal-origin foods would reach a peak. Then a 'behavioral change' stage would open, in which consumers would seek to correct the excesses resulting from excessive nutritional transition. In later reformulations of this approach, this new inertia could coexist, however, with growing problems of nutritional health because the income effect, accompanied by an inappropriate preference structure, could lead to an increase in the demand for all kinds of unhealthy but attractive foods (Fabiosa, 2011; Grigg, 1995, 1999; Popkin, 2009).

This narrative focused on consumer income has been supported by a mass of historical evidence that, in parallel, has found that the nutritional transition was started by high-income groups, later spreading downwards in the social pyramid (Chiapparino, 1995; Crawford, 1995; Kjaernes, 1995; Logan, 2009; Nelson, 1993; Oddy, 2003). It is not surprising, therefore, that those economic historians closest to mainstream economics have concluded that the 'change in diet patterns is related to income elasticities for different types of food … As people got richer, they spent extra income on non-grain products' (Floud et al., 2011: 317).

A second narrative shifts the focus of explanation from affluence to the food system. Beyond its original focus on international political economy, the neo-Marxist theory of food regimes, originally proposed by geographer Harriet Friedmann and sociologist Philip McMichael, has developed ramifications that present the transformation in diets as a result of changes in the 'system of provision' of food. Changes in the Western diet in the decades after the Second World War are presented as a derivative of the formation of agro-industrial complexes with Fordist features, which would have made possible a significant reduction in the consumer prices of various foods, especially those that, like meat, had traditionally been characterized by relatively high prices. This would have allowed the working class to be incorporated into a more abundant and diversified diet. However, the logic of food industrialization would have continued to this day. Under the current neoliberal (or 'corporate') food regime, what McMichael calls 'food from nowhere' would have become very cheap, which would have contributed to the spread of an excessive and unbalanced diet. High-income groups could afford a 'quality turn' and buy 'food from somewhere' from organic, local, or differentiated quality circuits. But, in a historical era of rising social inequality, lower classes would be subject to the fearsome impacts of the 'neoliberal diet' (Dixon, 2009; Fine et al., 1996; Friedmann and McMichael, 1989; Goodman and Redclift, 2005; McMichael, 2013; Otero, 2018).

In this case too, there is much historical evidence that, while not directly linked to food regime theory, fits well with it. The structure of the diet in different parts of the world has been seen as influenced by the specific characteristics of local and international production chains (Francks, 2009, 2019; Langthaler, 2018; Presa and Román, 2023). During the second half of the twentieth century, the triumph of the 'green revolution' in agriculture and the incorporation of farmers into a chain dominated by processors had major impacts on the consumer price of food and on dietary change (Bairoch, 1999; Brassley, 2009; Oddy, 2003; Oddy and Drouard, 2013; Otter, 2020). In a way, this historical work, especially when it has focused directly on consumption patterns, has done much to provide a more thorough understanding of the integration of food within the capitalist circuit.

The third narrative, finally, emphasizes the role of consumer culture. The rise of good diets would have had much to do with consumers' increasing exposure to scientific, political, and business messages that urged them to reform their habits and diversify their diet, giving greater weight to foods rich in proteins, vitamins, and minerals. Another key factor was that, especially in the post-war decades, Western consumers developed a trust relationship with mass-produced foods. On the other hand, the subsequent decline of good diets would reflect the extent to which the cautionary messages of nutritional science, increasingly focused on reducing the consumption of critical foods, clashed with other influences that weighed heavily on consumer decisions. These included the effective advertising seduction designed by producers of ultra-processed foods, a growing popular interest in service foods that reduced preparation time at home, the pleasure derived from the consumption experience, and the search for novelty and exoticism. It has been argued, however, that the persistence of a broadly shared food culture across all social strata, as might be the case in France or Southern Europe (but less so in the Anglosphere), could cushion some of the worst consequences of this dynamic (Bentley, 2013; Díaz Méndez and Cardon, coords., 2022; Gavrilova, 2005; Levenstein, 2003; Oddy, 2003; Petrick, 2012).

The overall picture is disorienting. We witness a fragmentation that may reflect broader academic dynamics towards division of labour and specialization, but also a more specific dynamic in the field of the history of food consumption: the premature decline of the research programme driven by the Annales school under the leadership of Fernand Braudel in the 1960s and 1970s. Braudel's (1979: 75–221) ambition was to identify 'dietary regimes' and explain their evolution through a combination of macroeconomic, microeconomic, and cultural factors, and perhaps the best application of this approach to the study of long-term dietary change has been that of the economist Louis Malassis (1997). Malassis proposes the existence of four 'models of food consumption': a mass poverty model before 1850, a 'diversified-merchant' model between 1850 and 1950, an agro-industrial model of mass consumption between 1950 and 1980, and a model of 'qualitative substitutions' after 1980. His explanation of each of these models revolves around the type of combination of variables that Braudel outlines in his own study of the early modern period: the 'demand capacity' of consumers, the 'supply capacity' of the food system, the 'objective conditions of consumption' (for instance, urbanization and patterns of household organization), and the 'cultural framework'. Much of the work we have reviewed in this section can be read, in fact, as illustrations and extensions of the role played by each of these factors. While the first two factors are the pillars of the first and second narratives, respectively, the third narrative focuses on the other factors, which Malassis sometimes groups together as a 'third factor' of preferences and orientations (Malassis and Padilla, 1986).

This research programme, however, declined before it could thoroughly investigate the post-1945 period. It is fair to recognize the work of some historians to combat fragmentation, especially those linked to what eventually became the International Commission for Research into European Food History (den Hartog, 1992, 1995; Scholliers, 2014; Teuteberg, 1982, 1992). Oddy's (2003) history of the British diet in the twentieth century, which we have cited as empirical support for each of the three narratives, can be seen as the best illustration of how the British tradition of economic and social history could lead to terrain not very different from that cultivated by Braudel and his followers across the Channel. But in general, research trends have gone in another direction. In the world of the Annales, the history of food consumption turned early, already in the 1980s, towards culture and mentalities as a study object in itself, rather than as a piece for the study of successive consumption models. The tradition of economic and social history, on the other hand, was gradually supplanted by the retrospective econometrics of the so-called cliometricians, as rigorous in their statistical search for alleged causal relationships between quantitative variables as lacking in interest in qualitative variables and in the argumentative styles of the humanities. Meanwhile, outside the historical profession, interest in the *longue durée* has dwindled. Both economists and sociologists have tended to abandon Braudel's structural time, which barely a generation ago seemed indispensable to understand changes in diet. Today, however, it does not seem to be very operative to apply the techniques and methods that define their respective disciplinary identities (Clark Burnett and Ray, 2012; Craig, 2016; Pilcher, 2012; Watts, 2012).

As a result, the empirical problems that we identified in detail in the previous section for the case of Spain are equally evident on the international scene. There is much talk of affluence as the cause of deteriorating diets, the ability of the modern food system to cheapen products, or the difficulties of poor consumers to turn to quality and buy 'food from somewhere', but few reliable measurements have been made of how these different causal factors have evolved over time and how this evolution fits with that of observed consumption patterns in different population groups. This, in turn, makes it difficult to properly assess the role of qualitative variables. Meanwhile, even the description of the facts that need to be explained begins to blur. In the 1990s and early 2000s, a surprising variety of researchers from different fields with little connection with one another found evidence of a rupture in food consumption models in the final stretch of the twentieth century (Grigg, 1995, 1999; Magnan, 2012; Malassis, 1997; Montanari, 1993; Oddy, 2003; Popkin, 1993), but it never became very clear what the most recent consumption model consisted of. Following the terminology proposed by Goodman et al. (2012), the available characterizations did not quite capture the 'regime' of consumption after 1980: either they were too restrictive, capturing more of a 'niche' than a 'regime' (as in Popkin's 'behavioral change' or the contrast between 'food from somewhere' and 'food from nowhere' in McMichael's case), or they were so broad that they were equally applicable to previous regimes (as in the case of Malassis's 'qualitative substitutions'). Meanwhile, the vision of a rupture at the end of the twentieth century was fading as an alternative narrative of great acceleration spread, in which the so-called 'Western diet' and food industrialization triumphed from 1945 (or even earlier) onwards (Otter, 2020; Pollan, 2008).

As in the case of Spanish research, these empirical issues partly reflect a fundamental theoretical question. It is by no means evident how we can combine the neoclassical economics that informs the developmental narrative, the neo-Marxist political economy that informs the narrative about food chains, and the anthropological concepts that (perhaps more loosely) inform the cultural narrative. Malassis is undoubtedly the researcher who comes closest to offering an integrative theoretical framework, with his consideration of demand capacity, supply capacity, and that 'third factor' of orientations and preferences of consumers, but he proceeds by juxtaposition. The result is largely vulnerable to the kind of criticism that Braudel himself sometimes received: having many individual theories, each acting on its own empirical material, does not equate to having an overarching theory (Arrighi, 2009; Tilly, 1984). In a sense, this criticism extends to the fragmented state of the question about the transformation of diets in the West, even if we take the sum of its parts as the whole it really is not.

Conclusion: What vision?

In his *History of Economic Analysis*, Joseph Schumpeter (1954: 78) asserts that every analytical endeavour is necessarily preceded by some form of 'vision': a 'pre-analytic cognitive act' that provides the raw material for the analytical effort. The vision informing this book is essentially the one outlined by Fernand Braudel (1979) and systematized by Louis Malassis (1997): that studying dietary change involves examining successive consumption models whose reproduction and transformation involve a wide variety of economic, social, and cultural factors, the study of which needs to be framed in long chronologies. This may seem like an obvious premise, but, as we have reviewed in this chapter, it has become marginal among researchers.

In this book, we will focus on the case of Spain and, within it, on a very specific group of foods: milk and dairy products, the choice of which will be justified in Chapter 3. Descending to this reduced scale seems to us as the best way to confront the demanding empirical challenges ahead, both in Spain and internationally. However, as argued in this chapter, the advancements we need are not only empirical but also theoretical. It is to this theoretical task that we dedicate the following chapter, where we present an approach based on the socio-economics of (precisely) Schumpeter.

2

A neo-Schumpeterian approach

A team of researchers led by Benjamin Wood has recently turned to Joseph Schumpeter in a study on the world's largest producers of ultra-processed food, referring to a 'creative destruction of diets' (Wood et al., 2023). Schumpeter may seem like an unusual figure to inspire a theoretical approach to the study of dietary change; after all, the renowned scholar of innovation and business cycles had little to say about the realm of consumption, let alone food consumption. However, Schumpeter grounded his contributions in an approach of 'reasoned history' that can be read as a general framework for the social sciences, not just a specific framework for the study of economic growth (Freeman and Louçã, 2001). Since Schumpeter's 'reasoned history' emphasizes the articulation of various variables, this is a perspective that can help us overcome the theoretical and empirical fragmentation in which research on dietary change has been operating.

Schumpeter and his followers

The most distinctive feature of Schumpeter's theoretical framework is its orientation towards the description and explanation of processes of change. In contrast to the emphasis of the neoclassical school of economic thought on equilibrium situations, Schumpeter focuses on the evolution of capitalism as an economic and social system. Capitalism is presented as an inherently unstable system that 'is by nature a form or method of economic change and not only never is but never can be stationary' (Schumpeter, 1942: 102). Consequently, the object of analysis is the 'unique process in historic time' through which the dynamics of capitalism incessantly transform economic and social life. This is why the Schumpeterian school is often labelled as 'evolutionary'.

For Schumpeter (1939, 1942), the evolution of the economic system is unpredictable and chaotic, partly because it is embedded in a social and natural environment that is also evolving and, therefore, modifies the circumstances of economic action. Nevertheless, economic evolution also follows a certain pattern, manifested in a succession of 'long waves' triggered by the emergence of technological revolutions and their subsequent assimilation by the economic and social fabric. In the expansive phase of the wave, the proliferation of closely related innovations induces an extraordinary transformation and increases the growth potential of economies. The exhaustion of this impetus gives way to the contractive phase of the wave, in which economic life becomes dominated by pressures towards 'rationalization' and structural adjustment. Viewed with sufficient temporal perspective, the history of capitalism becomes a sequence of 'creative destructions':

> [These industrial revolutions] impart the fundamental impetus that sets the general tone of business; while these novelties are being set in motion, spending is easy and 'prosperity' prevails …; but, at the same time as these achievements are completed and their fruits begin to flow in, the outdated elements of the economic structure are removed, and 'depression' prevails …. This process of creative destruction is the essential fact of capitalism. (Schumpeter, 1942: 120–1)

Although Schumpeter emphasizes the variable duration of long waves, his empirical approach aligns with the result that the Russian economist Nikolai Kondratiev had previously found: that the entire long wave, with its expansive and depressive phases, would last between forty and sixty years.

We do not intend to evaluate the merits and limitations of Schumpeter's empirical approach at this point, but it is important for our study to identify its methodological foundations. For Schumpeter (1954: 47–57), economic analysis must be supported by four instruments: theory, history, statistics, and economic sociology. The latter two instruments can be seen to a large extent as oriented towards the quantitative and qualitative aspects of inquiry, respectively. Statistics provide a precise measure of the system's major trends and are essential for describing and explaining its dynamics. However, this approach must be complemented with what Schumpeter calls economic sociology, which, in his hands, is a qualitative analysis of the reasons why individuals act the way they do, thus reproducing and transforming the structures of the system. Given the evolutionary nature of the object of study, this combination of quantitative and qualitative materials must be approached from a long-term historical perspective. Not surprisingly, the lack of 'historical sense' is what Schumpeter (1954: 48) considers the main source of error among economists. In turn, since history is a collection of facts and connections potentially overwhelming in its extraordinary complexity, theory is crucial for structuring the material, stylizing key facts, and providing a corpus of possible explanatory hypotheses. This is what Schumpeter, reacting against a type of historical research still very much alive in the early decades of the twentieth century, calls a 'reasoned history' approach.

This methodological approach is followed in this book, but our framework is better labelled as 'neo-Schumpeterian' because it aligns with Schumpeter's followers in three subsequent developments. The first is the relaxation of Schumpeter's separation between 'endogenous' and 'exogenous' determinants of change. Schumpeter makes a great effort to separate the purely economic engines of evolution from the rest of the changes that may be taking place in the 'social and natural environment'. However, there are moments when he admits that there are different 'distinguishable spheres of social activity', each with 'a life and mechanisms of its own that enjoy many degrees of freedom' (Schumpeter, 1939: 305). This perspective has led neo-Schumpeterians like Chris Freeman and Francisco Louçã (2001) to propose a more open approach in terms of the co-evolution of five social subsystems: science, technology, economy, politics, and culture. Each of these spheres is influenced by the others but also retains a considerable degree of relative autonomy. Consequently, the key to economic evolution lies in the historically contingent way in which the respective paths of evolution of these spheres are combined. Beyond the specific typology of subsystems established by Freeman and Louçã (an issue that, as we will see later, needs to be adapted to our purposes), the crucial question is the openness of the 'reasoned history' approach to a combination of histories about different aspects of social reality:

> Our approach … does not attempt to assign primacy in causal relationships to any one of the five spheres … It emphasizes rather the relative autonomy of each of the five spheres …, each with its own selection environment. It is this co-evolution that generates the possibility of mismatch between them and, periodically, of radical institutional innovations, which attempt to restore better coordinated development … [This provides] a framework for analysing and reconciling the research data, case studies, and generalizations emerging from the various subdisciplines of history: the history of science and technology, economic history, political history, and cultural history. (Freeman and Louçã, 2001: 125)

This leads us to a second neo-Schumpeterian elaboration: the conceptualization of change in terms of 'punctuated' dynamics. Drawing inspiration from the notion of 'punctuated equilibrium' in evolutionary biology, neo-Schumpeterian economists have emphasized that evolution does not take place gradually but is structured around paradigms whose rise and fall correspond to an alternation of phases of gradual and radical change. Building on an original formulation by Giovanni Dosi (1982), Freeman and Louçã (2001) identify successive 'techno-economic paradigms' that pattern a particular path of change until the accumulation of disruptive dynamics leads to its decline and eventual replacement by a new paradigm, following a phase of turbulence and transition. Because different social subsystems are relatively autonomous from each other, and precisely because, as a result, 'reasoned history' is a history of co-evolution, there will be periods when developments in different subsystems are very congruent with one another, facilitating the consolidation of a paradigm. There will also be periods of much less coherence in which elements of a declining paradigm coexist with those of its eventual successor.

If these two elements, co-evolution and punctuated dynamics, develop the original Schumpeterian approach, our third and final neo-Schumpeterian element constitutes a clear break with the master. Although Schumpeter was hostile to the incorporation of ethics into economic analysis, some of his modern followers, especially Mariana Mazzucato, have approached innovation and evolution from a perspective more sensitive to the social meaning of economic activity. For Schumpeter (1939: 50, 439), as for an increasing number of economists of his time, the activity of the 'capitalist machine' had no more social meaning than satisfying consumers' desires. For Mazzucato (2018, 2021), however, economic growth is not just a rate but also a direction. Technological innovation should be assessed not only in terms of its growth-driving capacity but also in terms of its capacity to address relevant societal challenges. Mazzucato's 'capitalist machine' is as unstable and fluctuating as Schumpeter's, but it is subject to ethical scrutiny: its problematic nature does not only lie in the existence of cycles, each with its fearsome depressive phase, but also in the direction that the deployment of economic and social energies will take during the expansive phases. Obviously, there is a huge political distance between Schumpeter's defence of capitalism and Mazzucato's advocacy for a 'mission-oriented' economy, the 'entrepreneurial state', and purpose-driven innovation.

Understandably, some readers may be wondering: What does all of this have to do with changes in diets? Schumpeter's theoretical analysis of capitalism virtually pays no attention to the world of consumption, and it cannot be said that his modern followers have done much about it either. Wood et al. (2023), whose interest is mainly in studying large multinational producers of ultra-processed foods, do not delve deeply into the analysis of what they describe as the 'creative destruction of human diets'. Nevertheless, the neo-Schumpeterian approach offers a theoretical framework that can be adapted to study a variety of processes of change, including changes in diets. Our goal is to adapt the neo-Schumpeterian approach to the world of food consumption. To achieve this, we will proceed in three steps: the description, evaluation, and explanation of changes in diets. For the first, we will retain paradigm thinking; for the second, the ethical assessment of the direction of economic behaviour; and for the third, the notion of co-evolution of social subsystems relatively autonomous from each other. In all cases, we will use the Schumpeterian framework as a structure for the articulation of additional theoretical perspectives, such as political economy and institutionalism.

Long waves of dietary change

In the same way that neo-Schumpeterian economists have conceptualized the history of capitalism as a succession of 'techno-economic paradigms,' we will conceptualize the history of dietary change as a succession of what Malassis (1997) calls 'food consumption models'. Although Malassis is not very explicit in his definition of the components of a food consumption model, he is including three groups of interrelated patterns here (Collantes, 2015). The first is the evolution of the aggregate level of food consumption, measurable in terms of calories or nutrients. The second is the change in the composition of that consumption according to the biological characteristics of foods, their degree of processing, or associated consumption practices. This leads us to identify contrasts between plant-based and animal-based foods, between natural and processed or ultra-processed foods, and between home and out-of-home consumption. Finally, a third group of patterns relates to differences among consumers based on their income level, social class, or any other variables that, such as education, settlement, or age, might be suspected of shaping differentiated consumer profiles.

Based on this, Malassis (1997) defines four models of food consumption in the contemporary era. Two of them would unfold during the period of interest here, after the Second World War: the 'agro-industrial mass consumption' model between 1950 and 1980, and a post-1980 model, tentatively called 'agro-industrial mass restoration' but perhaps better described by Malassis's notion of 'qualitative substitutions'. Without prejudice to this empirical application, what we want to emphasize now is the conceptual utility of the notion of a food consumption model: it forces us to go beyond averages and generalizations to also incorporate changes in the types of products consumed and the different consumer profiles involved.

Although Malassis does not make this connection, the essence of his consumption models, like that of the techno-economic paradigms of evolutionary economists, does not consist in suggesting a static image of the diet over periods of several decades but rather a stable path of change, as well as the latter's periodic renewal. We are dealing with structures that emerge and unfold over time, finding internal coherence in the combined evolution of their three major elements. The transition of some of these elements to disruptive paths of change is what would precipitate the fall of the food consumption model and the eventual emergence of a new model. Around 1950, for example, Malassis finds that the transition to a highly industrialized food system opens the door to a model marked by the diffusion of processed foods with increasingly lower prices. Around 1980, on the other hand, we would have a society of 'average satiety'. As a vast majority of consumers are already biologically satiated, the type of change embodied by the post-war 'mass agro-industrial' model runs out of steam. A new consumption model takes shape based on qualitative changes within each major food group.

Although Malassis's proposal is a theory of stages, we find it more useful to read it in an evolutionary key as punctuated dynamic in which periods of change along stable directions alternate with periods of turbulence and rupture. Precisely for this reason, it also seems more convenient to replace Malassis's type of temporal ontology with another closer to the original conception of Schumpeter and Braudel. Instead of Malassis's implicitly flat ontology, we will study the history of successive food consumption models from two differentiated temporal scales. In his history of business cycles, Schumpeter (1939: 15–16) intuits that studying evolution requires two different temporalities:

> If we consider, for example, the organism of a dog, the interpretation of what we observe can easily be divided into two branches. We may be interested in the vital processes taking place in the dog, such as blood circulation, its relationship with the digestive mechanism, and so on. But no matter how well we master all these details and how satisfactorily we manage to relate them to each other, this will not help us describe or understand at all how things like dogs come

into existence. Obviously, we are dealing with a different process here, involving different facts and concepts such as selection or mutation, or, in general, evolution.

This intuition was, of course, taken up and elaborated in a much more systematic way by Braudel (1958) when he proposed distinguishing three historical scales: structure, conjuncture, and events. In this book, we will handle two different temporalities. There will be a structural time, manifested in periods lasting several decades, which will be useful for identifying successive models of food consumption, establishing contrasts between them, and reflecting on transitions. And there will be a shorter-term temporality, in which each food consumption model unfolds, possibly under the influence of critical events. Throughout our analysis of dietary change, we will consequently combine both scales.

At this point, it is worth clarifying the positioning of this proposal in the current state of the art. What does Malassis's notion of food consumption models contribute compared to the more frequently used alternative of Popkin's (1993) 'nutrition transition'? In our view, the models of food consumption capture well everything that has made the nutrition transition a successful concept. Both the described facts and their chronology are quite similar: after all, Popkin's original nutrition transition corresponds to the sequence composed of Malassis's second and third models, while Popkin's sense that a new stage of 'behavioral change' was starting in the late twentieth century fits well with the emergence of Malassis's fourth model. However, Malassis's conceptualization allows us to go further because it is based on a more systematic definition of the different dimensions of dietary change according to the characteristics of foods and according to consumer profiles. Hence, for example, Malassis divides Popkin's nutrition transition into a before and after the triumph of processed foods, even though in both cases the biological dimension of change (the reorientation from a predominantly plant-based diet to one where animal-based foods gain prominence) is the same. This is also why Malassis's model of consumption after 1980 encompasses a richer variety of paths of change than suggested by Popkin. Alongside the 'behavioral change' oriented towards the reduction of fats and sugars (once again, the predominant biological dimension in Popkin), Malassis identifies the role of differentiated quality foods, exotic foods, or service foods. These are paths of change whose unifying theme is consumers' willingness to spend more money than necessary to ensure a basic food basket.

What is a good diet?

Certainly, the basic criterion for evaluating successive models of food consumption is nutritional health. Our bodies depend on food consumption to function properly and have enough energy to carry out tasks vigorously. Alongside energy, a good diet also comprises a handful of additional nutritional values that are equally important for different subsystems of the body to function harmoniously and sustainably over time. If we agree with Amartya Sen (1999) that well-being requires individuals to have a core of basic capabilities, few will doubt that adequate nutrition is part of this. Nutritional science provides us then with dietary references to evaluate observed patterns of food consumption according to this biological perspective.

However, we consider it necessary to accompany the nutritional dimension with another of a socio-economic nature. Consumers make monetary expenses that open a different angle of evaluation. As Sen himself has pointed out, consumer spending should not be seen as an end but simply as a means to obtain well-being. Precisely for this reason, the money metric allows us to assess how efficient consumers are from an economic perspective in accessing a certain set of nutritional values (Stigler, 1945). A practical illustration of what we want to convey is provided by the reflection of the Spanish nutritionist Carmen Sanjosé in a lecture given around the turn of the millennium. At a time when more and more probiotic foods were appearing on the market accompanied by complex health claims from their manufacturers, one of the attendees asked if these foods were effective or not. Sanjosé replied that it was not easy to know, but that 'what is certain is that their consumption is not harmful, at worst neutral' ('Probióticos', 2001: 32). This is a plausible response in nutritional terms, but it obscures the socio-economic side of the issue: since probiotic foods are more expensive than conventional ones, what the nutritionist sees as neutral, the economist sees as inefficient.

This presents a significant analytical possibility as it allows us to evaluate what, inspired by John Stuart Mill (1848) and the Cambridge political economy tradition (Martins, 2014), we will term 'surplus spending'. Mill (1848: 70) distinguishes between two types of consumption: productive consumption, which enables consumers to '[keep] up or [improve] their health' and ensure the proper reproduction of the socio-economic processes in which they are involved, and unproductive consumption, focused on 'pleasures or luxuries' that do not give 'any support to life or strength, but what would equally be given by things much less costly'. We will not retain Mill's labels, which must be understood within a previous tradition of economic thought that cannot be incorporated into the current debate without profound recontextualization. Instead, and no less faithful to the school of political economy in which Mill is situated, we will speak of basic consumption and surplus consumption.

Mill is ambivalent about this second type of consumption. It is undoubtedly inefficient expenditure from an economic point of view, as we have just seen, but this does not mean that its existence or hypothetical expansion is necessarily bad news for society. On the contrary, it can be an opportunity to address higher-level issues in human development, such as moral advancement and cultural enrichment. The problem for Mill (1848: 72) lies not in surplus spending itself but in 'the little worth of the objects to which the greater part of it is devoted'. Mill is thus taking us to the territory of ethics, which, despite the rejection it has traditionally aroused among empirically oriented researchers, is indispensable for evaluating consumption patterns (Offer, 2012). The fact that nutritional science provides a certain objective reference with which to define basic spending makes things easier because it restricts the need for an ethical anchor to the evaluation of surplus spending. Even so the task is arduous, and we think it is best to make explicit the ethical position that we will adopt, framed in the terrain defined by three scholars: John Maynard Keynes, John Kenneth Galbraith, and Mariana Mazzucato.

Keynes (1930) believed that economic growth and the adoption of consumption patterns sufficient to satisfy 'absolute needs' (those independent of other people) would open the door for individuals to have more time and resources to pursue the rest of the components of the good life. Once the economic problem was solved, the time would come to cultivate more intensely personal relationships or new interests that, from art to nature, would renew those orientation codes towards meaning that had traditionally been associated with religion. Post-Keynesian economists like Robert and Edward Skidelsky (2012) have made a critique of consumer society based on this idea. The realization of all kinds of what we call 'surplus spending', following the erosion of a traditional philosophy of sufficiency in favour of one oriented towards the pursuit of unlimited material wealth, would have led affluent societies down a path of high consumption, persistently long working hours as a means to sustain consumer spending, and, as a result of all of the above, poor performance in the other constitutive capacities of the good life. But 'We need the good life …, not sushi boxes and pre-washed salad leaves' (Skidelsky, 2012): consumers' fixation on all sorts of what Keynes called 'relative needs' would have prevented them from progressing in the cultivation of the non-monetary dimensions of the good life.

This view converges with the type of criticism that institutional economists have been making of consumer society since the late nineteenth century. In the hands of Thorstein Veblen (1899), conspicuous consumption represents a regrettable diversion of energies and resources, both personal and collective, towards the dubious end of signalling status. His most prominent disciple from the post-war decades, John Kenneth Galbraith (1973), produced a consistently critical portrait of what he called the 'affluent society'. In it, once the basic needs of the population are satisfied, businesses seek to restore some kind of scarcity: to induce new needs among consumers so that a new cycle of growth may begin. The problem for Galbraith is, as for Keynes and his followers, a problem of priorities. Surplus consumer spending ends up being directed towards the satisfaction of non-urgent, if not openly superfluous, needs, while in the process, investment in the provision of public goods such as education and health would remain chronically below what would be desirable.

If Keynes was sceptical about surplus spending as a path to the good life, Galbraith was sceptical about the use that was being given to surplus spending in America's consumer society. We will take both names to label two possible empirical scenarios. We will call 'Keynes situation' one in which consumers achieve a sufficiently good nutritional state through a basic food basket that absorbs only the resources that are strictly necessary. In the Keynesian situation, all consumption spending is basic, and there is no surplus spending. On the other hand, we will call 'Galbraith path' one in which surplus spending contributes little to social progress and can even act against it. When a society ventures down this path, monetary indicators overestimate the real well-being of the population.

But is all surplus spending doomed to lead us towards what Stiglitz (2008) calls 'excessive consumerism'? Or can there be excess spending oriented towards genuine human flourishing? To the Keynes situation and the Galbraith path, we will add a third possibility: what we will call the 'Mazzucato path'. As we saw at the beginning of this chapter, Mazzucato (2018, 2021) has advocated the need to align economic change with relevant social purposes. For Mazzucato, it is not just about taking the economy out of the stagnation that Schumpeter called 'circular flow' but ensuring that the innovation that does so is oriented towards 'missions' that embody goals of social progress. This implies, of course, breaking with the idea that all possible paths of economic growth are equally valid. On the contrary:

> Deciding which activities are more important than others is critical in setting a direction for the economy: put simply, those activities thought to be more important in achieving particular objectives have to be increased and less important ones reduced. (Mazzucato, 2018: 43)

Although the argumentation has primarily focused on the supply side, it is straightforward to extend it to the demand side to obtain the inverted image of what we have termed the 'Galbraith path'. On the Mazzucato path, surplus spending, instead of deviating towards superfluous ends, fosters the cultivation of the good life by consumers and contributes to social progress.

What could this mean in the realm of food consumption? Throughout the book, we will identify the Mazzucato path with some form of notion of values-driven consumption. We will follow Albert Hirschman's (1985) distinction between tastes, which are not subject to discussion, and values, which result from deliberation and reflection aimed at guiding consumer behaviour. An example could be the consumption of organic foods whose production and distribution have had a moderate environmental impact. Another example is the shift to a food consumption pattern that incorporates cultural heritage values. Consuming these types of foods is more expensive than consuming their conventional counterparts, requiring mobilization of surplus spending that may not be strictly necessary to ensure good nutritional health. However, this type of surplus spending, oriented towards relevant social missions, cannot be lumped together with the consumerist deviations denounced by Galbraith.

It is important to underscore the role that social missions and individual values aligned with them play in defining the Mazzucato path. As the theory of conventions suggests, a variety of alternative definitions of quality and value will coexist in tension, each reflecting a certain coordination among the interpretative frameworks of the individuals and social groups involved in economic life (Boltanski and Chiapello, 1999; Goodman et al., 2012; Hamilton, 2023). However, only some vectors of this 'economy of qualities' lead us down the Mazzucato path. Drawing on a long tradition of economic thought that encourages distinguishing between *complacibilitas* and *virtuositas*, subjective utility and objective utility (Roncaglia, 2005, 2019), we do not believe that hedonism offers an umbrella that legitimates any possible orientation of surplus spending. Following Skidelsky and Skidelsky (2012), we are also very sceptical about the social value of consumer spending on what some biomedical researchers have called the transition from 'adequate nutrition' to 'optimal nutrition' ('Panorama', 2000: 71): once a criterion of sufficiency is abandoned in the health domain and the possibility of maximization is introduced, what sociologists call the 'medicalization of nutrition' takes place (Díaz Méndez and Gómez Benito, 2004), with essentially healthy populations aiming for the dubious goal of improving their health. In summary, although we do not adopt the extreme position that all surplus spending is superfluous, we also reject the equally extreme position that all surplus spending reflects some kind of progress.

At this point, it seems inevitable to clarify here that our approach diverges from the common belief widely prevalent in academic and public debates that dietary change, particularly the 'animalization' of diets, is responsible for serious environmental impacts. It is evident that, unlike other consumptions such as gasoline consumption for driving a car, the mere act of consuming certain foods does not cause environmental impact. By then, the impact has already been generated by actors further up the food chain, from farmers and livestock breeders to industrialists or supermarkets, including transporters. Only some activities related to food consumption, such as cooking or managing waste, can reasonably be incorporated into the inventory of environmental impacts (Teisl, 2011). However, in this case, a significant portion of the difference commonly attributed to the animal or vegetable origin of the food is dissolved, and much more generic factors come into play. In our case, we incorporate the environmental dimension through a different route: that of a socially progressive direction in which consumers, inspired by their ethical values, can channel some of their potential surplus spending.

Why?

In a manner analogous to Freeman and Louçã (2001) in their neo-Schumpeterian explanation of economic growth, our explanation of dietary change will revolve around the co-evolution of a series of social subsystems. For Freeman and Louçã, who aim to identify variables with an indisputable impact on economic growth, these are the scientific, technological, economic, political, and cultural subsystems. Our equivalents for the study of dietary change will be the macroeconomic, microeconomic, and cultural subsystems, and our justification for this derives again from the agri-food economics of Malassis (1997; Malassis and Padilla, 1986).

Malassis (1997, II: 167–8) explains the rise and decline of successive models of food consumption as a result of the historical combination of four groups of factors. The first is what he calls 'demand capacity' and refers to the level of disposable income in households. The second is 'supply capacity', that is, the capacity of production chains to bring a wide range of foods to the market and do so at affordable prices. Thirdly, Malassis refers to changes in the 'objective conditions of consumption', such as urbanization or the shift to household structures with two income earners instead of one. Finally, food consumption would also be influenced by changes in 'cultural models', which shape the orientations and dispositions of consumers. These last two factors, the 'objective conditions of consumption' and the 'cultural model', are sometimes grouped together as a single 'third factor' that covers everything that cannot be encompassed as demand or supply capacities (Malassis and Padilla, 1986: 274–82).

Our interpretation of this approach, informed by the state of the art reviewed in the previous chapter, is that we can identify three social subsystems with a direct influence on dietary change. The first is the macroeconomic subsystem, whose results in terms of higher or lower growth will determine the level of income available to consumers (Malassis's 'demand capacity'). The second is the microeconomic subsystem: the food chain, whose business dynamics explain both the relative price structure that consumers are facing and the configuration of the choice space in which they have to make their decisions (Malassis's 'supply capacity'). Finally, a third subsystem is the cultural one, understood in a broad sense as a variety of influences on the orientations and preferences of consumers, including the production of images and social meanings of different foods (Malassis's 'third factor'). Our history of dietary change will, essentially, be a story about the co-evolution of macroeconomic history, the history of the food chain, and cultural history.

Once this neo-Schumpeterian framework is established as a general approach, we can integrate the perspective of evolutionary economics with other theoretical perspectives for the specific analysis of each subsystem. Obviously, our macroeconomic history will be heavily influenced by the evolutionary approach we have already discussed when presenting the basic ideas of Schumpeter and his followers: the punctuated dynamics resulting from the deployment of technological revolutions and their interaction with other social spheres. There will also be significant doses of Schumpeterian economics in our history of food chains, especially regarding how entrepreneurial innovation reconfigures what Malassis (1997) calls the 'field of possibilities' for consumers.

Our theoretical expectation, following Schumpeter (1939), is that the choice space of consumers is cyclically reshaped by the innovation strategies of food industries. The initial phase of the cycle would be a 'transformation' phase, during which key innovations are implemented, and market expansion makes enterprises of various sizes and characteristics viable. Later, we would enter a 'rationalization' phase, during which a structural adjustment is unleashed that concentrates economic activity in the most competitive business units. These rationalization conjunctures, featuring what Schumpeter sometimes calls 'vigorous competition', generate particularly intense pressure for the generation of innovations that allow leading companies to start a new transformation phase. These cycles of entrepreneurial 'creative destruction', especially when triggered by successful product innovation strategies, will reshape the choice space of consumers, whose purchasing decisions are less a *primum mobile* of business activity than a potential ratification of the direction taken by it.

However, our history of the food chain will also, following Malassis's conceptualization of 'supply capacity', be a story about relative food prices, a field where we will depart from the Schumpeterian view to rely on the perspective of classical political economy (Martins, 2014; Roncaglia, 2005). Although the behaviour of relative prices in the short term may reflect supply or demand shocks in the style described by neoclassical economists (or, at this point, by Schumpeter himself on many occasions), we think that their long-term trend is better explained in terms of the classical notion of 'relative difficulty of production'.

This is regarding macroeconomic history and the history of food chains, but how to approach the history of consumer culture? Here, the Schumpeterian approach will be of little help, and we will refer to the approach of institutional economics and economic sociology. The basic idea is that consumer behaviour is rooted in a matrix of social relationships that pre-exist any individual, conditioning their behaviour and, at the same time, depending on individual behaviour for its reproduction or transformation (Chai, 2017; Warde, 2016). In contrast to what, following Granovetter (1985), we could call an 'under-socialized consumer', food preferences are shaped by the influence of various actors, from companies and public administrations to the media and scientists, as well as by the interaction that occurs between consumers both horizontally and vertically. In contrast, however, to what Granovetter would call an 'over-socialized consumer', it is the agency of consumers that ends up reproducing or transforming social structures. A fundamental aspect in this regard, and of particular importance for the case of food consumption, is how individuals' sensory experiences shape over time a specific structure of preferences, tastes, and habits. There is also the possibility, as we have outlined in the previous section, that structures of values emerge around food.

How to make this conceptual framework operational for empirical research? Given the heterogeneity of factors explaining the rise and fall of food consumption models, our empirical strategy will develop at two levels, responding to Schumpeter's (1954) call to combine statistics and economic sociology. At the first level, we will seek to identify the statistical evolution of consumers' purchasing power for specific foods. This will lead us to work with a synthetic indicator that, in the tradition that Braudel and Malassis themselves inherit from the economist Jean Fourastié, incorporates simultaneously the evolution of the income level and the relative prices of the foods under study, so that we can measure how tight the budget constraint that consumers are facing is. We will perform these calculations not only for the average consumer but also for a variety of profiles according to social status, geography, and other relevant variables. The second level concerns the preferences and orientations of consumers, as well as the definition of their choice space. This will lead us to delve into qualitative factors such as cultural environment, consumption experiences, or business strategies.

The link between both levels of analysis will be the calculation of what we will call 'response factors', an approximation to the greater or lesser sensitivity with which consumers react to variations in their purchasing power to buy a particular food. To do this, we compare the change in consumption with the change in purchasing power. The latter is the change in disposable income, deflated by the general price index and additionally corrected for the evolution of the price level of the food we are studying, so that an increase in the relative price of that food deteriorates the consumer's purchasing power and a decrease strengthens it:

$$R_i = c_i/(y - p_i)$$

where R is the response factor, i is the product under study, c is the consumption growth rate, y is the consumer income growth rate, and p is the price growth rate. In all cases, the growth rates are compound annual rates.

This indicator will allow us to organize the use of qualitative material, especially regarding consumer orientations. High response factors will draw our attention to the possible existence of great consumer interest in a particular product, as there has been a noticeable increase in consumption in relation to the increase in purchasing power. Low (or even negative) factors, reflecting situations where notable increases in purchasing power do not lead to much more consumption (or perhaps even less), will suggest the opposite. It can be speculated that each product would be subject to a life cycle in which, tendentially, these response factors could gradually decrease. Although the interpretation of the concept moves in a terrain similar to the elasticity of demand in mainstream economics, it is a simpler calculation that, without assuming any functional forms or a scarcity-centred theoretical framework, simply compares the orders of magnitude of the change in consumption and the change in purchasing power. Unlike the elasticity of demand, however, the response factor needs to be applied over periods of some duration, so that variations in prices that enter into its calculation can be taken, in the spirit of classical political economy, as indicative of the fundamental transformations taking place in the food system and its integration into the overall economic system. These periods of some duration seem, however, the most reasonable scale to study changes in consumer orientations when, as is the case with food, habit plays an important role and consumer reorientations take hold only gradually (Warde, 2016).

Although we have identified macroeconomics, the food chain, and consumer culture as the three key spheres, this does not mean that our 'reasoned history' will do without other spheres that are connected to them through multiple channels. It is evident that political history, for example, has a notable impact on macroeconomic outcomes or the dynamics of food chains, in the latter case through policy impacts on relative prices, business capabilities for innovation, or the definition of quality standards (Stanziani, 2005). Even the evolution of consumer cultures can be significantly influenced by political history, especially through the rise of projects aimed at politicizing consumption, either as a support for the existing political order or as alternatives to it (Glickman, 2012).

Social history, understood in its narrowest sense as a study of social stratifications and hierarchies, is also essential to, for example, introduce the dimension of inequality into our macroeconomic understanding. It is crucial to delve into the analysis of differentiated consumer profiles, conducting a reading of macroeconomic, microeconomic, and cultural changes that go beyond the deceptive notion of the average consumer. Finally, the history of science plays a very important role in opening new possibilities for the design of business strategies at the microeconomic level, both in terms of process innovations aimed at producing food more efficiently and in the research and development of product innovations. In addition, in the case of food, the emergence and consolidation of nutritional science can play a fundamental role in shaping social images and cultural frameworks about the foods that make up our diet (Biltekoff, 2012). Our emphasis on the macroeconomic, microeconomic, and cultural spheres does not in any way seek to exclude the spheres of the political, the social, and the scientific, but rather to clarify the channels through which they develop their influence.

Conclusion: A Schumpeterian route towards … Braudel and Malassis?

In a recent assessment of the historiographical project led by Fernand Braudel, Jan de Vries (2018: 325) laments that '[it] was a strong vision that did not become anything more; it is now visible only to those old enough to know where to look'. In this chapter, we have proposed a novel theoretical route to revitalize that project, framed within Joseph Schumpeter's socio-economics. The result conceptualizes dietary change by identifying models of dietary consumption, evaluates these models based on nutritional as well as socio-economic criteria, and explains the rise and fall of successive models as a punctuated co-evolutionary process in various spheres relatively autonomous from each other. This approach, due to its focus on the social context in which consumer choices are made (and the field of possibilities in which these take place), differs from that of mainstream economics. It also distinguishes itself from Marxist political economy and political ecology by emphasizing the combination of dynamics within the food chain with other relatively autonomous spheres, such as the macroeconomic sphere. Finally, it differs from the implicit approach in numerous studies of cultural history by conceptualizing dietary change in terms of successive models of consumption and advocating for the incorporation of quantitative variables into the analysis.

However, precisely because of this, our neo-Schumpeterian approach can be seen to a considerable extent as an alternative route to the destination to which Fernand Braudel and Louis Malassis were leading us before their research programme entered a premature decline. Their focus on the long term and their combination of quantitative and qualitative empirical materials have much in common with Schumpeter's call for a 'reasoned history' supported by theory, statistics, and economic sociology. Braudel's famous idea of different historical temporalities also finds a precedent in the way Schumpeter tried to fit paradigms and cycles of different durations and natures. In a manner that anticipates the neo-Schumpeterian approach, both Braudel and Malassis keep relatively autonomous social subsystems connected, preventing their explanatory focus from disproportionately concentrating on any one of them. Braudel (1977: 77–8) is, in fact, as explicit as Freeman and Louçã later would be regarding the need to abandon the premise that any of these subsystems could have primacy over the others. Braudel (1979: 150) even anticipates the ethical ramifications of the debate when, in a way that connects him with Mazzucato's ideas about the directionality of economic change, he states that luxury consumption in modern Europe was a 'disease of the *Ancien Régime*', made possible by an 'unfair, unhealthy, brilliant, uneconomic use of surpluses'. For all these reasons, we believe that Schumpeterian socio-economics offers a fantastic opportunity to revitalize the kind of vision that inspired the contributions of Braudel and Malassis, providing it with a more integrated theoretical framework.

3

Spain's two models of dairy consumption since 1950

'Indeed, it is the rare, seemingly forlorn plant today that does not have its own historian', asserts Peter Coclanis (2019: 193) when commenting on the recent rise of the 'commodity studies' genre among historians. Our choice of a case study in this book is motivated not so much by the desire to contribute to this genre but by the need to adopt a manageable scale to address the empirical challenges faced by research on the Spanish and Western diet. But why milk and dairy products? Wouldn't olive oil, wine, or oranges, for example, provide a more recognizable basis for a case study focused on Spain? Yet, as we will see in this chapter, this is perhaps the group of products whose history best illustrates the drastic sequence of the rise and fall of good diets in the country.

Milk and dietary change in the West

The diffusion of liquid milk consumption has been repeatedly identified as one of the central vectors of dietary change between approximately 1850 and 1980. Liquid milk transformed from being a food that was rarely consumed by most households, whose diet perhaps included modest amounts of cheese or butter, into a mass-consumed commodity. Still in the early twentieth century, there was a noticeable social gradient: the upper classes regularly and abundantly consumed milk, while the working classes scarcely did. However, as the twentieth century progressed, milk ceased to be a status marker and became a staple in the overwhelming majority of Western households, regardless of their social status (Burnett, 1999; DuPuis, 2002; Kjaernes, 1995; Smith-Howard, 2014; Valenze, 2011; Velten, 2010; Wiley, 2011).

This popularization of milk in the Western diet has been attributed to economic causes, such as an increase in consumer income and a reduction in the relative price of the product. Rising incomes made it possible for an increasing number of consumers to afford the regular purchase of an expensive food product that had a considerable price relative to its caloric contribution. This developmentalist perspective is consistent with the fact that, as numerous studies have found, the incorporation of milk into the Western diet was led by the upper classes and the more developed countries, with a gradual diffusion down the social and international scale occurring later. The decline in relative prices, on the other hand, resulted from the formation of an agro-industrial production chain. Milk production was initially subject to significant technological and business limitations that kept its price high, thereby hindering the social diffusion of its consumption. Some agro-industrial transformations had already taken place since at least the late nineteenth century, but it was mainly after 1945 that the type of production chain armed with high-yielding cows, capitalized farms, and mass production technologies triumphed, leading to a substantial reduction in the price of milk (Burnett, 1999; den Hartog, 1992; DuPuis, 2002; Felice, 2004; Fine et al., 1996; Knittel, 2023; Lanero et al., 2023; Valenze, 2011; Vatin, 1990; Velten, 2010; Wiley, 2011).

Alongside these economic factors, the significance of consumer culture has also been emphasized. During the 'short' twentieth century, coalitions of actors sought in every Western country to improve the social image of milk. They aimed to encourage the adult population to consume more of what had hitherto been considered primarily a children's food. This 'gospel of milk', as Deborah Valenze (2011: 206) calls it, had a scientific component as nutritional science began extolling the health benefits associated with regular milk consumption – its proteins, vitamins, calcium, and its status as a 'protective food' capable of correcting other potential dietary deficiencies. However, it also had a clear political component, as most states eventually mobilized this message in propaganda campaigns that were connected to policies supporting the concurrently emerging livestock industry. Policies aimed at improving consumer perceptions of milk also included school milk programmes and quality standardization programmes. Over time, as large-scale dairy industries emerged, these actions were accompanied by advertising campaigns launched by processing companies. Significant resources were devoted to the 'gospel of milk' and its triumph was definitive once companies refined their processing methods so that the natural flavour of the product was not greatly compromised (Atkins, 2010, 2017; Martiin, 2010; Moser and Brodbeck, 2007; Smith-Howard, 2014; Valenze, 2011; Vatin, 1990; Velten, 2010).

Almost everyone agrees that the diffusion of milk improved the nutritional health of consumers. Milk not only provided its share of calories or proteins but also carried incorporated vitamins and minerals, such as calcium, which were not as easily obtainable through other foods. However, some doubts persist about the extent to which nutritional recommendations, designed within an intellectual tradition largely unaware of the biological variability of human organisms in different cultures and geographical environments, may have exaggerated the magnitude of these health benefits (Levenstein, 2003; Mendelson, 2023). Moreover, questions have been raised, at least for countries with higher levels of consumption, about the socio-economic appropriateness of such high milk consumption. For example, Melanie DuPuis (2002: ch. 5) acknowledges that milk contributed to improving the health of Americans for much of the twentieth century but argues that it also absorbed a disproportionate share of consumer spending. She suggests that it would have been more beneficial for consumers to allocate some of that spending towards foods like fruits and vegetables.

Regardless, at some point in the second half of the twentieth century, a turning point was reached. In country after country, first in northwestern Europe and North America and later in their peripheral European followers, consumers began to reshape their shopping baskets. Even in countries with a strong dairy tradition, people started abandoning liquid milk in favour of a highly varied range of dairy products, including domestic and international cheeses, yogurts with various flavours and textures, fermented 'functional' milks with probiotics, and a variety of refrigerated desserts. As had happened during the previous wave of milk consumption diffusion, this shift was led by households with higher socio-economic status but nonetheless had some tendency to social generalization (Fine et al., 1996; Kjaernes, 1995; Smith-Howard, 2014; Stewart et al., 2013; Wiley, 2011).

The consumer culture that had prevailed for much of the twentieth century began to crumble. Consumers were exposed to scientific messages that, instead of extolling the potential virtues of milk, raised concerns about the saturated fats it contained. In science, the 'newer nutrition' paradigm, with its emphasis on increasing the consumption of healthy foods, was replaced by the 'negative nutrition' paradigm, with its emphasis on reducing the consumption of unhealthy foods (Bilketoff, 2012; Levenstein, 2003). The advertising strategies adopted by dairy industries to promote their new low-fat milks only served to amplify these attitudes. Furthermore, a greater scientific and subsequently cultural space was opened for the recognition of lactose intolerance as a feasible biological condition. This was compounded by a certain loss of consumer confidence in what had hitherto been perceived as absolute truths of nutritional science that now seemed, at the very least, relative. If drinking milk was indeed so important, why were there not more health disorders observed in such a large part of the world's population that, for various reasons (including lactose intolerance), did not consume it? On the other hand, the culture of beverage consumption was undergoing a significant transformation, especially among children and young people, towards carbonated soft drinks and industrial juices – a competition that was challenging for a product like milk, which offered less pleasurable sensory experiences (Atkins, 2010, 2017; Burnett, 1999; Kjaernes, 1995; Stewart et al., 2013; Valenze, 2011; Velten, 2010; Wiley, 2011).

Meanwhile, the culture of dairy consumption was evolving towards ultra-processed and gratifying products, favouring a shift of consumers away from milk towards complex yogurts and ice creams. Yogurt took off, especially once corporate advertising shifted its focus from dietary values to promoting images of a tasty and convenient snack. Ice cream, on the other hand, faced the current against fats, but the promise of gratification was more than sufficient to counterbalance it (Smith-Howard, 2014; Spiekermann, 2009; Vatin, 1990).

These cultural dynamics operated in significantly reconfigured economic spaces. The dairy chain underwent decisive transformations for the emergence of a new consumption pattern. The agribusiness complex began to shift from process innovations, focused on producing milk more cheaply, to product innovations, centred on creating possible new market niches. This made it possible for the consumption pattern to shift from whole milk to low-fat milks and, even more so, towards cheese, yogurt, and various refrigerated desserts (Felice, 2004; Fine et al., 1996).

Whether this new consumption pattern was beneficial for nutritional health is, however, questionable. While avoiding the saturated fats of a simple food like milk, consumers were becoming increasingly dependent on ultra-processed dairy products. Although none of these products was by itself a definitive threat to health, each contributed to constructing the kind of diet rich in ultra-processed foods that was increasingly identified as problematic. On the other hand, this problem coexisted with another striking trend: dragged down by the decline of milk, the aggregate consumption of dairy and calcium intake was dropping below the dietary references in many countries. While research on developing countries continued to reveal a positive association between dairy consumption and nutritional health (Haile and Headey, 2023), consumers in the affluent world faced potential (although not entirely proven) consequences for their bone health. It was also unclear whether this new pattern of dairy consumption could be subject to a particularly benevolent socio-economic assessment. Ann Mendelson (2008: 52), for example, has criticized consumers for rejecting milk and instead spending more money on 'crude artificial mimicries of the dreaded offender' as a result of an 'endless chorus of commercial persuasions to buy more and more … of this or that added-value niche product targeted to real, imaginary, or highly misrepresented needs and deficiencies'.

The *Longue Durée* of Spain's dairy consumption

Before delving into the Spanish case, it is pertinent to introduce the sources that will be utilized in this chapter and throughout the rest of the book. Our two main statistical sources employ direct methods to estimate dairy consumption. The first of these, available since 1958, is the Household Budget Survey (*Encuesta de Presupuestos Familiares*) from the National Institute of Statistics. Through a representative sample of several thousand households, this survey provides information on the quantities consumed of major types of dairy products, such as milk, cheese, and yogurt. It also furnishes data on the expenditure consumers incurred to buy these products. The information is disaggregated for different consumer profiles based on their socio-economic status, regional area, urban/rural settlement, and other relevant variables. This source is highly reliable, grounded in well-founded procedures, and consistent over time. Its main weakness lies in the fact that what consumers buy may differ from what they actually consume, as there might be waste. However, a specific study on dairy waste in Spain as late as 2017 revealed that the percentage of milk wasted by Spanish consumers was only 1 per cent ('Crece', 2018: 10), making it reasonable not to be overly concerned about this detail.

A second statistic based on direct estimations is the Food Consumption Panel (*Panel de Consumo Alimentario*) managed by the Ministry of Agriculture, Fisheries and Food since 1987. Similar to the Household Budget Survey, the Panel gathers information on food purchases by a representative sample of households and provides estimates of consumption and expenditure for different consumer profiles. Its significant advantage over the Household Budget Survey is that it offers much more detailed information on various types of consumed products. What the Household Budget Survey considers simply as cheese becomes distinct categories in the Panel, including cured cheese, semi-cured cheese, fresh cheese, or melted cheese, also taking into account skimmed cheese or, on occasion, the differentiation between domestic and imported cheeses. Another contribution of the Panel, especially in its classic version until 2006, is that it allows the estimation of dairy consumption outside the home. While this is an indirect estimation based on purchases made by a sample of restaurants and bars, it still provides an idea of the magnitude of consumption outside the home.

Our main sources will be the Household Budget Survey and the Food Consumption Panel, but occasionally we will resort to indirect estimations of dairy consumption, especially those conducted by the Ministry of Agriculture and the FAO using the 'balance method'. This method involves calculating the residue obtained by subtracting the net foreign trade balance from production, converted to equivalent units of primary production. In the absence of direct estimation methods, as is the case before 1958, these calculations are undoubtedly useful. However, it is noted that for recent historical periods when both methods are applicable, direct estimations appear to be more reliable, reducing the margin of error (Collantes, 2014; Smil, 2001). In direct estimation, the error primarily stems from waste in households and foodservice establishments. In contrast, indirect estimation carries additional errors from waste and losses across other links in the food chain, as well as potential errors from fluctuations not captured in the conversion coefficients that supposedly apply to the transformation of raw materials into the foods purchased by consumers. We do not share the conclusion of Cerrillo et al. (2023) that the difference between their results based on indirect methods and the information provided by the Food Consumption Panel reflects the latter offering 'questionable data'. These supposedly questionable data are consistent with those provided by the Household Budget Surveys, conducted by another institution using different methods and different population samples, while the indirect results of the authors rely on unproven assumptions about the waste coefficients that are truly applicable in the Spanish case. Additionally, it should be noted that, to some extent, the balance method serves to provide a general idea of what demand trends may mean for farmers and livestock breeders working at the beginning of the food chain, rather than studying the consumer's perspective at the end of the chain. Indeed, indirect estimations do not allow for consumer profile disaggregation and do not identify the variety of foods consumed.

To complement this quantitative analysis, various qualitative sources aimed at better understanding consumer orientations and preferences, as well as their evolution over time, are employed. The most important among them are the two major professional journals in the dairy sector: *Revista Española de Lechería* (Spanish Journal of Dairying) and *Industrias Lácteas Españolas* (Spanish Dairy

Industries). The former began publication in 1952, precisely when the Francoist dictatorship implemented its policy to promote the dairy industry, and the latter in 1978, shortly after the country's transition to a democratic regime. The target audience of both journals consisted mainly of industry professionals, politicians, officials, and farmers linked in one way or another to the sector. In different combinations depending on the stages and circumstances, these journals provided information ranging from purely technical aspects of dairy production to a generous dose of economic, social, and political information, always from a perspective dominated by the interests of dairy industry stakeholders. Although scattered and impressionistic, this information gives us a good portrait of the consumer – their preferences, experiences, behaviour – as perceived by the sector's actors.

For similar reasons, we will also track the advertising announcements used by industrialists to communicate with consumers. In line with other studies (Díaz Méndez and González, 2008; DuPuis, 2002), we will interpret these advertisements as suggestions about consumers' desires and concerns regarding dairy products. Obviously, this approach is conditioned by the unequal involvement of different producers and products in the world of advertising. Nevertheless, studying the advertising strategies of major producers, often with significant market shares, will provide a reasonably reliable perspective.

In some cases, our sources will even allow direct access to the voice of the consumer, expressing their orientations and commenting on their experiences. However, our interest is not so much in conducting a deep dive into the world of a few consumers of unknown significance as in capturing the overall picture. This is where statistical sources, a reflection of the behaviour of all consumers without exclusion, and qualitative profiles, identified at each historical moment by industrialists seeking to understand consumers as best as possible, become fundamental.

Now is the time to immerse ourselves in our case study. The starting question is: What models of dairy consumption can we find in Spain between 1950 and the present? If we reconstruct statistical series on aggregate dairy consumption and its breakdown by product types and consumer profiles, the image emerges of a succession of two models of dairy consumption between 1950 and the present. The breakpoint between them is around 1990, and in a sense, this rupture in the path of dairy consumption change constitutes the central theme of this book. Additionally, we can observe that the 1950s, far from being a spurious starting point for our research, also represent a rupture from previous dynamics.

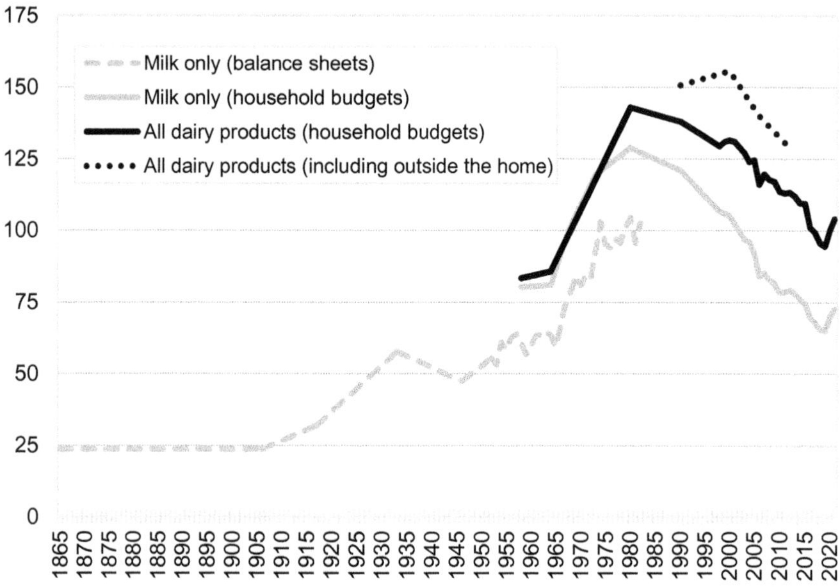

Figure 3.1 Consumption of milk and dairy products in Spain (kilograms per person and year), 1865–2020.
Sources: 1865–1935: Hernández Adell (2012: 190); 1950–2020: Collantes (2015), updated with INE (2023a) and MAPA (2023a). See Appendix Table A3.

This is demonstrated, to begin with, by the aggregated consumption of dairy products (Figure 3.1). The available data show an initial wave of expansion in milk consumption during the early decades of the twentieth century, a wave that was, however, disrupted by the Civil War and post-war period. The 1950s marked a rupture because they witnessed the start of a new wave of expansion. This accelerated sharply between 1965 and 1980, after which it began to lose momentum. The rupture was consummated in the late 1990s when dairy consumption started to decline for the first time since the war and post-war years. The precise moment of the trend change is difficult to pinpoint because it is only from 1987 that we can have estimates of consumption outside the home to add to estimates of domestic consumption. Nevertheless, these data suggest that consumption outside the home is likely to play a modest role in our story: its proportion within total dairy consumption tended to increase in the two decades leading up to the Great Recession that began in 2008, but it barely exceeded 15 per cent, and post-recession, it rapidly declined.

Aggregated data conceal the deployment of successive life cycles of individual products (Figure 3.2). The beginning of our period was a break not only from the decline in consumption that had occurred in the war and post-war years

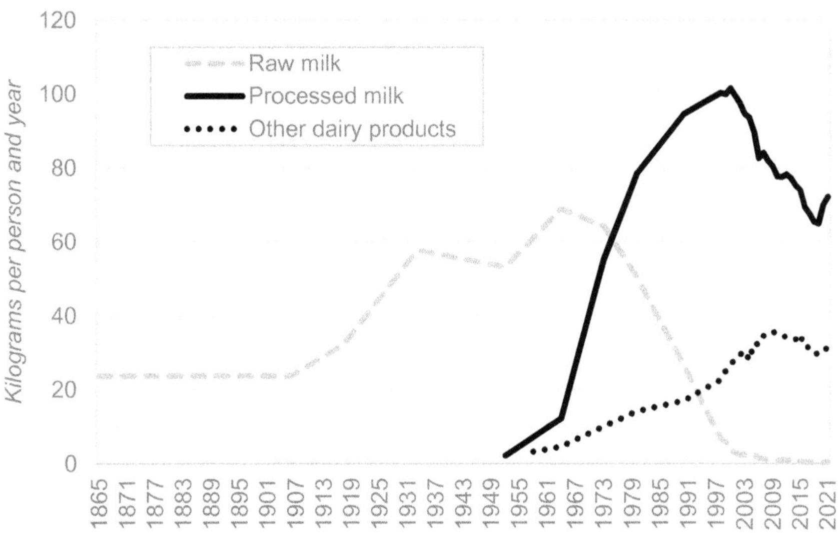

Figure 3.2 Three waves of expansion in dairy consumption, 1865–2021.
Sources: 1865–1935: Hernández Adell (2012: 190); 1950–2020: Collantes (2015), updated with INE (2023a). See Appendix Table A4.

but also from the type of expansive wave witnessed in the early decades of the twentieth century. This wave had been based on raw milk, but the new wave taking shape from 1950, and especially from the following decade, was led by processed milk. In turn, the rupture at the end of the twentieth century was not only in the aggregate trend but also in the composition of the dairy basket. The cycle of processed milk exhausted itself and dominates the aggregate trend, but simultaneously, there was a notable increase in the consumption of cheese, yogurt, and other dairy products such as shakes, and ice cream. Although this third wave of expansion never compensated for the contraction in milk consumption and has even shown signs of exhaustion in recent years, it undoubtedly deserves our attention.

The breakdown by consumer profiles also reveals a rupture in the final stretch of the twentieth century (Figure 3.3). During the first part of our period, the trend was towards equality. Still around 1965, there were significant social and territorial differences in milk consumption, which was higher among the upper classes and in a few regions with Atlantic climates in the northern part of the country. This inequality was undoubtedly not as pronounced as what had been recorded a generation earlier, at the beginning of the diffusion of milk in the diet (Hernández Adell, 2012: 201), but it remained very significant. By the 1980s, in contrast, milk consumption had become similar across different

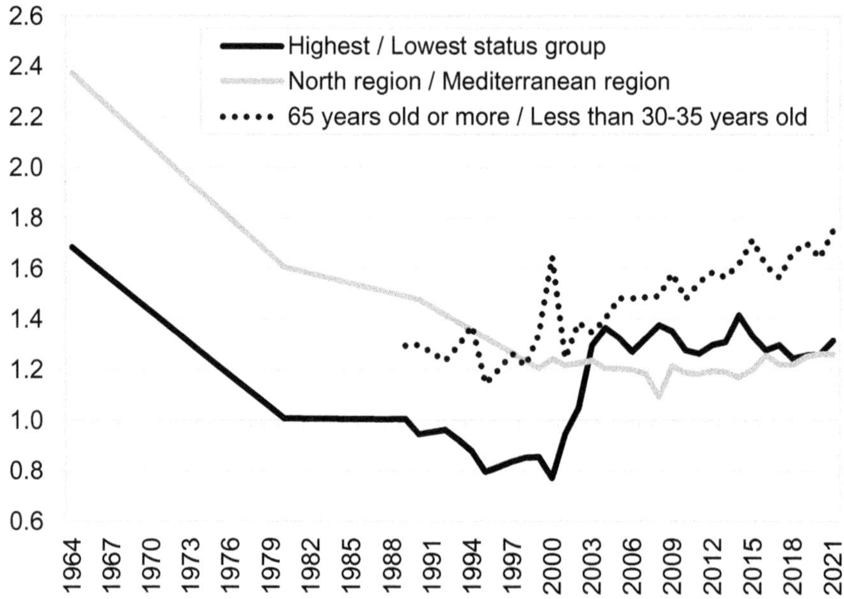

Figure 3.3 Differences in dairy consumption between consumer profiles, 1964–2021. *Sources:* Collantes (2015), updated with MAPA (2023a). The highest and lowest status groups are the highest and lowest quartiles, respectively. North region: Asturias, Basque Country, Cantabria, and Galicia; Mediterranean region: Balearic Islands, Catalonia, Murcia, and Valencian Community. Age refers to the household member in charge of purchasing food and drink. See Appendix Table A5.

strata of the social ladder. Regional differences had also softened considerably. In the final stretch of the twentieth century, however, as the milk cycle gave way to that of dairy products, the consumption pattern re-hierarchized. It was the upper classes that led the transition towards a dairy consumption more oriented towards cheese, yogurts, and other fresh desserts. Although, over time, the middle and even lower classes also made transitions in that direction, there remained a noticeable social gradient. Another significant factor of consumer segmentation, age, also tended to intensify in this period, as the gap between households of older individuals and young households widened. Territorial gaps, on the other hand, did not become as pronounced as those in the previous period, but it is interesting to note that regional convergence halted.

These Spanish trends fit well with what was happening simultaneously in other Western countries, but two particularities are still noticeable (Collantes, 2015). The first is that the chronology of the Spanish waves of dairy change was notably delayed. By around 1980, when milk had finally become a mass-consumed food in Spain, it had been so for decades in other countries in Atlantic Europe and

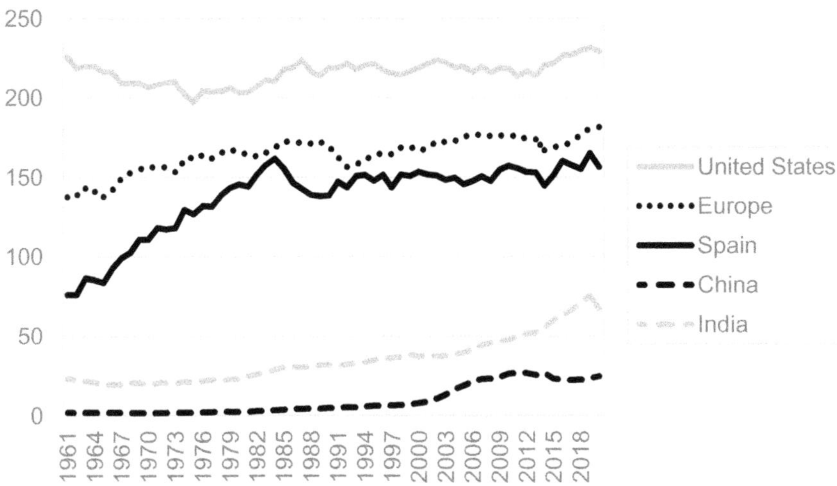

Figure 3.4 Apparent consumption of milk and dairy products (equivalent kilograms per person and year), 1961–2020.
Source: FAO (2023). The current methodology, starting in 2010, has been retained. Data taken from the old methodology have been corrected according to the average of the deviations observed for the period 2010–13, in which data from both methodologies are available. See Appendix Table A6.

North America. However, Spain, despite being late, went through stages at an extraordinary speed (Figure 3.4). Nowhere else did such rapid and widespread growth in milk consumption occur as in Spain between approximately 1965 and 1980. Partly because of this, the rupture towards the second consumption model did not occur much later than in other countries and, certainly, generated a much more abrupt contrast in Spain.

A second particularity of the Spanish case is that, although its trends were similar to those of other countries, the levels on which these trends unfolded were much lower. This aligns well with some historians' recent emphasis on the existence of differentiated variants of dietary change in different countries and regions (Langthaler, 2018; Pujol and Cussó, 2014). Spain started from a level of dairy consumption that was clearly lower than that typical in Atlantic Europe or North America. It tended to converge later, but, by the time its rapid growth phase ended around 1980, the latter had barely lasted a decade and a half. Consequently, Spain's convergence was incomplete. From the late twentieth century onwards, as we have seen, Spain experienced the same type of decline in aggregate dairy consumption as in other countries, so the gap persisted. It is true that, for reasons that have not yet been systematically analysed, this is something that indirect consumption estimates such as those presented in

Figure 3.4 do not capture well. Indirect estimates produced by the FAO from production and trade data consistently offer higher figures than direct estimates based on national sources on food purchases by consumers themselves, probably because they incorporate losses and waste accumulated throughout the entire production chain, as well as dairy products used as secondary ingredients in the manufacturing of other types of processed foods. Once we extract these effects, we find the type of decline described at the beginning of the chapter.

Dairy consumption and the good diet

There is no unanimity among biomedical researchers regarding the recommended level of dairy consumption. In fact, dairy products are one of the food groups whose position is most variable in official dietary guidelines in the Global North when comparing different historical periods or countries (Aranceta et al., 2019: 5; Comité Científico AESAN, 2020). Advocates of dairy emphasize its contribution to nutrition in terms of calories, proteins, vitamins (A and D), and especially calcium. They recommend a daily intake ranging from two to three–four servings, where one serving equals a cup of 225 millilitres of milk, 70 grams of fresh cheese, 35 grams of aged cheese, or 125 grams of yogurt (Comité Científico AESAN, 2020; Valero et al., 2020). Sceptics, on the other hand, argue that this recommendation, prevalent throughout the West for much of the twentieth century and still present in many countries, including Spain, exaggerates the benefits of dairy. Their reading of the evidence leads them to propose a range of one–two servings per day (Willet et al., 2019).

Throughout the rest of the book, we will retain the reference of two servings per day, which represents the intersection between the lower limit of one range and the upper limit of the other. Alongside this reference of two servings, we will also consider a slightly lower one, at 1.5 servings. This is motivated by our desire not to make our argument dependent on an overly stringent definition of what a good diet is. History teaches us that more than a few malnutrition claims made in twentieth-century societies were based on exaggerated dietary references, more focused on maximizing nutritional values than on identifying sufficiently good diets (Levenstein, 2003). We also want to avoid making our argument vulnerable to a long-debated issue among specialists: the distinction between calcium ingested with the diet and calcium absorbed by the body. This is particularly important in Mediterranean countries like Spain, where high sun exposure would lead to more efficient calcium absorption than in, for example, Nordic countries.

We will establish differentiated references based on age. The Spanish Nutrition Foundation (*Fundación Española de la Nutrición*) sets a range of two–three servings for the adult population but suggests it should increase to three servings for children and four for adolescents (Valero et al., 2020). These proportions will be applied to our range of 1.5–2 servings, so the average recommendation will not remain constant over time but will change as the age composition of the Spanish population changes.

The results indicate that the first model of dairy consumption tended to improve the nutritional health of Spaniards, while the second model tended to worsen it (Figure 3.5). Around 1950, the average Spaniard was well below the recommended intake. Given the level of social inequality in milk consumption, most Spaniards were significantly below that average. In a country emerging from post-war hunger, the deficiency of proteins, vitamins, and calcium remained a persistent problem. Calcium deficiency, in particular, affected most families and was widespread across almost all regions of the country (Casares, 1958; Cussó, 2001: ch. 7). By 1965, when milk consumption was still low, calcium deficiency had likely become the most notable deficiency in a diet that,

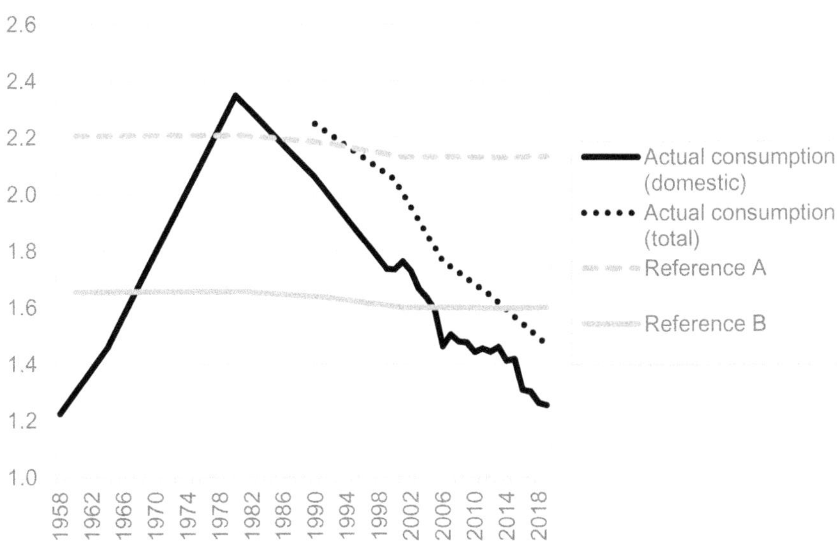

Figure 3.5 Dairy servings per person and day, 1958–2019.
Sources: Consumption: INE (1959, 1965–95, 2023a), MAPA (1988–91, 1992–2006, 2023a); references A and B: Valero et al. (2020) and Willet et al. (2019), adapted to age structures with INE (2023b). See Appendix Table A7.

otherwise, had completed most of the classical nutritional transition. A move towards widespread consumption of milk, supported by modest supplementary portions of powdered milk (reconstituted at home with water), cheese, and simple yogurts, addressed this issue. Between approximately 1980 and 2000, the average Spaniard managed to stay within the recommended consumption range.

However, this was short-lived: the subsequent decline in dairy consumption pushed the average Spaniard out of that range again. The key factor here was the decrease in milk consumption, only partially compensated by additional servings of cheese or yogurt. This resulted in a significant portion of the Spanish population once again facing a calcium deficiency problem. We should interpret Figure 3.6 with caution, as it is based on a demanding dietary reference – a recommended calcium intake that falls on the higher end of proposals by nutritionists and applies equally to all countries, regardless of their varying degrees of sun exposure. What is more relevant in this figure is the extent to which dairy consumption predicts calcium intake. In other words, although other foods also contain calcium, the calcium intake of Spaniards is closely linked to dairy consumption. As Spanish nutritionist Rosa María Ortega (2020: 9–10) puts it, it is easier to consume a glass of milk every day than 240 grams of chard or 80 grams of canned sardines. Consequently, those segments of the population consuming fewer dairy products are at a higher risk of calcium deficiency. According to the demanding reference in the figure, this problem would affect no less than three-quarters of the Spanish population today. Even with very undemanding references, it would still be a quarter of the population.

Additionally, we need to consider another issue in recent trends: the growing prevalence of ultra-processed products in the dairy basket. According to the increasingly influential NOVA classification created by nutritionist Carlos Augusto Monteiro, ultra-processed foods are 'formulations of ingredients, mostly of exclusive industrial use, typically created through a series of industrial techniques and processes' (Monteiro et al., 2019: 8). The NOVA scale starts with natural or minimally processed foods, followed by 'processed culinary ingredients', then processed foods, and finally ultra-processed foods. The latter have faced increasingly strong criticism from scientists, who accuse them of severely deteriorating nutritional health because of their contribution to excess intakes of energy, fats, sugars, salt, and other additives. Some dairy products, such as plain milk and yogurt without added sugars, fall into the first category of the NOVA classification, while others, such as butter and simple varieties of cheese, fall into the second and third categories, respectively. However, a significant portion of the most popular dairy products in recent times, especially

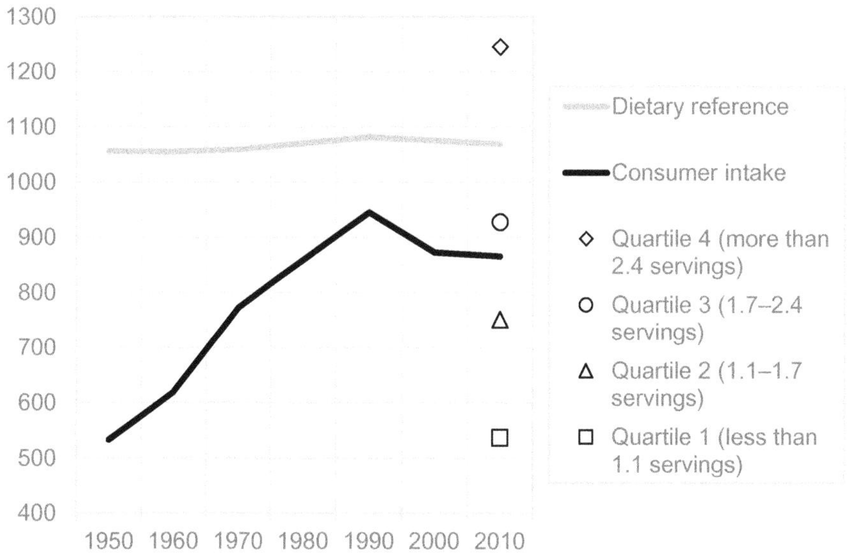

Figure 3.6 Dietary calcium intake: Recommended, observed, and disaggregated by quartiles of dairy consumption, 1950–2010.
Sources: Dietary reference and consumer intake: Cussó et al. (2018: 14–15); quartiles of dairy consumption: Valero et al. (2020: 51), scaled to the average level reported by Cussó et al. See Appendix Table A8.

many yogurts and desserts, belong to the fourth category of ultra-processed products (Sánchez Perona, 2022).

This implies that, while the first model of dairy consumption revolved around natural or minimally processed foods, the second model has largely revolved around ultra-processed foods (Figure 3.7). A common criticism levelled by nutritionists against ultra-processed dairy is that any potential nutritional benefits from their milk content are more than offset by the adverse effects of their sugar content (Popkin, 2009: 48). Data from the Spanish Association of Manufacturers of Yogurt and Fresh Dairy Desserts acknowledge that consuming a yogurt already represents almost half of the sugar level that the World Health Organization recommends not exceeding in a day ('La realidad', 2018: 5).

If we evaluate dairy consumption from a socio-economic perspective, we also find a rupture: the emergence and consolidation of 'surplus spending'. As discussed in Chapter 2, this refers to spending that exceeds what is necessary to ensure a nutritionally adequate basket. But how do we define such a basket? One option, inspired by Stigler's (1945) efforts to identify the cost of a 'minimum diet', is to define it in purely biologically terms: take the midpoint of

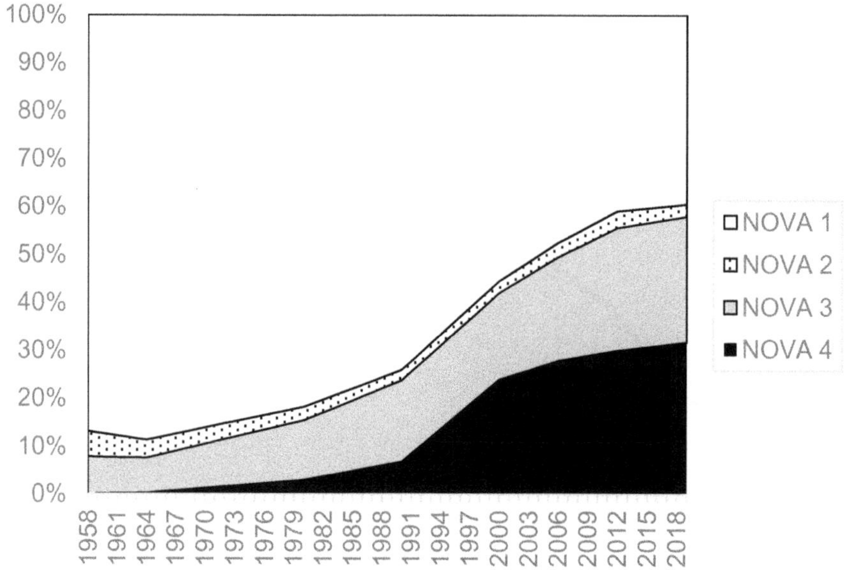

Figure 3.7 Composition of the dairy basket according to NOVA categories (energy intake shares).

Source: INE (1959, 1965–95, 2023a). NOVA 1: Unprocessed and minimally processed foods; NOVA 2: processed culinary ingredients; NOVA 3: processed foods; NOVA 4: ultra-processed foods. For more details about the NOVA classification, see Monteiro et al. (2019). See Appendix Table A9.

our range of 1.5–2 servings (adjusted for the changing age composition of the population) and calculate, for each date in our analysis, how much money the consumer would have needed to access these 1.5–2 servings in the cheapest possible way. This leads to a calculation on the cost of drinking 1.75 cups of 250 millilitres of milk each day of the year. Any spending beyond this is considered surplus spending. Another option, which we find more interesting, is to take the basic dairy basket that prevailed in 1990, that is, at the dividing point between both models of consumption. As seen, the 1990 pattern can be considered nutritionally adequate, and compared to the other alternative, it has the advantage of leading to an estimation of surplus spending that is not based on a comparison with a basic basket that only exists in the researcher's mind but with a basic basket that actually existed and was widespread at a certain point in the past. In this basic basket, some leeway is given for milk, the product that allows compliance with nutritionists' recommendations in the most economical way, to be accompanied by modest supplements of dairy products, such as cheese and simple yogurts.

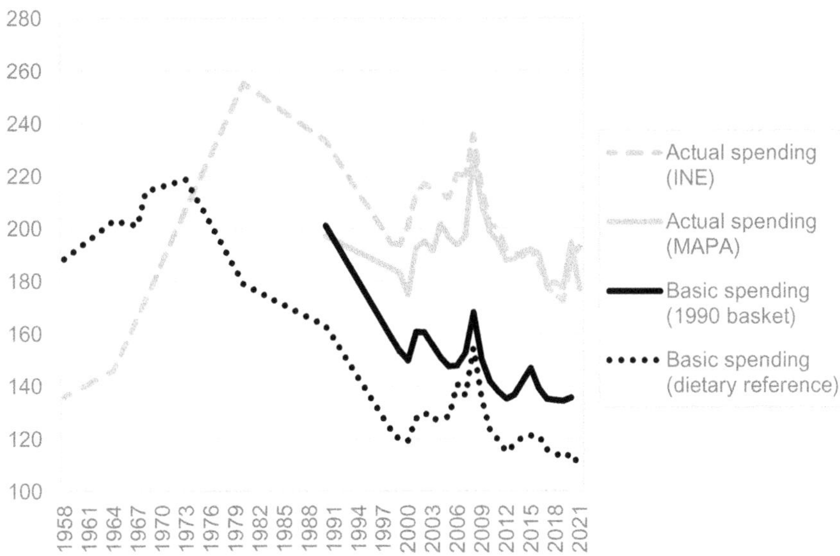

Figure 3.8 Consumer domestic spending on dairy products, 1958–2021: Actual and 'basic' (constant 2019 euros per person and year).
Sources: Nominal spending: INE (1959, 1965–95, 2023a), MAPA (1988–91, 1992–2006, 2023a); deflator: INE (2023c). Dietary reference is the average of references A and B in Figure 3.5. See Appendix Table A10.

The results are, however, similar with either basic basket (Figure 3.8). Initially, consumers did not spend enough to ensure the basic basket. By the final stretch of the twentieth century, the consumer made such expenditure, but not much more. In the last three decades, however, a striking gap has opened up between the actual level of spending and the level that would be sufficient to ensure a basic basket. The period between 1990 and the Great Recession was particularly significant for the emergence and consolidation of this surplus spending. At its peak, more than a quarter of dairy spending was, in fact, surplus spending, and this is still a conservative estimate (Figure 3.9). What had been a reasonably efficient consumer in converting money into nutritional values gradually became an inefficient consumer who, despite mobilizing more resources than in the past towards the purchase of dairy, was now unable to ensure such values. A product breakdown reveals that the core of this inefficiency was in the growing consumption of yogurts, other fresh desserts, and, in general, ultra-processed products with high prices per serving.

Even though the evidence is fragmentary, it seems clear that neither of the two social missions that could most embody what we have called a 'Mazzucato path', organic food and heritage food, channelled a significant fraction of this

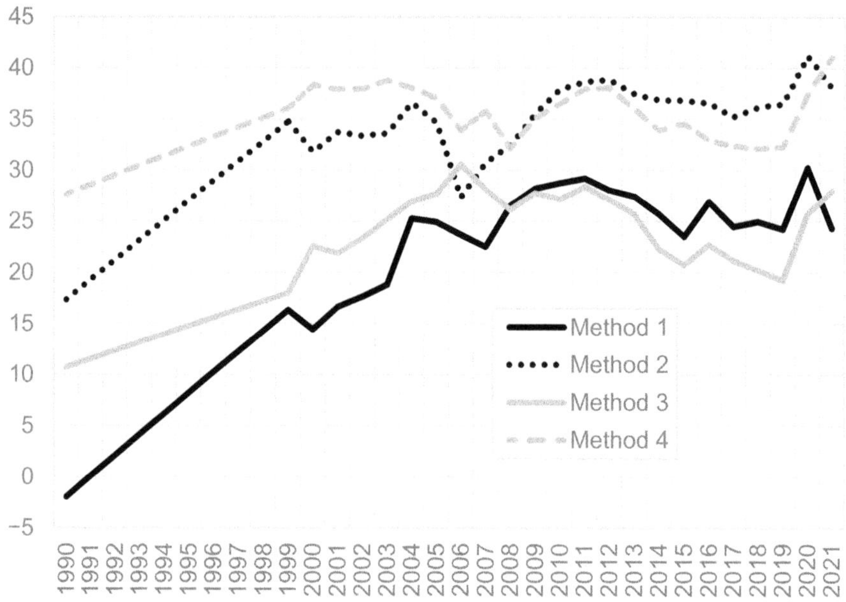

Figure 3.9 Surplus spending as a percentage of total dairy spending: Alternative methods of calculation.
Method 1: Total spending: MAPA; basic spending: 1990 basket.
Method 2: Total spending: MAPA; basic spending: dietary reference.
Method 3: Total spending: INE; basic spending: 1990 basket.
Method 4: Total spending: INE; basic spending: dietary reference.
Source: Figure 3.8. See Appendix Table A11.

surplus spending (Table 3.1). When the Food Consumption Panel started reporting about organic milk in 2021, it was found that the market share of organic milk was lower than 1 per cent. The most important heritage dairy food, cheese with protected designation of origin (henceforth, PDO cheese), was also marginal. Although the number of designations climbed up to almost thirty, even an upward-biased estimation such as the one presented in Table 3.1 gives them not more than a joint 5–6 per cent share of the total cheese market. Most Spanish consumers were so uninterested that the producers of PDO cheese became increasingly oriented towards export markets, whose share in total sales rose from 21 to 42 per cent between 2000 and 2016 (MAPA, 2018: 27). Consumers moved away from the 'Keynes situation' to something more akin to the 'Galbraith path' than to the 'Mazzucato path'.

The nutritional problems identified at the beginning and end of the period affected a broad majority of Spanish society, but more severely as we descended the social pyramid. Even around 1965, milk consumption

Table 3.1 Market Share of Organic Milk and Cheese with Protected Designation of Origin

Product	Metric	Market share (%)			
		2000	**2012**	**2016**	**2021**
Organic milk	Kilograms				0.6
PDO cheese	Euros	5.5	5.3	6.2	

Source: MAPA (2018, 2023a). The estimation for PDO cheese is biased upwards because it considers all sales made by producers but only the total home consumption of cheese. Because the average price of PDO cheese was substantially higher than that of conventional cheese, a physical metric of its market share would also lead to lower figures.

remained highly segmented by social class, with lower-middle and lower classes being the farthest from nutritionists' recommendations. Mass consumption made it possible for all social strata, with no significant differences between them, to eventually align with these recommendations. However, the resurgence of under-consumption in the twenty-first century was concentrated again in the lower classes. Although dairy consumption contracted in all social strata, it did so to a lesser extent among the upper and upper-middle classes, which deviated less from the zone recommended by nutritionists. Furthermore, although we lack specific data on dairy in this regard, it is plausible to think that the higher prevalence of eating out among the upper classes (Rama, 1997) widened the gap even more with the lower classes. These results confirm the contrast between a first model of consumption that improved nutritional health and social equality and a second model with opposite implications.

Just as nutritional problems tended to hit the lower classes especially, the rise of dubious surplus spending was particularly visible among the upper classes. They were the ones who quickly, from the 1990s onwards, led the way in spending beyond what would have been necessary to ensure a basic basket (Figure 3.10). The middle classes joined somewhat less vigorously, but they clearly participated in the trend and intensified their surplus spending in the years leading up to the Great Recession. The lower class, on the other hand, remained on the sidelines in the 1990s. Nevertheless, around the turn of the millennium, even the lower class began to make some surplus spending, and the latter continued to increase during the toughest years of the Great Recession. Even after the adjustments that followed the recession, again led by the upper class, surplus spending was especially striking as we ascended the social pyramid, and yet noticeable in all social strata.

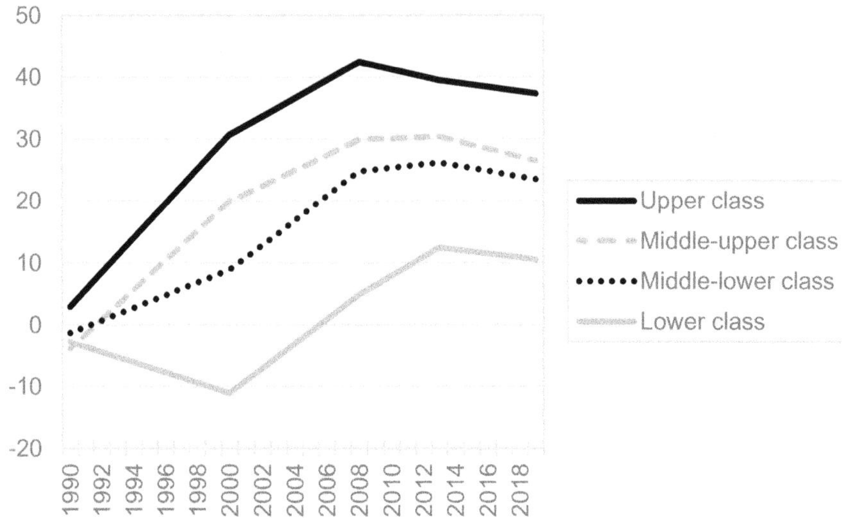

Figure 3.10 Surplus spending on milk and dairy products (method 1) by social class (%).
Source: MAPA (1988–91, 2023a). See Appendix Table A12.

Two protagonists

The longitudinal analysis conducted in the preceding sections reveals the emergence of two major protagonists in our narrative. These protagonists are not individual consumers but rather models of dairy consumption, each characterized by distinct features and implications. It is pertinent to chronologically integrate the contrast between them before delving into their analysis.

Our first protagonist, the dairy consumption model of 1950–90, shows a reasonably benign profile. Around 1950, dairy products had a small presence in the Spanish diet. The average Spaniard fell below the nutritionists' recommended intake and, given the level of social inequality in milk consumption, a significant portion of the Spanish population lagged below this average. Calcium deficiency was a notable and widespread nutritional health issue in the country. Despite the introduction of liquid milk into the diet in the early twentieth century, substantial segments of the population either did not consume milk regularly or did so in minimal quantities. These pockets of under-consumption were concentrated among the lower and lower-middle classes, especially in regions like the Mediterranean coast and Andalusia. Unlike other Mediterranean countries such as Italy or Greece, where milk consumption was also lower than in the rest of Western Europe, the compensation through alternative dairy

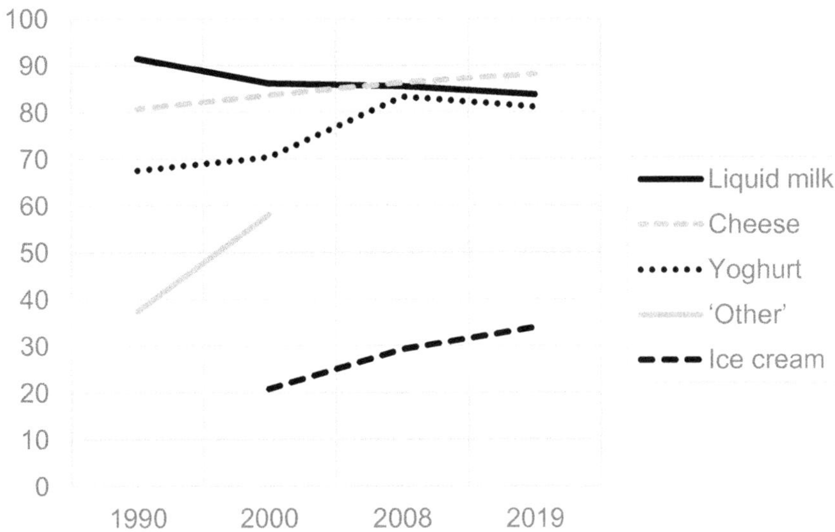

Figure 3.11 Percentage of households that purchase milk and dairy products.
Source: MAPA (1988–91, 2023a). See Appendix Table A13.

products like cheese and yogurt was relatively insignificant in Spain (Collantes, 2015; Hernández Adell et al., 2019).

The consumption model deployed between approximately 1950 and 1990 corrected this problem. Its trajectory was driven by milk consumption, especially processed milk. While the hitherto dominant raw milk was relegated to marginal niches, processed milk turned populations that were previously non-consumers into regular consumers. With over 90 percent of households regularly consuming milk (Figure 3.11), we can borrow from Moser and Brodbeck's (2007) work on Switzerland to describe this era as the 'milk for everyone' period.

By 1990, widespread milk consumption had enabled a broad majority of Spaniards to align with the nutritionists' recommendations regarding dairy and calcium. Considering these recommendations as reference ranges rather than discrete thresholds, the dairy consumption pattern of Spaniards was generally satisfactory. The number of servings consumed was close to the recommended levels, and, given that Spaniards are more exposed to sunlight than other Europeans, they were probably more efficient in absorbing their diet-related calcium. Biological indicators of well-being, such as height, had significantly improved (Martínez Carrión, 2016). The essentially satisfactory nature of the dairy consumption pattern around 1990 was further confirmed by its orientation towards minimally processed foods, such as liquid milk, traditional varieties of cheese, and plain yogurts.

Signs of exhaustion of this consumption model began to manifest around 1990, combined with indicators hinting at the possible rise of a new model. This new model, the second major protagonist of our narrative, effectively took shape in the 1990s and extends to the present day. The model comprised two trends: a nutritional trend towards the contraction of dairy consumption and a socio-economic trend towards its sophistication. The key to the contraction was the increasing abandonment, either totally or partially, of the product that had hitherto been relied upon to a greater extent: liquid milk. While consumers also incorporated increasing quantities of cheese, yogurt, and other dairy desserts, products that were among those whose consumption grew more rapidly during these years along with prepared dishes, juices, and sodas (Langreo and Germán, 2018: 191–2), this was insufficient to prevent most Spaniards from falling outside the dairy consumption bands recommended by nutritionists. This problem rapidly and profoundly affected the lower classes but soon spread upwards through the social hierarchy. In an era where nutritional health problems were increasingly associated with excesses, a classic scarcity problem such as calcium deficiency re-emerged. Furthermore, the new consumption pattern that was consolidating also contributed to another trend identified by nutritionists as problematic in the evolution of the Spanish and Western diet: the growing dependence on ultra-processed foods. While all Western countries recorded similar trends, the Spanish dairy basket shifted in a particularly intense way towards refrigerated desserts and to a lesser extent towards simpler dairy products like cheese (Langreo, 2005).

This, in turn, leads us to the sophistication of the new dairy consumption model. From a socio-economic perspective, the crux was that consumers were reorienting their pattern from whole milk, supplemented with modest amounts of dairy products, towards a variety of more complex dairy products that they considered superior and were willing to pay higher prices for. The time had come for 'surplus spending' that would go beyond the basic consumption basket already achieved by 1990. Surplus spending, however, was channelled to a limited extent towards relevant social missions, such as substituting conventional industrial dairy products with ecological and short-chain alternatives, or alternatives that embodied a commitment to the preservation and revitalization of local food heritage. These were, so to speak, loose ends from the mass consumption model of the previous period: perhaps secondary at the time in relation to improving the nutritional health of the population, but with the potential now to guide a new consumption model towards new objectives. This was not the case, and surplus spending actually allowed consumers to access a dairy basket that was not even capable of maintaining the nutritional achievements of the previous period. Our second historical protagonist illustrates well the nutritional and socio-economic dimensions of the return of bad diets to affluent societies.

Conclusion: A 'fundamental break with the past'

Spanish dairy consumption illustrates the 'fundamental break with the past' that geographer David Grigg (1999: 11) identified in the recent history of diets: the rupture between the consumption model of the decades following the Second World War and the model that began to take shape in the final stretch of the twentieth century and extends to the present day. Precisely because dairy consumption was initially low in Spain and its diffusion took place later than in other European countries, the move towards massive milk consumption was something like the closing chapter in Spain's history of escaping hunger and classical malnutrition. However, while the dairy world travelled at the tail end of the nutritional transition, it was at the forefront of the subsequent model of food consumption. This makes the contrast between the two food consumption models sharper than in other countries with an earlier tradition of both sustained economic growth and mass dairy consumption.

How could a dynamic that had improved nutritional health lead to another that facilitated the return of bad diets? We will study now the history of our two protagonists. Our goal is not to produce a commodity biography, in the style popularized by anthropologist Sidney Mintz (1985) on sugar and cultivated by various researchers since then. In the case of milk, we have comprehensive studies of this type with interests ranging from technological aspects (Atkins, 2010) to environmental considerations (Smith-Howard, 2014), encompassing global perspectives (Valenze, 2011), anthropobiological aspects (Wiley, 2011), and the historical sociology perspective (DuPuis, 2002). We will simply take milk and dairy products as a study case to address the considerable empirical challenges we face in better understanding the transformation of diets in Spain and the West, with the hope that this may also open the door to future research that incorporates more products and countries into the analysis.

Part II

The Mass Consumption Model (1950–90)

4

Massification

'Unfortunately,' pointed out Juan Manuel Palacios (1968: 77), director of the EDALNU programme for education in food and nutrition, still at the end of the 1960s, 'in Spain, little milk is consumed, especially in some regions and among the less affluent classes.' This part of the book is devoted to the study of the historical trend that changed this situation and made mass milk consumption possible between 1950 and 1990. We begin with a structural, statistical chapter, and then we will have two conjunctural chapters based on qualitative material. To a considerable extent, this chapter aspires only to present a deliberately concise skeleton of the argument that, in a more contextualized manner, will be constructed in the following two chapters.

Going massive

The key driver of the dairy consumption model that unfolded in Spain between 1950 and 1990 was the extraordinary increase in the consumption of liquid milk (Table 4.1). The best way to view this increase is as a process of massification through which a food item that was not firmly embedded in the diet of much of the population became so. Massification had a social dimension, as at the beginning of the period only the upper classes engaged in regular milk consumption that was in line with nutritional recommendations. Outside this small world of entrepreneurs, landowners, or highly qualified professionals, milk was infrequent in the diet of peasants and workers. As a paediatrician summarized on a television programme of the time, 'milk in Spain is a luxury food, used only by wealthy people' ('Leche', 1958: 196). By 1990, however, even among lower-status groups, now mainly composed of the less qualified working class, milk had become a common part of the daily diet. There were still some class differences in the composition of the dairy basket, with the lower classes

Table 4.1 Domestic Consumption of Milk and Dairy Products Per Person and Year

	1958	1964/5	1980/1	1990/1
Consumption				
Liquid milk (L)	77.9	78.7	125.1	117.6
Canned milk (kg)	1.2[a]	2.8	3.7	1.8
Cheese (kg)	1.5	1.5	4.3	5.7
Butter (kg)	0.5	0.4	0.4	0.3
Yogurt (kg)			5.7	7.6
Other (kg)				1.6
Share of consumer spending on dairy (%)				
Liquid milk	70	71	57	54
Canned milk	9	9	8	6
Cheese	15	14	22	26
Butter	6	4	2	1
Yogurt			9	11
Other		2	2	2
Total	100	100	100	100

Note: [a]Only condensed milk.
Source: INE (1959, 1965–95).

relying more on raw milk and less on processed milk, and the upper classes buying a somewhat more varied basket. But, compared to the social gap of 1950, which had profound implications for nutritional health, the gap in 1990 was insignificant (Table 4.2).

Massification also had a territorial dimension. At the beginning of the period, only a small strip of northern, Atlantic climate regions showed levels of consumption in line with nutritional recommendations (Table 4.3). In these regions, class differences did not weigh much, and milk consumption was widely spread among the population. So much so that, in fact, even by 1965, the consumption level in this northern region was clearly higher than that of the upper classes in the country taken as a whole. Outside the north, however, large pockets of the population either did not consume milk regularly or did so to a limited extent. It is interesting to note that these pockets could be found not only in poor regions with an agrarian economy and rural settlement, such as Andalusia, but also in rich regions with a strong industrial presence and dense city systems, such as Catalonia. The incorporation of these diverse regions

Table 4.2 Domestic Dairy Consumption Per Person and Year (kg), by Social Class

	Upper	Middle-upper	Middle-lower	Lower	Total
1964/5					
Liquid milk	101.6	85.2	67.6	60.4	81.1
Cheese	1.9	1.6	1.2	1.0	1.5
1980/1					
Liquid milk	130.2	130.4	124.8	129.7	128.9
Preserved milk	2.9	3.5	4.1	4.8	3.7
Cheese	4.9	4.2	4.2	3.8	4.3
Yogurt	5.5	6.4	6.0	4.6	5.7
1990/1					
Liquid milk	111.0	120.7	125.6	133.3	121.1
Preserved milk	1.5	1.5	2.1	2.4	1.8
Cheese	5.9	5.6	5.8	5.3	5.7
Yogurt and other	9.0	9.0	9.6	9.0	9.1

Source: INE (1959, 1965–95).

Table 4.3 Domestic Dairy Consumption Per Person and Year (kg), by Region

	North	Interior	Mediterranean	Andalusia	Total
1964/5					
Liquid milk	142.3	86.9	51.6	53.6	81.1
Canned milk	0.6	1.3	6.2	2.3	2.8
Cheese	1.4	1.2	2.1	1.1	1.5
1980/1					
Liquid milk	172.8	145.9	99.7	123.1	128.9
Canned milk	1.0	2.3	4.1	3.7	3.7
Cheese	5.0	4.0	4.5	3.5	4.3
Yogurt	4.5	5.0	5.7	7.8	5.7
1990/1					
Liquid milk	153.1	132.5	99.3	117.5	121.1
Canned milk	0.7	1.3	1.8	1.7	1.8
Cheese	6.3	5.0	6.2	4.8	5.7
Yogurt and other	9.8	7.5	8.4	11.6	9.1

Source: INE (1959, 1965–95). North: Asturias, Basque Country, Cantabria, and Galicia; Interior: Aragón, Castile and León, Castile-La Mancha, Extremadura, La Rioja, Madrid, and Navarre; Mediterranean: Balearic Islands, Catalonia, Murcia, and Valencian Community.

into regular milk consumption was crucial for the rapid increase in average consumption in Spain. By 1990, the footprint of these regional gaps was still present, and milk consumption was somewhat higher in the north than in the extensive Mediterranean region stretching from Catalonia to Murcia, including the Valencian Community and the Balearic Islands. However, these were much smaller gaps and lacked the relevance they once had for nutritional health.

In addition to these social and territorial dimensions, massification also had an important technical dimension. Although we have only talked about liquid milk so far, it has to be noted that the milk Spaniards consumed in 1990 was very different from what they had consumed in 1950. In 1950, around 95 per cent of the milk consumed was raw, meaning consumers drank exactly the same liquid that had come out of the cow's udder. By 1990, around 80 per cent of the milk consumed by Spaniards was processed milk. Initially, the rise of processed milk was led by pasteurized milk, but later, from around 1970 onwards, sterilized or UHT processed milk ('ultra-high temperature') began to prevail. The engine of the great expansion of milk consumption was, therefore, not the type of natural food that had been dominant until then, but a processed and standardized food, subjected to heat treatment and other possible transformations (e.g. homogenization of fat in the case of UHT milk). Mass consumption and mass production went hand in hand.

Although liquid milk was the centrepiece of the consumption model deployed between 1950 and 1990, other dairy products also played complementary roles of some importance. Especially during the first part of the period, consumers turned to different types of canned milk to complement their consumption of liquid milk. Condensed milk and powdered milk were the most important. Both canned milks could be 'reconstituted' by adding hot water, producing a liquid that still bore some resemblance to liquid milk. As the period progressed, consumers also incorporated increasing amounts of cheese into their diet. The most common cheese was what, somewhat imprecisely, was called *Manchego*, referring to the extensive region of Castile-La Mancha (south of Madrid) and its tradition of making cured cheeses from sheep's milk. However, most of the *Manchego* that reached the tables of Spaniards was a mixed cheese that combined variable proportions and types of sheep's, goat's, and cow's milk. All in all, the cheese landscape was quite fragmented, and consumers turned to a variety of local specialties. Finally, as the consumption of liquid milk was becoming massive, yogurt and other fresh desserts were also becoming moderately popular. At the beginning of the period, yogurt was more of a medicine for digestive pathologies that, as such, was bought in pharmacies. By 1990, it had become an everyday food. It was still a simple processed food, whose main varieties were natural yogurt, flavoured yogurt (especially strawberry-flavoured), and yogurt with pieces of fruit (e.g. peach). More elaborate fresh desserts began to spread, especially among higher-status groups. Some of them, such as flans and custards, were processed versions of dairy desserts that had a tradition of homemade preparation. Others, such as ice cream cakes, were industrially created foods. However, by 1990, their consumption level remained very moderate.

None of these dairy products had a truly outstanding level of consumption. Only in the very exceptional regional case of the Canary Islands did powdered milk play a central role in the massification of consumption. In general terms, the dairy basket of Spaniards was centred on liquid milk, whose remarkable expansion had allowed most consumers to align with nutritional recommendations. By 1990, in fact, Spain was one of the European countries with the highest consumption of liquid milk at a time when it had begun to decline in the United Kingdom, France, Germany, or Scandinavia (Collantes, 2014). Powdered milk, cheese, and yogurt accompanied this expansion, but their role was secondary.

The anatomy of mass consumption

The economic basis of growth in milk consumption was the extraordinary increase that took place in the purchasing power of Spanish households, shattering what had long been a severe budget constraint. At the beginning of the period, buying the basic dairy basket, reasonably aligned with nutritional recommendations, required a remarkable economic effort from the average Spanish household. Table 4.4 illustrates this, taking as the basic basket the dietary references established in the previous chapter, but also showing similar results if, instead, we take as the basic basket that which the average consumer reached in 1990. Buying a basic basket in the 1950s would have absorbed resources well above what households had the capacity to reasonably allocate to dairy. Even around 1965, we observe the severity of the budget constraint weighing on the broad populations of low consumers. To buy the basic basket that would become common just a quarter of a century later, households in the southern region would have had to spend almost 9 per cent of their income, and low-income households almost a (clearly) prohibitive 18 per cent. By 1990, however, accessing a basic dairy basket required households to spend little more than a perfectly manageable 2 or 2.5 per cent of their income. Even among low-income

Table 4.4 Share of Household Income Required to Purchase a Basic Dairy Basket (%)

	1958	1964	1980	1990
Dietary reference basket[a]				
Aggregate[b]	7.6[d]	6.6	2.8	1.9
By social class				
Upper class		3.4	1.8	1.0
Middle-upper class		6.0	3.0	1.9
Middle-lower class		9.3	4.0	2.6
Lower class		18.2	5.2	4.4
By region				
North		4.4	2.4	1.8
Interior		5.5	2.6	1.8
Mediterranean		6.7	2.7	1.9
Andalusia		8.6	3.6	2.5
Actual 1990 basket[c]				
Aggregate[b]		6.3	3.5	2.5

Notes: [a]Average of dietary references A and B, as defined in Chapter 3.
[b]Corrected by provincial differences in prices in 1964, 1980, and 1990 (not in 1958 due to lack of data).
[c]Without yogurt and 'other' dairy products in 1964 and without 'other' dairy products in 1980.
[d] Not corrected by provincial differences in prices and, therefore, biased downwards.
Sources: consumption, prices, and income in 1964–90: INE (1959, 1965–95); income in 1958: Carreras et al. (2005: 1372), interpolated and scaled to the 1964 level reported by INE (1965–95); deflator: INE (2023c).

households, the figure became already less than 5 per cent, quite close to what had been the required effort for affluent high-income households forty years earlier. The economic conditions had been created for all types of households to be able to buy dairy products regularly.

The other pillar of massification was the orientation that consumers showed in using these economic possibilities to buy more milk. This point is more complex than one might imagine: the evolution of the response factor, our statistical approach to consumer orientation, was remarkably volatile throughout the period (Table 4.5). We find nothing like an inherent characteristic of the product: more than a stable property, what we find is continuous change. Between 1958 and 1964, the response factor was very close to zero: despite the strengthening of their purchasing power, consumers decided not to buy much more milk. There is reason to believe that the figure would have been higher if we had data throughout the range from 1950 to 1964 (since consumption grew somewhat

Table 4.5 Consumption, Purchasing Power, and Consumer Response

	Annual compound rate of change (%)		**Response factor**[b]
	Consumption	**Purchasing power**[a]	
1958–64			
Milk	0.2	3.9	0.05
Cheese	0.1	5.4	0.01
1964–80			
Milk	2.9	5.3	0.56
Cheese	6.7	3.8	1.75
1980–90			
Milk	-0.6	3.1	-0.20
Cheese	2.8	4.4	0.63
Yogurt	2.9	4.4	0.65

Note: [a]$r\ (PP) = r\ (Y) - r\ (P)$, where r is annual compound rate of change, *PP* is purchasing power, *Y* is household income, and *P* is the nominal consumer price deflated by the general price index.

[b]$r\ (C)/r\ (PP)$, where r is annual compound rate of change, *C* is consumption, and *PP* is purchasing power.

Source: See Table 4.4.

more in the early years of the period), but even then it would have been a factor close to zero. It was nothing like the high value, close to two, calculated for the years before the Civil War, in the first wave of milk consumption diffusion in Spain (Collantes, 2017a).

If this consumer orientation had persisted in the following years, the massification of milk consumption would not have taken place. However, the response factor turned clearly positive between the mid-1960s and 1980: consumers were more inclined to use their increases in purchasing power to buy more milk. According to a complementary estimate, this reorientation was particularly pronounced between 1964 and 1973 (Collantes, 2019a). The reorientation was, in any case, brief. By the 1980s, the response factor entered negative territory: despite having seen an increase in their purchasing power, consumers not only did not continue to increase their milk purchases but even began to reduce them. This is a somewhat extreme view, which we should qualify to consider the more than likely increase that was simultaneously occurring in milk consumption outside the home. However, it is clear that the window of interest in dairy products that had opened in the mid-1960s began to close again in the 1980s.

The image provided by dairy products is intriguingly similar. The most important milk-based product was cheese, and it is actually the only one for which we have data that allow us to reconstruct the response factor of its consumption. In this case too, the first part of the period is characterized by a consumer who, despite seeing their purchasing power increase, does not buy more cheese. On the other hand, from approximately 1965 onwards, we perceive the deployment of a conventional life cycle, starting from a response factor that is quite high and then declining.

An important difference between cheese or yogurt, on the one hand, and milk, on the other hand, is that the life cycles of the former did not seem to be exhausted in any way by the 1980s. Both in the case of cheese and yogurt, the response factors were still comfortably above zero. Unlike what was beginning to happen with milk, consumers were still interested in channelling their increases in purchasing power towards buying more cheese and more yogurt. This would deeply mark the character of the new consumption model that would take shape during the 1990s.

But, returning to the massive model that unfolded between 1950 and 1990, we have identified the two central pieces of its anatomy: the softening of the budgetary constraint and the orientation of consumers towards milk. What was behind each of these two proximate causes?

A softer budget constraint

The increase in consumers' purchasing power was mainly a consequence of the rapid increase that took place in their income levels (Table 4.6). From the early 1950s onwards, the income of the average household grew very quickly. Despite some tendency towards deceleration, the underlying trend was clear growth in each of the three subperiods of our statistical analysis. By 1990, the average Spanish household had a significantly higher income level than four decades earlier. Furthermore, this average Spanish household was more than just a statistical abstraction. Around 1950, there was indeed a highly unequal income distribution. However, inequality moderated in the subsequent decades (Prados de la Escosura, 2008) and a middle-class society emerged. The lower classes saw their income grow at a rate that was actually well above the country's average. The rise in consumer income was widespread and opened up new consumption possibilities, including milk and dairy products, for all types of households.

Table 4.6 Decomposition of Growth in Purchasing Power

	Annual compound rate of change (%)			Contribution to growth (%)	
	Purchasing power	Household income[a]	Relative price[b]	Income[c]	Price[d]
1958–64					
Milk	3.9	5.2	1.2	133	−33
Cheese	5.4		−0.2	95	5
1964–80					
Milk	5.3	3.7	−1.6	70	30
Cheese	3.8		−0.1	96	4
1980–90					
Milk	3.1		−0.6	79	21
Cheese	4.4	2.5	−1.9	56	44
Yogurt	4.4		−1.9	56	44

Notes: [a]Per adult equivalent (Luxembourg scale).

[b]Corrected by provincial differences in prices in 1964–80 and 1980–90 (not in 1958–64 due to lack of data).

[c][*r* (*Y*)/*r* (*PP*)] * 100, where *r* is compound annual rate of change, *Y* is household income, and *PP* is purchasing power.

[d][−*r* (*P*)/*r* (*PP*)] * 100, where *r* is compound annual rate of change, *P* is relative price, and *PP* is purchasing power.

Source: See Table 4.4.

The growth of household income was the driving force behind the improvement in purchasing power, but its effect was complemented by the behaviour of consumer dairy prices. The data show that the relative price of milk followed a somewhat bell-shaped curve (Figure 4.1). Initially, in particular until the mid-1960s, the price of milk grew significantly more than the general price index, so that the purchasing power of consumers to buy milk did not actually grow as much as their income. Around the mid-1960s, the price of milk began to align more closely with the general price index and only grew slightly above it. Moreover, most of this differential is a statistical illusion resulting from the effect of incorporating new consumer segments in regions characterized by relatively high prices into regular milk consumption. Once we correct for this effect, the picture is one of relative stability. Lastly, during most of the 1970s and the entire 1980s, the relative price of milk clearly declined. This bell-shaped pattern implies that, just as at the beginning of the period the evolution of milk prices was offsetting part of the formidable increase in consumers' income levels, at the end it was a complementary source of increased purchasing power.

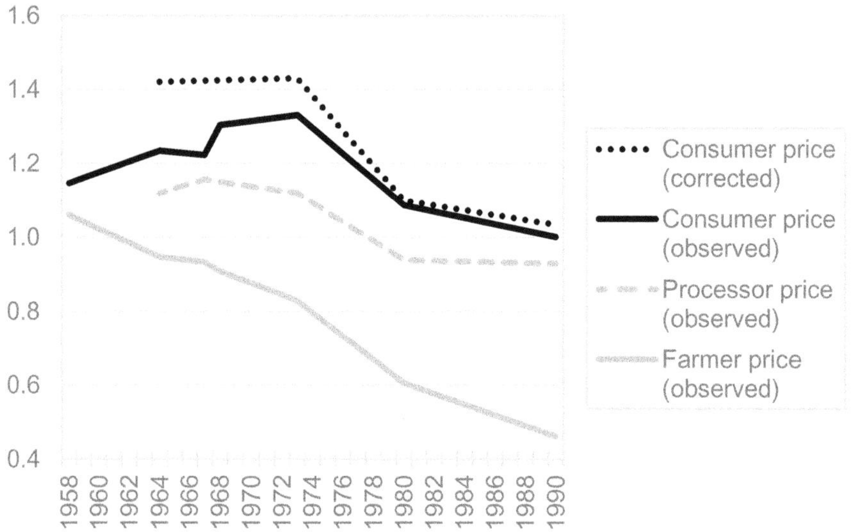

Figure 4.1 Milk prices (constant 2013 euros per litre), 1958–90.
Sources: Collantes (2017a: 135; 2019a: 964, 969). The 'corrected' consumer price is an average of province-level prices weighted by the population of each province, whereas 'observed' prices are unweighted national-level prices. See Appendix Table A14.

If we analyse the price transmission within the chain, the key to this bell-shaped evolution is not to be found in farming but lower down: in the processing and retailing links of the chain. After all, the price that farmers perceived for their sales of raw milk decreased steadily. If the price paid by consumers for their milk had depended only on that, it would have been declining since the beginning of the period. The bell-shaped form is more due to the widening gap between the price of milk (raw) received by the farmer and the price of milk (increasingly, processed milk) paid by the consumer. Although this may suggest notions of imperfect competition and market power on the part of industries or retailers, the fact that prices throughout the chain were influenced by state regulations compels us, for now, to be cautious. Let us retain an obvious reason for this widening: as consumers substituted raw milk for processed milk, the price they paid had to be sufficient to allow the economic reproduction of the new link in the chain. The costs and profits of processing were transmitted downwards along the chain, creating a kind of 'step' upwards in the evolution of the consumer price, at least until the substitution of raw milk for processed milk was completed. The dairy chain, with its growing production capacity, ended

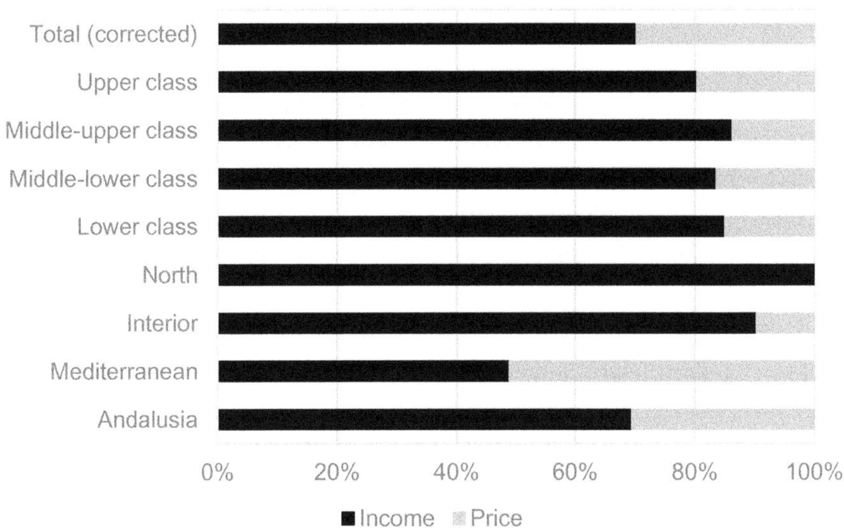

Figure 4.2 Relative contributions of income and price to increases in the purchasing power for milk (%), 1964–80.
Source: INE (1965–95, 2023c). See Appendix Table A15.

up generating price reductions for consumers, but it took some time to reach that point.

The evolution of milk prices was, therefore, a kind of late complement to the formidable increase taking place in consumers' income levels. Only in very specific regions and situations did it play a role comparable to this (Figure 4.2). For example, in some traditionally less-consuming areas, especially those in the Mediterranean, the relative price of milk had become so high by 1965 that its subsequent fall had an impact equivalent to the increase in disposable income.

The price histories of the dairy products that modestly accompanied milk in the formation of the new consumption pattern are similar. Purchasing power to buy cheese increased because household income did as well, and only in the 1980s did price reductions begin to play a notable role. In the case of yogurt, we can only reconstruct the calculation for the 1980s, and although we find that the product became substantially cheaper, the magnitude of the increase in household income was even greater. Canned milk does not even seem to have seen its relative price reduced, at least during the long period after the mid-1960s for which we have reliable information.

Responsive consumers

The volatility of the response factor in milk consumption is intriguing because it does not align well with a conventional product life cycle. Under conventional life cycles, products typically exhibit initially high response factors that gradually diminish over time. At the outset of the cycle, the product is novel, and as a result, its consumption has ample room for growth, often outpacing the purchasing power of consumers. However, as the cycle progresses, consumers lose interest in directing their increases in purchasing power towards a product that already holds a significant place in their shopping basket. By the end of the life cycle, consumers redirect their purchasing power increases towards other, more novel products, but not towards the initial product. The response factor tends to approach zero if consumers decide to keep their purchases of the product stable, or it may even become negative if consumers start abandoning the product.

Some segments of the timeline suggest something akin to this type of life cycle. In the decades before the Civil War, for instance, milk was a novel product generating keen interest among (at least) a certain segment of consumers, eager to incorporate it into their diet at a faster pace than their purchasing power was growing. The post-1964 evolution fits this pattern as well. The response factor for 1964–80 is not as high as that for 1917–33, reflecting the greater diffusion achieved by the product. Nevertheless, it remains a clearly positive factor, consistent with the interest that purchasing more milk generated among large population segments that were previously low consumers. The subsequent gradual decline in the response factor aligns with the fact that, as milk consumption became more widespread, these segments became increasingly smaller.

This interpretation is also supported by results obtained from a more detailed study of response factors from the mid-1960s onwards (Table 4.7). The response factor tended to be higher as we moved down the social pyramid. The middle and lower classes, with initially low consumption levels, enthusiastically embraced the new economic opportunities to purchase more milk. The upper classes, starting from a higher consumption level, reacted more moderately. A similar pattern emerges when studying territorial differences in the response factor: it tended to be higher in regions that, like the Mediterranean, concentrated populations with low consumption, and lower in those regions where, as in the north, milk already had a significant presence in the diet.

The blind spot of this life cycle interpretation is that, according to it, the response factor for 1958–64 (or, if that is the case, 1950–64) should have fallen somewhere between the extremely high value reached before the Civil War

Table 4.7 Breakdown of Response Factors

	Liquid milk		Cheese		Yogurt
	1964–80	**1980–90**	**1964–80**	**1980–90**	**1980–90**
Average[a]	0.56	−0.20	1.75	0.63	0.65
By social class					
Upper	0.43	−0.45	2.02	0.44	0.59
Middle-upper	0.65	−0.20	1.71	0.57	0.31
Middle-lower	0.73	0.02	1.58	0.66	0.57
Lower	0.61	0.07	1.07	0.65	0.92
By region					
North	0.34	−0.44	2.08	0.70	1.33
Interior	0.73	−0.29	1.97	0.50	0.55
Mediterranean	0.72	−0.01	1.60	0.76	0.31
Andalusia	0.99	−0.15	2.18	0.63	0.40

Note: [a]Corrected by provincial differences in prices.
Source: INE (1965–95, 2023c).

(1917–33) and the still positive value we observe for the years after 1964. Yet, we find an empirical anomaly: the response factor for 1958–64 was much lower than that, and it actually dropped to almost zero. We will have an opportunity to delve deeper into the qualitative variables that explain these response factors, but the data allow us to take a revealing step. If, instead of working with milk as a whole, we calculate the response factors for raw milk and processed milk separately, these indeed depict something resembling two conventional life cycles unfolding at different points in time (Figure 4.3).

Before the Civil War, and still in the 1950s, almost all the milk consumed in Spain was raw, and this milk followed a rather accelerated life cycle. Raw milk went from having an extremely high response factor in 1917–33 to an almost zero factor in 1958–64, eventually entering clearly negative factors after that. In just two generations, raw milk shifted from being a product that sparked avid interest among consumers, willing to increase their purchases more quickly than their purchasing power was growing, to being a product consumers shunned despite their reinforced capacity to buy it. On the other hand, processed milk shows all the signs of a product at the beginning of its life cycle around the mid-1960s, with a splendid response factor reminiscent of what raw milk had achieved at the outset of its pre-war diffusion. This conventional life cycle unfolded gradually and by the 1980s it began to show signs of exhaustion.

Figure 4.3 Response factors of milk consumption.
Source: Collantes (2019a: 967–8). See Appendix Table A16.

The statistical reason why the 1958–64 period (or, if data for the calculation had been fully available, the entire 1950–64 span) appears as an empirical anomaly is straightforward: it is a period in which the life cycle of raw milk was exhausted but the life cycle of processed milk had not taken off yet. At the beginning of our period, the lack of consumer interest in using their increased purchasing power to buy more milk was a lack of interest in raw milk. The subsequent recovery of this interest was, in fact, the result of consumer reorientation towards processed milk as a new product. In the next two chapters, we will have the opportunity to study the reasons why the life cycle of raw milk concluded some time before that of processed milk took off.

The available statistical information does not allow for a similar disaggregation in the case of the main dairy product: cheese, whose response factor also rebounded (and even more vigorously) from the mid-1960s onwards. We will have to rely solely on qualitative evidence to understand what was behind this result.

Conclusion: A bumpy road towards 'integration'

Mass dairy consumption was part of a broader movement towards well-being and an enhanced quality of life in Spain. Between 1950 and 1990, the country's 'augmented human development' index grew rapidly, reflecting significant progress in health, education, income levels, as well as the successful political transition from a dictatorship to a parliamentary democracy. Other indicators of well-being, such as height, also showed undeniable improvements, partly due to enhancements in nutrition, as studied in this chapter. As the country rapidly completed industrialization and urbanization, everyday life was revolutionized by the rise of a mass consumer society, with the memories of the tragic 'years of hunger' in the post-war period becoming increasingly distant (Alonso and Conde, 1994; Maluquer de Motes, 2005; Martínez Carrión, 2016; Prados de la Escosura, 2022).

The road to the massification of dairy consumption was bumpy, though. Massification did not gain momentum until the mid-1960s because only then did the increase in consumer income combine with a decrease in the price of milk, and, above all, with a reorientation of consumers towards milk and dairy products. Beneath the statistical data used in this chapter, one can sense underlying movements in the macroeconomic, microeconomic, and cultural spheres. The period between 1950 and 1965 emerges as a turbulent time, marked by incongruence among developments in different social subsystems. In contrast, the post-1965 period appears as a time when these developments harmoniously converged to produce the rise of the mass consumption model of dairy products. A similar sequence is suggested by neo-Schumpeterians Chris Freeman and Francisco Louçã (2001: 127) in the presentation of their 'reasoned history' approach:

> The *relative* autonomy of each of these five [subsystems] … can give rise to problems of lack of synchronicity and harmony or, alternatively, of harmonious integration and virtuous circle effects … It is thus essential to study both the relatively independent development of each stream of history and their interdependencies, their loss of integration, and their reintegration.

That is precisely our task in the following two chapters.

5

Losing the battle for milk (1950–65)

Alberto Ullastres has gone down in Spanish history as one of the reformers who transformed the political economy of Franco's dictatorship, redirecting towards the market what had originally been an autarkic experiment with fascist undertones (Maluquer de Motes, 2014). However, in 1960, while serving as minister of Commerce (one of the key departments in that reorientation), when addressing an audience largely composed of housewives to comment on the country's situation, he chose an analogy with echoes of Mussolini. Drawing inspiration from Italy's *battaglia del grano* in the 1920s, he declared, 'the battle for milk is still far from being resolved'. Ullastres explained that fresh liquid milk was not easily amenable to foreign trade and that 'it is not the same, because you do not accept it in the same way, that milk is produced as powder'. The dictatorship had adopted a policy of milk centrals as a solution, which, according to Ullastres, was a globally followed approach. 'It is only through centrals,' Ullastres continued, 'that we can ensure a specific price and deliver true, quality milk to the Spanish consumer, all that is needed' ('Información', 1960: 206). Milk was still not a mass-consumed food, and in that sense the situation was not very different from what it had been about ten years earlier, at the starting point of our study.

The situation around 1950

Around 1950, the consumption of dairy products in Spain was significantly lower than in Europe. In the UK, France, and Scandinavia, milk had already become a mass-consumed and regular food item. In these countries, as well as in the United States across the ocean, what had been irregular and class-segmented consumption during the early modern period became one of the most striking vehicles of the nutritional transition during the second half of the nineteenth century and the beginning of the twentieth century. Once the initial stage of industrialization, where the working classes did not benefit much from the macroeconomic progress of their countries, was overcome, continued economic growth expanded consumption possibilities for most households. High-income households had the purchasing power necessary to incorporate milk as a regular element in their diet without causing significant disruptions to the family budget. Middle- and low-income households gradually followed. After all, milk was by no means the most efficient option for obtaining calories (its price per calorie was significantly higher than that of cereals or potatoes), so that reaching a certain income threshold was necessary for consumers to consider incorporating it into their diet. However, in these early developed countries with an Atlantic climate, the relative price of milk was not particularly high. Especially since the late nineteenth century, when the agricultural crisis provoked by the integration of international agricultural markets forced numerous European farmers to seek alternatives to grain production, the high levels of both rainfall and urbanization allowed many farmers to shift towards intensive dairy farming, largely sustained by the meadows, pastures, and cereals of their local area. Combined with the rapid expansion of railway lines, this made it possible for consumers to have access to milk at reasonable prices. Beyond the increasingly favourable economic calculations that households could make, there was also a decisive shift in consumer preferences. Emerging nutritional science began to outline the paradigm of 'newer nutrition' and, among other things, enthusiastically recommended abundant consumption of milk as it was a food rich in proteins, vitamins, and calcium. Milk could compensate for other dietary deficits, and it could also strengthen the health benefits of consuming other foods. Doctors and scientists began to present milk as an almost perfect and indispensable food. Over time, especially during the interwar period, states would become enthusiastic preachers of this 'gospel of milk'. Milk was firmly entrenched in the nutritional social contract of these states amid turbulence such as world wars or the economic crisis of the 1930s (Levenstein, 2003; Oddy, 2003; Valenze, 2011; Velten, 2010; Wiley, 2011).

All of this had also happened in Spain, but nothing had occurred on a comparable scale. Firstly, in Spain, unlike Atlantic Europe or North America, there was not even a certain prior tradition of consuming dairy products. Even a relatively optimistic view of the role of dairy in the pre-industrial diet, such as Braudel's (1979: 172–3), depicts a rare case of 'proliferation of dairy products' as a 'particularly uncommon luxury in Spain'. Towards the end of the nineteenth century, not only did the diet continue to revolve around cereals, legumes, and potatoes, but its main animal-origin complement was meat. Meat actually had a secondary presence in the diet and was almost absent from the daily lives of many households, especially those of the lower class. However, this laid the groundwork for the possibility of meat becoming a vehicle for the nutritional transition. Milk was different because in much of the country it was seen less as a regular food item and more as a kind of medicinal food for occasional consumption by people with digestive ailments. Furthermore, although the Spanish population was generally tolerant to lactose, it is likely that the population segments with some degree of intolerance were somewhat larger than in those parts of the continent where the genetic mutation that turned Europeans into potential milk drinkers originated long ago. It is true that the social image of milk began to transform as Spain also received messages from the 'newer nutrition'. Like in other countries, various local institutions (e.g. the *Gotas de Leche* or 'Milk Drops') contributed to spreading the gospel of milk, a task in which the work of doctors with their patients was also decisive. In any case, when the Spanish Civil War broke out in 1936, this transformation of the social image of milk was not as advanced as in other countries. The nutritional message had reached urban populations more than rural ones and, among the urban population, it reached the business and professional elites more than the working classes (Carreras and Tafunell, 2020; Hernández Adell, 2012; Hernández Adell and Pujol, 2017; Nicolau and Pujol, 2007; Pujol et al., 2007).

Moreover, in Spain, households faced a more severe budget constraint than in the UK, France, or the United States. Although Spain had already launched a process of industrialization similar to these countries in the central part of the nineteenth century, allowing for a sustained increase in income, the formation of a middle-class society remained a more distant prospect. This alone was enough to hinder the transition of numerous households to regular milk consumption, but it was also reinforced by the fact that milk was relatively more expensive than in other countries. Spain did not have such favourable environmental and socio-economic conditions. Except for a small strip of regions located in the northernmost part of the country, rainfall levels were low, making it not so easy to mobilize resources for the feeding of animals, especially in the demanding case of cattle. It was not so easy for many farmers to specialize in milk production and reap the associated productivity gains because, although Spain was urbanizing, its urban markets were neither as large nor as deep as those in England, France, or the United States. Considering both the income effect and the price effect, the conclusion is clear: throughout the first third of the twentieth century, the budget constraint was softening, but it was doing so slowly and unevenly. The budget constraint remained a substantial obstacle to the possible diffusion of milk consumption among many households (Carreras and Tafunell, 2020; Hernández Adell, 2012; Nicolau and Pujol, 2007; Pujol et al., 2007).

The situation in 1950 was, on the other hand, greatly influenced by the disastrous effects of the civil war and the long post-war period of the 1940s. During the first third of the twentieth century, after all, the life cycle of milk as a consumer good had at least started, but the war and the post-war period drastically interrupted this trend. In 1950, Spain had not yet recovered the GDP per capita it had reached in the years before the war, and the gap separating it from the leading European economies was greater than ever before. The substitution of the democratic regime of the Second Republic for a fascist-inspired dictatorship had led to the cancellation of many social and labour policies that had helped reduce inequality. If the Spain of the first third of the twentieth century, despite its progress, had been a backward economy and a remarkably unequal society, around 1950 these features were more pronounced than ever. Although the evidence is somewhat incomplete, it seems that, throughout the 1940s, the Francoist project to create a highly intervened autarkic economy by the state, whose failure was evident in various sectors of the national economy, may also have had a negative impact on the dairy chain, especially on its farming link. Thus, the relative difficulty of production, with its effects on the price of milk, was still present around 1950. In other words, if by 1936 the budget constraint on households was still considerable, by 1950 it had hardened. Milk was even further from being a mass-consumed food item (Carreras and Tafunell, 2020; Domínguez and Puente, 2009; Langreo, 1995).

Household economies under pressure

Over the subsequent fifteen years, until 1965, milk consumption experienced some resurgence in Spain. However, this growth was remarkably slow. Many households went on facing severe budget constraints, even if these were gradually softening. Notably, this period marked a phase of rapid economic expansion for Spain. Emerging from the profound impacts of the war and the post-war autarkic economic experiment, the country began integrating into the fantastic wave of European economic growth often referred to as a 'golden age' (Maddison, 2001). Starting from a backward position, with a substantial portion of the population still engaged in low-productivity agriculture and other low-tech activities, Spain managed to accelerate its industrialization by assimilating innovations previously generated in more advanced countries. This process was facilitated by the entrepreneurial and labour capabilities forged over the pre-war period of gradual modernization. A pivotal factor in this transformation was the shift in the Francoist political economy. Beginning in the 1950s, the autarchic experiment gradually evolved towards a form of 'coordinated capitalism', to take Barry Eichengreen's (2007) expression, combining significant state intervention with expanded space for market mechanisms through a dual process of external and internal liberalization. A milestone in this dual process was the Stabilization and Liberalization Plan of 1959, after which the Spanish economy entered a phase of accelerated growth (Calvo-González, 2021; Carreras and Tafunell, 2020; Collantes, 2017b; Maluquer de Motes, 2014).

The improvement in household income levels during these years was significant, surpassing any previous period. Moreover, a gradual reduction in income inequality began to take place. While the social and labour policies of the democratic era did not return, market forces conducive to social cohesion started to emerge from the mid-1950s onwards. The most significant of these forces was undoubtedly the revival of rural-to-urban migration. Rapid industrialization not only increased the demand for labour in cities, encompassing industrial activities, construction, and services, but also, in conjunction with the greater difficulties faced by remote rural populations in accessing basic services, prompted a substantial shift of people from low-productivity agriculture to occupations offering higher income opportunities. The progress of urbanization was thus linked to an expansion of the middle classes (Collantes and Pinilla, 2011; Prados de la Escosura, 2008).

However, the fact that Spain in 1965 was no longer mired in the economic and social crisis of the post-war period did not mean that most households attained income levels comparable to their Western European counterparts. The average income of a Spanish individual in 1965 remained actually much lower. Furthermore, income distribution continued to be more unequal. The Francoist dictatorship was barely implementing the pro-equality policies commonplace in Western Europe at the time, especially in areas such as labour regulation, social public expenditure, and progressive taxation. For most households, most income growth served primarily to regain pre-war levels and reconstruct a consumption pattern disrupted by subsequent events. The margin for pursuing new objectives, such as buying more milk, was modest (Maluquer de Motes, 2005, 2014).

In the case of milk, another complicating factor was its increasing cost. The purchasing power for buying milk grew less than the overall income level because, since at least the late 1950s (data for earlier periods are unavailable), the relative price of milk tended to rise. In a rapidly expanding Spanish economy, where technological absorption and efficiency gains were boosting productivity across various sectors, the dairy chain showed signs of difficulties. As in the past, the constraints affecting dairy farming remained significant. A considerable portion of the milk was produced on very small farms by unspecialized peasants who combined dairy cows with other activities on and off the farm. Most of the cows were of indigenous breeds, well adapted for multitasking (including fieldwork) but with much lower milk yields compared to a Frisian or Swiss cow. The diet of these animals primarily consisted of local meadows and pastures, combined with locally produced corn or other agricultural products. This made dairy farming highly sensitive to climatic conditions: most cows were concentrated in the narrow strip of Atlantic climate regions whose agroecosystems allowed suitable animal nutrition. Beyond that strip, maintaining dairy cows was a much more costly activity, requiring integration into broader commercial networks to source supplementary feed due to the limited possibilities of the local agroecosystem, which, in contrast, might have been more suitable for productions such as wine, olive oil, oranges, or vegetables. Some of these networks had slowly developed in Mediterranean regions like Valencia before the war, but the autarchic experiment of the early Francoist period proved fatal to them (Calatayud and Medina-Albaladejo, 2017; Domínguez, 2001; Fernández Prieto, 2001; Gallego, 2001).

Nevertheless, despite these long-standing obstacles that had already driven the price of milk to higher levels than in other countries, clear advances in the productivity of milk farmers occurred during the 1950s and early 1960s. In fact, the price received by these farmers for the sale of their raw milk decreased. The vision that the Francoist regime had for the sector involved what was then seen as technological modernization: the introduction of high-yield Frisian cows, the transformation of farmers into specialized breeders, and the resizing of their operations to capitalize on economies of scale (Calcedo, 1996; Fernández Prieto and Lanero, 2019; Langreo, 1995; Otero, 2022). Although none of this happened at a breakneck pace or on a sweeping scale, the beginnings of dairy farming's integration into the 'green revolution' allowed for a sustained reduction in the relative price of raw milk at the farm gate. In other words, what drove the cost of milk higher for consumers in the late 1950s and early 1960s was not the price charged by the farmer but the widening gap between that price and the final product price.

Considering that most milk purchased by consumers (approximately 85 per cent still in 1965) was raw milk, the focus should be on the commercial chain connecting farmers to consumers. This was a highly heterogeneous chain, where various economic actors operated in diverse circuits (Calcedo, 1996; Fernández Prieto and Lanero, 2019; Langreo, 1995; Otero, 2022). In some cases, farm families conducted periodic routes to sell their milk as itinerant vendors in nearby cities. Other times, they sold milk to a small-scale commercial intermediary. If the milk had to travel a greater distance, a somewhat larger intermediary could come into play. There were also small urban shops that sourced milk from these diverse circuits and sold the product to consumers in their establishments. In turn, these shops could be specialized stores originating from an old urban dairy (where only the commercial function remained) or common stores. The unifying feature of these circuits was that, in any of their versions, they were characterized by an atomized business structure and rudimentary technologies. They also faced the demanding challenge of incorporating into the commercial circuit a myriad of small farmers scattered throughout the territory. Atlantic Spain, where most cows were concentrated, was not the Netherlands: its topography was extremely rugged, further exacerbating the difficulties and costs required to connect farmers with consumers. The cost of commercial intermediation then proved to be much higher than in the Europe north of the Pyrenees (Collantes, 2017a). At a time before supermarket chains and processing industries' systematic networks for milk collection, these commercial circuits were the primary source of milk inflation for consumers. In a Spanish economy with significant advances in various sectors, it was in these types of circuits that one could find greater difficulties of production in relative terms.

It must be acknowledged that this increase in the cost of milk never completely offset the overall rise in household incomes. It did not even come close to doing so. Nevertheless, in combination with the other socio-economic factors discussed in this section, it contributed to many households continuing to face a significant budget constraint. Towards 1965, regularly buying milk still represented a considerable effort for lower-middle-class households and was unaffordable for lower-class households. In some regions, such as Andalusia and the Mediterranean coast, even the average household was subject to a significant budget constraint. There was a sense that, thanks to the ongoing wave of inclusive economic growth, this constraint would continue to soften until it became practically irrelevant. However, that moment had not yet arrived by 1965.

The limits of propaganda

The traditional economic barrier to the massification of milk remained significant, but during these years it became accompanied by another, more novel obstacle. Unlike what had happened before the war or what would occur after 1965, consumers in these years showed little interest in using their increased purchasing power to buy more milk.

But how could such a thing happen in Spain between 1950 and 1965? After all, many consumers had already been exposed to the gospel of milk during the first third of the twentieth century. Additionally, the Francoist dictatorship enthusiastically engaged in intensifying the dissemination of pro-milk messages, using more forceful means than it was the case before the war (Collantes, 2017c). Milk was part of the 'nutritional social contract' (Valenze, 2011: 263) that Francoism sought to reconstruct after the deprivations of the war and post-war period. Although in many aspects the dictatorship represented an anomaly within post-1945 Western Europe, nutritionally it aligned quite conventionally with the tenets of the 'newer nutrition' and ardently advocated for milk as an indispensable part of the basic basket that every Spaniard should be able to access.

As part of its increasing integration into international institutions in the Western orbit, the dictatorship implemented various initiatives aimed at communicating the health benefits of regular milk consumption. In 1954, it launched a school milk programme sponsored by the United Nations and supported by donations of powdered milk from the United States. Over the next decade, more than sixty thousand schools would have the opportunity to offer their children a cup of milk, often powdered milk donated by US aid reconstituted with hot water at the school itself. The goal was to promote the nutritional health of children and, more importantly, to instil pro-milk preferences in them that would accompany them throughout their lives and perhaps contribute to gradually redirecting the preferences of their parents (Langreo, 1995).

The National Dairy Committee, the corporatist agency created by the dictatorship for the coordination of dairy actors and interests, began organizing the International Milk Day in 1958, an activity promoted by the International Dairy Federation. For a few days, the main cities of the country were filled with promotional posters, while mass media carried enthusiastic pro-milk recommendations from various doctors. In a televised roundtable, paediatrician Juan Bosch recommended 'that all children and adolescents under twenty years of age drink a litre of sterilized, cold milk daily with their meals' ('Leche', 1958: 201). The slogan of the day, common to all member countries of the International Dairy Federation, was simple but very illustrative: 'Milk is health' ('Información', 1958a, 1958b).

In 1961, the regime launched a programme of Education in Food and Nutrition, EDALNU (*Educación en Alimentación y Nutrición*), whose orientation reinforced these types of messages. Led by prominent doctors such as Francisco Vivanco, various actions were taken to ensure that populations of all social groups and territories definitively became aware of the recommendations coming from nutritional scientists. Within what was a fairly comprehensive view of food consumption, Vivanco and his team's approach to milk was undoubtedly positive. Their recommendation, aligned with international standards, was to drink at least half a litre of milk a day. This was equivalent to doubling the consumption level that the country had actually reached by the end of our period, in 1965 (Trescastro-López et al., 2014; Vivanco et al., 1976).

One might be tempted to question the effectiveness of these initiatives. And, of course, there is no doubt that by 1950 Spain was a country with significant educational and cultural gaps. Many households, especially in rural areas and in the more backward regions, had remained unaware of the messages and guidance that spread in the early decades of the century. However, it is by no means evident that this continued to be the situation by 1965. The scale and intensity of milk propaganda had increased significantly. The school milk programme and the organization of events such as the International Milk Day had amplified the reach of pro-milk nutritional messages on a national scale. An increasingly extensive network of doctors enthusiastically prescribed milk consumption to their patients. In fact, those who reported symptoms of lactose intolerance were encouraged to leave behind their complaints and get to work educating their bodies to drink the much-needed milk (Vivanco et al., 1976: 318). As the nutritional message became more forceful, Spanish society recorded an increase in its educational level and urbanization rate that could only favour a better absorption of the former.

The school essay contests organized on the occasion of International Milk Day allow us to get an idea of the success with which the gospel of milk was spreading among ordinary people. In 1959, when the essays had to respond to the title 'Why do I drink milk?' the winner of the contest was José Lozano, a teenager from the city of Alcalá de Henares in Madrid who formulated a decalogue. The ten reasons why Lozano said he drank milk ranged from 'because it has a pleasant taste' to 'because it is a complete food', 'because it has never harmed me', and 'because it is rich in vitamins', concluding with 'because its consumption increases the national economy' and 'because by drinking it daily, I will become a strong and useful man for my Homeland'. The second prize went to a girl from the Castilian town of Romanillos de Medinaceli, who referred to her mother's insistence that she drink milk and added that 'It tastes very good … Now that I am older, I drink milk to grow and become very tall, like the tower' (Garrido, 1959; Lozano, 1959).

The problem was not that consumers remained unaware of the gospel of milk. Generic interest in milk existed. What was fading, as we could infer from the statistical analysis in Chapter 4, was the specific interest in the type of milk that most Spaniards had at their disposal: raw milk, whose market share was 95 per cent in 1950 and had barely fallen to 85 per cent in 1965. Buying and drinking raw milk could have its drawbacks. The purchase of raw milk was always under suspicion that it might be adulterated by the addition of water. This was a common practice, and if it was also supplemented using some kind of colouring, it was easier to detect it at the moment of drinking the 'milk' than in the previous moment of buying it. There were also health risks. It is true that everything could go well: the cow had been a healthy cow, the milk had been hygienically milked, intermediaries had taken care to prevent the milk from staying too long at unrefrigerated warehouses, and, in any case, the housewife had boiled that milk a couple of times before she and the rest of the household members drank it. But obviously, one or more of these steps could go wrong. In that case, the milk was contaminated with bacteria and other microorganisms that caused discomfort, and this discomfort could be severe. Intoxications from drinking spoiled milk were frequent in Spanish cities, especially in the summer months (Ramos, 1955; Trueba, 1968).

Consumer interest in raw milk was waning before most of them could have access to processed milk. This, in turn, points to the failure of the Francoist policy of milk industrialization (Domínguez, 2003; Langreo, 1995), which was unable to substantially renew consumers' choice space. The idea, as concretized in the 1952 Milk Centrals Regulation, was apparently simple. In all cities of a certain size (more than twenty thousand inhabitants), processing industries had to be established that sold pasteurized milk. Since regulating the heterogeneous commercial circuits of raw milk was an unfeasible goal for the administration, the solution (already identified, for example, in the United States at the beginning of the twentieth century) was to make pasteurized milk available to consumers. The traditional sale of raw milk, which at that time represented around 95 per cent of the country's consumption, was, in fact, prohibited in cities equipped with a 'milk central'. The milk centrals would have a local monopoly to supply consumers in their urban area, or, in the case of larger cities, would share the market with other concessionaire companies like them. They would buy raw milk from the surrounding farmers, pasteurize it, and finally distribute it among urban consumers. Characteristically in Francoist Spain, coordination between these different actors would take place through top-down public regulations. The state would set the price at which centrals had to buy raw milk from farmers and the price at which they had to sell pasteurized milk to consumers. For example, in 1958, the dairy central in the Catalan city of Girona, one of the first to be established, had to buy milk from farmers at a price of 3.60 pesetas per litre, and then sell pasteurized milk to consumers at a price of 4.98 pesetas if it was done through sealed drums at home, or 5.45 if it was done through bottles sold in stores ('Información', 1958b: 51).

However, the milk centrals plan advanced with such disappointing slowness that even political leaders could not help but acknowledge it. In Spain, there were more than one hundred cities where, according to the twenty thousand inhabitants threshold set by the Regulation, dairy centrals should have been created, but by 1965, only sixteen existed. In a few cities, the first being Badajoz, everything more or less went according to the plan: competitions were proposed to acquire the concession for the dairy central, some proposals were presented, and finally, some company or agricultural cooperative received the concession and began to produce pasteurized milk for the city's inhabitants. But in most cases, this did not happen, and no competition was even formalized. Even where there was a competition, it was not uncommon for it to remain deserted. And even where there was a competition and an eventual winner, sometimes the concessionary ended up renouncing the licence. The difficulties in promoting the creation of milk centrals were particularly striking in some of the country's largest cities, such as Madrid and Seville (de la Calle, 1969; 'Información', 1956a: 65–6, 'Precios', 1965).

The business community was not very interested in participating in the type of public-private partnership that the Francoist state had designed because the expected profitability of investments was doomed to be low. Since centrals had to buy raw milk at a certain price and sell pasteurized milk at another, their profitability was roughly implicit in the prices set by the state. The gross profit had to be enough to cover costs, which not only included the purchase of raw materials from farmers but also the expenses involved in obtaining labour or packaging for the final product, as well as fixed costs that were also borne by the central, such as the construction of the factory or the acquisition of pasteurizing equipment and other industrial machinery. The dominant feeling among the business and cooperative groups that might have been interested in participating in the competitions was that the numbers did not look good ('Información', 1956b, 1962). The profit rate implied in price regulation was too low, and the period needed to adequately amortize the initial fixed costs would become too long.

As if business expectations were not pessimistic enough, they deteriorated even further by the late 1950s when it was proven that milk centrals, despite the rhetoric that made them valuable instruments for promoting public health, lacked advantages when dealing with foreign suppliers. Foreign trade was subject to strict administrative control: it was not possible to dispose freely of foreign currency, and companies or individuals who wanted to use foreign currency had to apply for a licence and explain their purposes (Martínez, 2001). At the time, getting one of these licences was key to the reasonable operation of a Spanish milk central, which (for example) needed to obtain pasteurizing equipment manufactured in places like the Netherlands or Germany. However, concessionaires soon discovered that their participation in a public-private partnership did not guarantee them facilities in obtaining the import licence. The managers of one of the centrals in Madrid found that, after investing the substantial amount of 10 million pesetas in buildings to build the plant, the Foreign Currency Institute denied their requests for import licences. While concessionaires became angry because they could not count on the support of the dictatorship for something as basic as buying pasteurizing equipment, the lesson for the rest of the country's entrepreneurs was clear: in a country whose economy had begun to grow above 4 per cent annually, there were better options to invest in than a milk central ('Información', 1958a, 1958b).

In hindsight, the 1952 public-private partnership was poorly designed, and this prevented the life cycle of pasteurized milk from taking off in earnest at a time when that of raw milk was running out. We even have reasons to suspect that the failed attempt to mass-produce pasteurized milk contributed to accelerating the closure of the raw milk cycle. The gospel of milk that the dictatorship preached enthusiastically focused on pasteurized milk and largely excluded raw milk (Díaz Méndez and Gómez Benito, 2010). In fact, propaganda, heavily influenced by the views and interests of the businessmen, farmers, politicians, and officials most closely related to the milk centrals plan, often emphasized the harms that consuming raw milk could cause. The focus of policymaking on pasteurized milk also meant that the raw milk market came to present characteristics of a black market. The 1952 Regulation, let us remember, had prohibited the sale of raw milk in cities with more than twenty thousand inhabitants once they were equipped with their central. The slow progress of the project made the activities of intermediaries who went house-to-house or neighbourhood-to-neighbourhood with their pots of raw milk into illegal or semi-legal endeavours.

Local authorities were generally understanding and interpreted that, as long as the centrals did not gain more momentum, they had to let it happen. But this sparked heated protests among the industrialists and, in combination with the problems of adulteration and intoxication we have discussed, sometimes led to fines being imposed on sellers of raw milk. In other words, a market that already suffered from problems of asymmetric information and distrust due to the nature of the product and the absence of institutions ensuring its quality found itself immersed in an atmosphere that could only exacerbate these issues.

The result of all this was a consumer who, while reasonably interested in the generic idea of drinking more milk, was not willing to use their growing purchasing power to buy more raw milk and, in most cases, lacked access to pasteurized milk as an alternative. A harsh editorial from the newspaper *La Vanguardia Española* on the occasion of International Milk Day in 1958 illustrated the situation in the city of Madrid:

> Many attractive posters have been put up proclaiming the excellences of milk as a food product … Let's suppose that the propaganda here for International Milk Day had been so effective that it had convinced everyone at Madrid of the necessity and convenience of consuming cow's milk. Let's suppose that such conviction was immediately manifested in the positive decision to consume more milk. What would happen? Nothing, simply nothing … The product sold as milk is subject to an abuse of denomination and … Madrid, more than the product's propaganda, needs the product itself. ('Jornada platónica', 1958)

The life cycle of raw milk was closing before that of pasteurized milk had truly taken off. Perhaps dairy products, such as cheese, could have come to the rescue of the Spanish consumer and bring them closer to the zone defined by nutritional recommendations?

'Recently we bought cheese…'

Spain differed from other Mediterranean countries where low milk consumption was, at least in part, compensated by a significant consumption of milk-based products. It should be noted that Mediterranean agroecosystems, with low rainfall and high temperature, may not have been best adapted to the production of cow's milk and its subsequent commercialization and consumption in liquid form. However, they imposed few limitations when it came to producing dairy products such as cheese. In fact, in most regions of Spain there was a certain tradition of cheese production from various types of milk, including those from animals like sheep and goats, which were not as demanding in terms of their feeding and, therefore, not as dependent on rainy weather. It is true that, for reasons still little explored by historians of the nineteenth and early twentieth centuries, cheese consumption in Spain was very moderate, certainly lower than in Italy, Greece, or France. But this could have started to change around 1950. Consumer purchasing power clearly increased, not only because of rising income levels but also because (unlike milk) cheese did not tend to become relatively more expensive. Yet, and similarly to milk, the consumer response factor to cheese consumption dropped to a level close to zero. Consumers simply did not seem to be interested in the product.

This lack of interest was largely due to the negative assessment that consumers, based on their experiences, made of the types of cheese they typically had access to. Most cheese was produced using rudimentary technologies and on a very small scale, either by semi-artisanal manufacturers or by the farming families themselves. However, within the same company or farm, the characteristics of cheese could vary astonishingly from one time of the year to another, or even within the same batch. This was due to rudimentary technologies, unsystematized production processes, lax producer quality controls, and the lack of some guild organization that could establish such controls for all producers in a given territory. It was also because cheese makers consciously made decisions that could only alter the taste, texture, and other characteristics of their product. A very common case was the use of volatile combinations of different types of milk. Pure cheeses made from a single type of milk, in fact, were less common than the so-called 'mixed cheeses', in which cow's, sheep's, and goat's milks were combined in proportions that by no means remained constant over time. This allowed cheese makers to flexibly adapt to the circumstances, not always synchronized with each other, of the markets for different milks, but certainly prevented them from producing a cheese with stable characteristics over time (Compairé, 1966; del Río and Matallana, 1966).

For consumers, the lack of standardization was a problem. The consumption experience was not always satisfactory. Actually, disappointments were frequent: the cheese bought today turned out to have a less pleasant taste and texture than another seemingly similar one bought a short time ago. Even if, on occasion, the opposite was true, consumers could not view the purchase of cheese as an operation as reliable as others. An article published in 1960 in the humorous magazine *La Codorniz* captures the consumer culture of the time well:

> We recently bought cheese … As soon as we tasted it, we went back to the store to buy more before the shopkeeper ran out. The reason was that the cheese was sensational … We assumed that it had turned out that way by chance, which is not very common. ('Quesos', 1998: 38)

This lack of reliability was exacerbated during most of the period by a parallel problem: it was not uncommon for cheese makers to enhance the fat content of their products by covertly adding vegetable fats such as margarine. According to one of the key figures of the National Dairy Committee, Santiago Matallana (1963: 136–7), these cheese makers were 'discrediting products that consumers desired and, in many cases, are already rejecting, aware of the low quality of much of what they find in the market'.

On the other hand, consumers had very limited choices. For most households, options were not many and often boiled down to two. The most common cheese was hard-cured cheese, which tended to be known as *Manchego* cheese. This referred to the tradition of the Castile-La Mancha region of producing hard-cured cheeses from sheep's milk, but the cheese most consumers truly had access to was more of a *Manchego*-like commodity produced from a mixture of different types of milk. The second option would be some local variety produced following peasant traditions under semi-artisanal conditions. Both options were clearly subject to the problems just presented, and the lack of greater variety may have contributed to keeping consumer interest in cheese low (Plaja, 1965; Sanz, 1992).

Yogurt, on the other hand, could not yet emerge as a mass alternative. It is true that some of the problems in the world of cheese disappeared in the world of yogurt: yogurt was manufactured in a standardized way and subjected to systematic quality controls by a very small number of large companies, the most important of which was the multinational Danone, located in Barcelona since 1919 (Castro, 2008). However, during this period, yogurt remained a product aimed at a very specific niche: consumers with a certain purchasing power who were suffering from digestive ailments. The product was relatively expensive, not only (like any dairy product) in relation to its caloric content but also compared to milk or cheese. Additionally, its social image was not yet that of a mass-consumed food for healthy populations. The nutritional discourse on the benefits of yogurt consumption had remained within very concise limits, outlined by the pioneering research that Ilya Mechnikov had conducted in the early twentieth century, which had emphasized the role of microorganisms involved in milk fermentation as protectors and repairers of the digestive system. Such was the restrictively medicinal nature of yogurt in Spain in the 1950s and early 1960s that, although it could be found in some dairies and grocery stores, its commercialization mainly took place in pharmacies (Díaz Yubero, 1984; Lacasa, 1981).

The product that most clearly emerged as a possible alternative to liquid milk was canned milk. Condensed milk and powdered milk differed from liquid milk in a key aspect for a country with the geographical characteristics of Spain: they were much better suited to interregional trade. Liquid milk was a heavy, bulky, and delicate product, but canned milks could become a reliable and reasonably affordable tool to transfer milk surpluses produced in the northern Atlantic regions of the country to the rest of the regions. Furthermore, for the same reasons, the option of obtaining canned milk through imports that complemented national production was realistic. In 1954, Spain became a recipient of American aid in the form of powdered milk, as part of the United Nations-sponsored school milk programme: once transformed into powdered milk, surplus milk from places like Wisconsin reached Spanish children across the ocean. They were soon accompanied by powdered milk produced in Spain. In schools, water was heated or boiled, and powdered milk was added. Considering that more than 90 per cent of liquid milk is actually water, the result of this 'reconstitution' was a drinkable food that had similarities with liquid milk (Lacasa, 1968).

It should be added that, unlike raw milk dominating the consumption of Spaniards, powdered milk and condensed milk had the advantage of being standardized products, manufactured by companies that could reliably vouch for their quality and the stability of their composition. As expressed vividly in yet one more critical editorial in the national press,

> Anything before continuing to pay, even if it's a few pesetas, for a litre of dirty milk. Many people from Madrid, many housewives in Madrid have decided to buy cans of condensed milk or powdered milk and dilute it more or less according to the household budget. In this way, the family is sure to be drinking milk and water, but clear tap water. ('El problema', 1964)

Everything fit … except the consumption experience. The recognition of this limitation was at the core of the speech delivered by Minister of Commerce Alberto Ullastres in 1960. In case anyone had imagined a Spanish path to mass consumption based on powdered milk, Ullastres admitted that consumers did not consider 'reconstituted' milk to be a food comparable to liquid milk. It could be a reasonable supplement, especially at times when the price of milk tended to rise or when consumers suspected that the raw milk sold in their neighbourhood was adulterated. But 'it is not the same, because you do not accept it in the same way, that milk is produced as powder. Therefore, the problem of milk in Spain remains unresolved' ('Información', 1960: 206). What Ullastres was noting in 1960 was that the milk that had become part of the nutritional social contract of the dictatorship could not be canned milk: it would have to be liquid milk, or it would not be.

Conclusion: Mismatch

In an article published in 1955, Manuel Ramos, the director of the SAM (*Sindicatos Agrarios Montañeses*) cooperative, one of the few dairy industries of a certain size in Spain, claimed that, despite the recommendation to drink half a litre of milk per day, 'eating habits, even more than the average Spanish income level, will prevent the achievement of this goal for a long time'. For Ramos, the life of the Spanish dairy processor was subject to the constant threat of overproduction. The average Spaniard consumed so little not because production was scarce but simply 'because they just don't want to' (Ramos, 1955: 39, 41). Although our analysis in this chapter has only partially aligned with this perspective, it is a testimony that well illustrates the nature of the problem before 1965: some conditions for the rise of the 'mass agro-industrial consumption' model were present, but by no means all. The macroeconomic situation, with the end of the post-war stagnation and the onset of a wave of rapid growth, was favourable. Furthermore, despite the absence of pro-equality policies in Franco's dictatorship, market forces such as rural-urban migration and occupational change had made growth inclusive. However, inclusive economic growth alone was not sufficient to drive the massification of dairy consumption. Parallel changes of sufficient depth were lacking in the production chain and in consumer culture. There were transformations in all nodes of the chain, starting with livestock farming, but there were also severe limitations, especially in commercial intermediation and in the type of processing industry that Franco's regime was trying to promote from 1952 onwards. The spread of the nutritional message favourable to dairy consumption was much wider and intense than in the past, but consumers showed little enthusiasm for the specific dairy products that were actually available in the market, such as raw milk and semi-artisanal cheeses.

In 1965, with the Spanish economy definitively incorporated into the 'golden age' of Western growth and reaping the benefits of the successful Stabilization Plan approved in 1959, the Spanish population was still far from the range recommended by nutritional science for dairy products. Milk was not yet a mass-consumed food, and for a reformist like Minister Alberto Ullastres, it had been inevitable to admit: the battle for milk still had to be won.

6

Winning the battle (1965–90)

In his 1960 speech on the battle for milk, Alberto Ullastres believed, unsurprisingly for a member of the dictatorship's government, that victory depended on the success of the milk centrals policy. 'It is only through centrals,' he asserted, 'that we can ensure a specific price and deliver true, quality milk to the Spanish consumer, all that is needed' ('Información', 1960: 206). For the reasons studied in the previous chapter, he was right that a new path of evolution in the production chain was required. However, as we will see in this chapter, the new path would turn out to be something different from what was envisaged in the milk centrals policy. Moreover, the massification of milk consumption would also require a combination of these microeconomic developments, with others taking place in the macroeconomic and cultural spheres. So much so that in the 1980s, signs began to emerge of a new decoupling of at least some of these pieces, outlining a horizon of dissolution of the mass consumption model that had triumphed so overwhelmingly in the previous fifteen years.

Cheaper milk for richer people

The key reason why households became less affected by economic constraints was the rise in their income levels. The first decade of the period, until 1975, witnessed the completion of the most significant wave of growth in the history of the Spanish economy. The industrial sector acted as the driving force, while agriculture, construction, and services played significant roles as complementary supports. Substantial improvements in productivity were observed in all sectors, made possible by the adoption of technology previously developed in other Western countries and the efficiency gains resulting from the liberalization of Franco's political economy. In a period characterized by rapid economic growth worldwide, Spain experienced particularly accelerated growth, narrowing the gap with leading economies. The fruits of this growth were distributed more evenly than in the past, with lower-income households (precisely those initially facing more severe budget constraints) experiencing income growth at a faster pace than the national average (Calvo-González, 2021; Collantes, 2017b; Prados de la Escosura, 2008).

While the wave of rapid growth concluded in 1975, when Spain began to feel the effects of the international economic crisis stemming from the oil shock, the collapse of the Bretton Woods regime, and the exhaustion of Fordism, the average income level did not decrease. Moreover, the establishment of a democratic regime after Franco's death led to the implementation of labour, social, and fiscal measures that favoured a continued reduction in income distribution inequality despite the crisis. Although it was a prolonged crisis, Spain, shifting its focus from industry to construction, finance, and connections with the European Economic Community (joined in 1986), initiated a new cycle of economic expansion in the mid-1980s. The result of these macroeconomic and social trends is evident: by 1990, the vast majority of Spanish households had an income level that made it possible to purchase milk regularly without causing significant disruptions to their budget (Collantes, 2017b; de la Torre and Rubio-Varas, 2022; Torregrosa, 2021).

What is noteworthy about this period, however, is that these forces did not act alone; their effect was reinforced by the evolution of the price of milk. If, in the years before 1965, there had been an increase in the price of milk, now a decrease occurred. It was not a sudden change: during the second half of the 1960s and the beginning of the next decade, the relative price of milk merely stabilized. From that moment on, however, there was a notable decline that would extend until the end of our period in 1990. Consequently, by 1990, a litre of milk was approximately 20 per cent cheaper than it had been a quarter of a century earlier. Overall, this price effect was less crucial than the income effect in expanding consumer purchasing power, but not always and not in all regions. During the economic crisis that began around 1975, for example, the price effect allowed consumer purchasing power to continue growing at a pace similar to the previous years, despite the drastic slowdown in their income levels. The price effect was particularly important in regions that had hitherto been characterized by high milk prices and low levels of consumption, such as Andalusia and (especially) the Mediterranean.

The cheapening of milk was made possible by a profound transformation in all links of the production chain. The most decisive change was the rise of an industry focused on the production of processed milk, which partly resulted from the adjustments that the dictatorship implemented in its milk centrals policy in 1966.

A revision of the state's intervention mechanisms in the pasteurized milk chain took place, leading to more flexible price-setting systems and, in general, better profit prospects for potential investors. In combination with a more general turn of Spanish trade policy towards the market, facilitating processors' access to machinery produced in other countries, this favoured the creation of a denser network of milk centrals, reaching a total number of sixty-five. In fact, some of the largest processors in the later part of the period, such as Uniasa or Clesa, were formed by accumulating centrals in different provinces and regions. The dictatorship's policy was also crucial for the consolidation of some other major groups, especially the nationalized La Lactaria Española (Langreo, 1995; Ramos, 1991).

However, the rise of a strong processing industry was mainly due to the convergence of entrepreneurial initiatives that, rather than adhering strictly to state guidelines, found niches in which to operate more autonomously. As in other sectors of the Spanish economy, it is not only that the Francoist technocracy was adjusting its policies, aligning its plans more closely with market signals, but also that it left ample space for initiatives to emerge outside of such plans. In our case, the decisive niche was that of sterilized milk, which later evolved into UHT milk. These were milks subjected to more drastic processing than pasteurization, allowing them to be stored for a long time outside the cold chain. Crucially for some investors, operating in this niche meant being subject to much less rigid regulations than those in force for pasteurized milk. Price controls were much more flexible, there was no need to obtain a licence to supply a particular city, and there was no local monopoly to respect. Much of the core of Spain's processing industry at the end of the period consisted of companies that, like Pascual or Central Lechera Asturiana, had started in the 1960s but had never been involved in the pasteurized milk chain. Instead, they had opted to become suppliers of sterilized milk on a national scale from one or two strategically located factories (Calvo-González, 2021; Domínguez, 2003; Langreo, 1995).

It is true that the industrialization of the production chain did not immediately reduce the price of milk purchased by consumers. If the network of milk centrals had become denser, it was because (at least in part) the state was improving its expected profitability, which was important to avoid returning to the times when industrialists complained that the consumer price of milk was too low to amortize their investments. Additionally, it should be noted that processed milk was more expensive than the raw milk that most consumers originally drank. Whether pasteurized or sterilized, processed milk incorporated into its final price the profit of processing industries, making its price higher. Consequently, each time a household replaced raw milk with processed milk, or each time a previously non-consuming household transitioned to regular consumption of processed milk, a kind of upward step in the average price paid for milk was generated (Collantes, 2017b).

Over time, however, the industrialization of the dairy chain produced the type of cost reduction one would associate with large-scale standardized production. The absorption of technological innovations improved the efficiency of the processing of raw milk into pasteurized milk. There were also clear productivity gains resulting from the adoption of organizational improvements within companies. Additionally, and this could be even more critical in pressing the final price paid by consumers, the rise of the processing industry radically transformed the livestock link in the chain (Domínguez, 2003; Langreo, 1995).

We had left some farmers engaged in a process of dairy specialization and incorporation of high-yield cows. This path of change reached much greater depth and diffusion from the mid-1960s onwards, as the rise of the processing industry multiplied the incentives for farmers to do so. The Friesian cow became widespread on dairy farms, along with an intensification of animal feeding systems that included the expansion of pastures and meadows at the expense of subsistence polycultures. Farmers also sought to strengthen the feeding base of their cows by purchasing increasing amounts of industrial feed, allowing them to have herds larger than what their local agroecosystems would have initially allowed. The specialization and capitalization of livestock farms were completed with the purchase of milk replacers that allowed feeding calves without resorting to their mothers' milk, which could then be sold entirely to the processing industry. Some of these investments were supported by public policies, which, as in other areas of the Spanish agricultural sector, provided information and incentives for the adoption of the so-called 'green revolution'. Others were directly supported by the industries themselves, which carried out an intense outreach effort among farmers and, in some cases, financed the investments made by them. A clear case of this was, in the final stretch of the period, the incorporation of refrigerated tanks in an increasingly large proportion of farms (Calcedo, 1996; Casado, 2005; Langreo, 1995, 1996; Otero, 2022).

The extraordinary productivity gains achieved by farmers made possible an equally extraordinary reduction in the price of the raw material purchased by the industries. No other link in the chain contributed as much to changing the trend of the final price paid by consumers as the reduction in the farmgate price. Thanks to the reduction in the price received by farmers, the industry was able to reduce its selling prices while increasing its gross margin. The market power enjoyed by some industries over the farmers who served as their suppliers could indeed accentuate this dynamic through unbalanced negotiations between them for the collection price. Clearly, the industrialization of the production chain opened the door not only to greater production possibilities but also to structural inequality between a plethora of family farmers and the (comparatively) small number of industries collecting their milk. From the consumer's perspective, these greater productive possibilities, regardless of how their fruits were distributed among the different links in the chain, allowed for a reduction in the price of the final product.

From the mid-1970s onwards, these pressures on the consumer price of milk were reinforced by transformations that began to occur in the commercial link of the chain. Although there were some precedents for self-service chains, it was now that large-scale supermarkets and hypermarkets began to be implemented in Spain. It was the start of a 'retailing revolution' that profoundly transformed the organization of the sector, with dairy being one of its spearheads. While small retailers retained a considerable market share for some fresh foods (meat, fish, fruit, vegetables), milk, increasingly transformed into a non-perishable product after sterilization or UHT treatment, was one of the markets earliest dominated by large-scale retailers. Supermarkets and hypermarkets implemented strategies of supply chain management that allowed them to offer consumers more advantageous prices than those of small retailers. Moreover, many of them implemented marketing strategies in which milk played a 'loss leader' role: in a way that would not be illegal in Spain until 1996, supermarkets set a price for milk that was lower than its cost, but that could be expected to attract customers, so that the losses incurred through milk sales would be more than compensated by increased sales of other products (Castro, 2010; Collantes, 2016; Maixé, 2009).

In summary, the industrialization of the dairy chain, the transformation of livestock farms, and the start of the retail revolution led to a clear reduction in the consumer price of milk. In combination with their increasing income levels, this meant that there were no longer any significant economic obstacles to the mass consumption of milk. But, as we saw in the previous chapter, the problem was not only economic: would consumers now be willing to use their growing purchasing power to buy more milk?

The return of consumers

The social image of milk as a healthy food continued to spread, reaching even those population segments that, for various reasons, from their low educational levels to their location in rural areas with little dairy tradition, might have remained somewhat on the sidelines of the intense propaganda of the previous decade. The main public measures to promote demand remained in place. The International Milk Day continued to be celebrated, with slogans such as 'Milk is vitality', 'Milk completes nutrition', 'Milk leads to triumph in life', or 'Dairy products = Energy and growth'. The Franco regime continued to manage a school milk programme, and, some years after the transition to democracy, various regional governments and city councils of large urban areas promoted similar initiatives. Above all, the EDALNU programme for nutritional education was more extensively developed.

EDALNU's recommendations regarding milk were clear: it was such a positive food for health that it was necessary to consume more, much more than what was actually being consumed in Spain. Francisco Vivanco, one of the doctors who played a leading role in EDALNU, recommended in the 1970s that around 150–170 litres of milk per person per year should be consumed. This could be achieved, explained Vivanco and his collaborators, by drinking milk every day for breakfast and introducing milk or cheese as dessert for dinner on four out of seven days of the week. Even in a society experiencing a rapid massification of milk consumption, the reality was still far from such thresholds, so there continued to be a horizon of nutritional recommendations encouraging greater consumption ('Información', 1968a, 1968b, 1974; Vivanco et al., 1976: ch. 29).

However, as we saw in the previous chapter, these recommendations had to align with the perceptions that consumers had of the milk that was actually available to them. This is where the industrialization of the dairy chain that took place from the mid-1960s became crucial. Dairy industrialization allowed consumers in cities and increasingly in rural communities to have the option to buy processed milk. This way, consumers could buy the type of milk that nutritional messages had been focusing on and be free from the economic and health problems associated with the consumption of raw milk. Processed milk was a standardized commodity that, in line with a more complex production process, actually had a higher price than raw milk. However, in return, it was a much more reliable product. Processing industries, by coordinating many of (if not all) the links in the chain connecting consumers with farmers, could provide guarantees that their milk was not adulterated or deteriorated. This standardization process was accompanied by the promulgation of public regulations, such as the Food Code of 1967 or the Technical-Sanitary Regulation of Milk and Dairy Products of 1974 (Collantes, 2020; Langreo, 1995).

Most consumers had a clear mind about this. Raw milk was more flavourful, and there were laments about the 'loss of that aged flavour' that the transition to an industrial milk, which some pejoratively saw as 'pure chemistry', entailed ('En Huelva', 1981; Trueba, 1968: 71). But processed milk was more reliable. Although the consumption of raw milk did not disappear overnight, it was increasingly confined to more marginal spaces. By the end of the period, it was mainly lower-income groups that, pressured by budget constraints or the desire to channel more resources to other foods or other consumer goods, still relied to some extent on the consumption of raw milk. However, some of these households were rural households that obtained raw milk through short circuits where most of the problems of asymmetric information and lack of trust that had plagued urban consumers did not occur. The mass of urban consumers, in any case, preferred to pay a 'quality premium' to access standardized and fully guaranteed milk (Collantes, 2019a; Nombela, 1984).

Sterilized and UHT milk played a decisive role in this process. The vision of the Franco regime of consumers supplied with pasteurized milk by milk centrals materialized only partially. An increasing proportion of the milk purchased by Spaniards became sterilized and, from the late 1970s, UHT milk. It was not evident that consumers would be interested in this type of milk. If pasteurized milk had a taste problem compared to raw milk, sterilized milk had an even more serious taste problem, given its more aggressive thermal process. Additionally, the perception that consumers had of sterilized milk had been greatly damaged by the way available packaging further deteriorated the sensory experience, creating a sense of cooked milk that displeased most of those who dared to drink it. UHT milk could thus have ended up where powdered milk, condensed milk, and the first versions of sterilized milk did: a possible complement to the dairy massification but by no means its driving force (Llona, 1962; Madrid, 1979).

And yet, UHT milk ended up taking centre stage, surpassing the market share of pasteurized milk. Although its processing was more aggressive than pasteurization, industries developed versions of UHT milk that at least mitigated the effect on taste. They also benefited from the development of new packaging, such as Tetra Brik, which improved consumers' sensory experience. With this somewhat improved product at their disposal, consumers soon appreciated its logistical advantages. Precisely because of its aggressive thermal treatment, UHT milk did not require refrigeration. Throughout our period, more and more households transitioned to having a refrigerator, but that was no longer the issue. The issue was that consuming a fresh product like pasteurized milk required buying it almost daily, while consuming UHT milk allowed households to manage their acquisition within the framework of a single large weekly purchase, increasingly made in supermarkets and hypermarkets. As the advertising of the leading UHT packaging company explained, 'buying 12 litres of milk at once, and placing 2 or 3 in the refrigerator and the rest in the pantry without storage problems, is already a reality today' (Tetra Pak, 1981: 16). By the 1980s, almost 90 per cent of households had switched to buying milk on a weekly or more frequent basis (Tetra Pak, 1982: 13). That is the moment when there was no turning back. When the president of the Association of Housewives and Consumers of Madrid had to give her opinion on the launch of the so-called 'certified milk', a short-lived attempt by some entrepreneurs to create a market for raw milk with full sanitary guarantees, she could only comment that 'after two days, this milk does not keep. As for the quality of the milk, yes, it is liked, but the major drawback is its short duration' (Trillo, 1988: 28).

Consumers converged here with industries and retailers who were even more enthusiastic about the logistical advantages of UHT milk. For industrialists, it meant a less delicate production process and, due to political circumstances, less subject to the annoying price regulations that conditioned the production of pasteurized milk. For supermarkets, not having to maintain the cold chain was a blessing that allowed managing milk like any non-perishable product. Supermarkets were, in fact, decisive in consumers' growing orientation towards UHT milk. Once consumers started signalling that they did not view the product with disdain, supermarkets began reducing their purchases of pasteurized milk, tended to focus on UHT, and went on using it as a 'loss leader'. If in 1960 Alberto Ullastres had to admit that the dictatorship had not been able to make consumers see powdered milk as 'true milk', by 1990, the industry and supermarkets had succeeded in making consumers consider UHT milk as such (Collantes, 2016; Langreo, 1995).

Whether pasteurized or UHT milk, consumers could have a reliable product that aroused their interest to a greater extent than raw milk had. The advertising communication of processors, reinforced in some cases by visits to factories by housewives and schoolchildren, emphasized time and again the quality of their milk, understood not so much in terms of taste but in terms of consumer safety. One of the companies that was positioning itself in the core of the sector, Uniasa, developed the Puleva brand, which literally meant 'Pure cow's milk' (*PUra LEche de VAca*). Another, Leche Pascual, armed with the slogan 'Quality, our reason for being', had no qualms about emphasizing that its product was more expensive than that of other brands, but encouraged consumers to notice that this was because their hygiene and quality standards (on farms, in milk processing, in logistics) were more demanding. By the 1980s, after a serious episode of food poisoning caused by the sale of bulk rapeseed oil, virtually all milk-producing companies that made significant advertising investments were emphasizing the reliability of their standardized product more than any other of its characteristics. When, in 1990, the main cooperatives in the northern regions of the Basque Country and Navarre merged to form the future giant Iparlat, they chose the corporate slogan 'Quality is our North'. Over time, moreover, the success of some of these brands worked a miracle that would have seemed impossible at the beginning of the UHT project: that consumers ended up assessing positively some of the sensory attributes that differentiated this type of milk. Blind tasting experiments revealed that the loyalty of consumers to Pascual, in particular, led them to give surprisingly high scores to milk with features such as browning or caramelized flavour (Barreiro et al., 2001; Collantes, 2019a; Lacasa, 1990; 'Lactonoticias', 1990: 8; Moreno, 1984: 12; 'Pascual', 1996: 54).

These are the qualitative foundations on which the processed milk life cycle took shape, sometime after the raw milk life cycle had shown signs of exhaustion. Once these social perceptions of pasteurized and UHT milk had spread, it was a fairly conventional life cycle. The response factor was remarkably high at the beginning of the period, when many households were starting to incorporate regular milk consumption. The response factor was especially high among the middle and lower classes and among populations in those regions with particularly low initial consumption levels. Once processed milk became available to most consumers, increases in their purchasing power were channelled back into larger purchases of the product. Among the upper classes and in regions like the north, where the social diffusion of milk consumption had been more widespread, the interest in further increasing milk purchases was not as vivid. Gradually, this became the more common situation throughout the country, as regular milk consumption was achieved in all types of households and territories. Spain was not heading towards a steady expansion of consumption up to the 150–170 litres recommended by doctors like Vivanco but rather towards stagnation around 100–120 litres. By the 1980s, consumers' interest in using their purchasing power gains to buy more milk was starting to stagnate, if not to decline. The processed milk life cycle was conventional in its pattern, but remarkably short in its duration.

The beginning of the end

Signs of change began to emerge in the 1980s. The consumption of processed milk continued to grow, but at a slower pace. Moreover, most of this growth resulted from consumers substituting raw milk with processed milk. The total consumption of liquid milk, in fact, ceased to grow as rapidly as in previous years, and if we focus exclusively on its domestic component, it even declined. The response factor of milk consumption not only continued to decrease (which could be expected according to the logic of conventional life cycles), but it even became negative. It was not that consumers, once the full diffusion of milk across all social strata and territories was achieved, had reached something akin to a saturation point; rather, they seemed intent on retracing some of the path they had rapidly gone through between 1965 and 1980.

It was not an economic issue. The purchasing power of Spanish households to buy milk continued to strengthen, albeit at a moderate pace compared to previous periods. However, the combination of macroeconomic, microeconomic, and social factors that had emerged from the mid-1960s remained in place. The real income of households increased clearly, especially once a new wave of economic growth based on construction, finance, tourism, and various stimuli from the country's entry into the European Economic Community in 1986 was underway. The consolidation of pro-equality policies favoured that growth was inclusive, with its effects on income levels unfolding across a broad range of households in all social classes. Meanwhile, the transformation of livestock farms, processing plants, and retail stores continued to generate productivity gains that, at least in part, were transferred to consumers in the form of lower milk prices.

However, consumers in the 1980s were no longer interested in using these increases in purchasing power to buy more milk. The social image of the product was changing due to the diffusion of the 'lipid hypothesis', which posited that excessive intake of saturated fats increased the risk of cardiovascular diseases and deteriorated nutritional health through the multiple impacts of obesity. As had happened in other Western countries before, milk was quickly singled out as a problematic food. In the paradigm shift taking place in nutritional science, the heroine of the 'newer nutrition' became the villain of 'negative nutrition' (Díaz Méndez and Gómez Benito, 2004; Valenze, 2011; Velten, 2010).

None of this was entirely new in the 1980s, but only then did the lipid hypothesis begin to gain significant traction in Spain. One cause, certainly, was that it had become more powerful in scientific terms. What had originally been some indications and hypotheses connecting them were increasingly becoming an organized constellation of results and prescriptions. But even more important than the scientific message was its reception by society. Spain's transition to what Malassis (1997) calls a society of 'average satiety' proved decisive in this respect. For these negative nutrition messages to have an impact, they required a society where food problems arising from scarcity were distant. As we saw in Chapter 1, these problems had marked Spain's history for a long time and would not be fully resolved until after the dramatic post-war nutritional crisis. Only in the 1980s, in a consumer society with remarkably high calorie intake, could negative nutrition messages begin to make a kind of impact that would have been unthinkable just a few years earlier.

The dairy industry did not stand idly by and tried to combat the advance of the lipid hypothesis. With the help of doctors and scientists who were part of its network, it designed alternative messages. Voices were given to those arguing that the lipid hypothesis was not scientifically correct, and also to those who claimed that, in the Spanish context, it was not as applicable as in others because the country had a relatively low level of dairy consumption. However, these communication actions did not achieve a forcefulness comparable to the pro-milk message that had been prevailing in previous years. In its early days in the 1950s, the International Milk Day, for example, had been a propaganda vector with multiple ramifications in events, media, and advertising campaigns. Now, however, it was a more modest event in which a speaker from the scientific world delivered a pro-milk message to an audience increasingly composed of those already connected to the dairy industry, using the event more as a meeting point for various business and political actors involved in the sector. The industry could no longer count on governments that would strongly voice support for a certain type of diet. The EDALNU programme that the dictatorship had initiated in 1961, in which milk had always played a significant role, declined in the last years of the dictatorship and the early years of democracy (Collantes, 2020; Díaz Méndez and Gómez Benito, 2010).

Regardless of whether the channels through which the industry sought to defend itself from the lipid hypothesis were effective, the industry itself contributed decisively to the triumph of the hypothesis. Taken as a whole, industrialists did not hesitate to criticize the lipid hypothesis and its implications. In his lecture at the International Milk Day in 1991, Antonio Lacasa of the National Association of Liquid Milk Manufacturers called on the collective to 'always be attentive to respond as they deserve to those who try to portray milk in a bad light … to consumers' ('La jornada', 1991: 18). However, each industrialist individually developed a business strategy that only affirmed and disseminated the hypothesis among the population. The first significant case was

Leche Pascual, one of the major UHT milk processors, which in 1980 introduced skimmed milk for the first time in the Spanish market. This was accompanied by an ambitious advertising campaign that emphasized its benefits for health and for consumer image, with the emphasis primarily on obesity prevention. All major milk-producing companies followed suit. It is likely that the prevailing spirit in the sector was described by a nutritionist who asserted that '[Milk] is more easily manipulable because today milk can have its fat removed better than a sausage. That's why milk is manipulated: because it's easy, not because it's guilty' ('La salud', 1993: 14). Guilty or not, the promotional campaigns for skimmed milk, with their implicit acceptance of the potential problems associated with whole milk consumption, probably did more to spread the lipid hypothesis than any public policy in place at that time (Collantes, 2015; 'Tomás Pascual', 2006).

However, removing the fat did not guarantee that consumers would continue to channel their increases in purchasing power into buying more milk. The initial response of consumers to skimmed milk was actually lukewarm (Extremo et al., 1992). It was a product with an unappealing taste and texture. Industrialists then introduced the option of semi-skimmed milk, which offered a more balanced way to combine nutritional and sensory aspects. Consumers showed a bit more interest in this product, but by 1990, over 80 per cent of the milk consumed in the country was still whole milk. The new launches were not a complete failure, but certainly they had not been able to sustain the wave of consumption growth that had been occurring since the mid-1960s. In fact, for some consumers, it might have made more sense to reduce their milk purchases rather than increase them. Especially in regions with higher consumption, such as the north, milk had ended up being present in various dietary spaces: not only as a breakfast staple but also as a supplement for snacks (like afternoon tea) or as a closer for dinner. Whether due to its association with the lipid hypothesis, the lesser appeal of low-fat milks, or simply because other alternatives unrelated to the dairy world were beginning to proliferate, milk was losing presence in some of these secondary spaces.

The 1980s, therefore, was the time when the model of mass consumption that had triumphed so strongly between approximately 1965 and 1980 began to run out of steam. An increasing number of consumers seemed to have settled into a level of milk consumption that was sufficient for them and, if we conduct a retrospective nutritional analysis, they were probably right. It is worth noting, moreover, that many households supplemented this with a growing consumption of cheese, yogurt, and other dairy products, thus reinforcing their alignment with nutritional recommendations.

'I trust *El Caserío*'

During the mass consumption wave that unfolded from the mid-1960s, the consumption of cheese and yogurt also increased. Their presence in the diet remained modest, but it is interesting to note that during the 1980s, while the great expansion of milk consumption was waning, the consumption of cheese, yogurt, and other fresh desserts continued to grow. Although dairy products played a complementary role within this consumption model, their subsequent rise to a central position in the next model was beginning to take shape.

Similar to milk, consumers were able to enjoy economic circumstances that favoured an increase in their purchases of cheese or yogurt. These products were understandably more expensive than milk, as they involved more complex production processes and, from a biological standpoint, represented a less efficient way to obtain the corresponding calories, proteins, vitamins, and minerals. Nevertheless, household budget constraints continued to ease, as had been the case in the years leading up to 1965. Economic growth and enhanced equality were joined, in these cases as well, by a clear trend towards the relative cheapening of products.

The cheese and yogurt production chains were very different from each other, but both underwent transformations that greatly expanded their potential. While much cheese continued to be produced in small dairies or on farms, a core of medium-sized cheese producers emerged. These proved capable of undertaking some technological innovation projects, especially in the standardization of production. Some larger business groups, especially the multinational Kraft, entered the processed cheese and melted cheese segment. The yogurt chain, on the other hand, was largely dominated by such large companies from the outset, with a special role for the multinationals Danone and Nestlé. These large companies leveraged the resources and know-how inherited from their parent companies, operated at an appreciable technological level, exploited the economies of scale derived from the manufacturing of large, standardized batches, and had efficient organizational systems that allowed them to coordinate a wide variety of functions and departments. It is worth noting that both cheese and yogurt producers benefited from a cheaper access to raw materials as a result of transformations in dairy farming, transformations that they also contributed to. They also benefited from the retailing revolution that supermarkets and hypermarkets were starting to bring about from the mid-1970s. The accumulation of these transformations along the cheese and yogurt chains generated productivity gains that, at least partially, were transferred to consumers in the form of lower prices in stores and supermarkets (Castro, 2008; Collantes, 2016; Domínguez, 2003; Langreo, 1995; López and Cebrián, 2005).

However, beyond economic factors, it was crucial that consumers became more receptive to cheese as a product. Cheese became a somewhat more standardized product, whose taste and texture could be more reliably anticipated than in the past. Cheese makers, especially those gaining in size and allocating resources to systematize their production processes, improved their ability to offer a product that did not undergo pronounced variations at different times of the year or from batch to batch. The logic of standardization could be taken to the extreme in some emerging segments, such as spreadable cheese and melted cheese. These were products that, in a sense, lent themselves better than traditional cured cheese to standardization, but it is also true that precisely for this reason, large companies with well-adapted organizational resources entered the niche. Nevertheless, even in the artisanal cheese segment, local varieties produced and marketed on a smaller scale, there were clear movements in that direction. In some of these cases, a certain collective capacity was even developed to promote the standardization process through PDO (protected designations of origin or *denominaciones de origen*) labels which, after having originated much earlier in the world of wine, developed quite vigorously in the 1980s for cheese (Bernardo, 1989; 'Dimensión', 1982; Yubero, 1972). The goal, for both these artisanal cheese makers and the more industrialized ones, was what Miguel Ángel Martín Villa (1986: 106), a technician from the regional government of Cantabria, considered to have been achieved for the designated origin cheese from his region in the mid-1980s: 'When someone buys a kilo of cheese, they are sure they are acquiring ten kilos of milk.'

Consumers shifted towards cheese because they could see that cheese was now a more reliable product, but also because cheese companies intensified their efforts to communicate this and other potential advantages of the product. An archetype is the advertising campaign launched by the Balearic company El Caserío, with its successful slogan 'I trust *El Caserío*' ('*De El Caserío me fío*'). The multinational Kraft also made a notable advertising effort to promote its spreadable cheeses, with a special impact on the child population. It is true that many cheese makers had too modest resources to deploy large-scale communication strategies. Nevertheless, collective initiatives aimed at improving consumers' generic perception of cheese began to emerge. Especially in the 1980s, as a result of collaboration between public administrations, cheese makers, and local groups, many cheese fairs and contests were held throughout the country. These events combined outreach with the tasting of various artisanal cheeses in a festive atmosphere that attracted numerous visitors (Arroyo, 1984; Duelo, 1987; 'El Caserío', 1996; 'Una apuesta', 1983).

The case of yogurt was different. Yogurt had always been a large-scale standardized production and, therefore, had not suffered from the perception problems that weighed down the consumption of some cheeses. The key in the case of yogurt was the advertising effort made by the major companies that dominated the sector to transform its social image, turning what was previously seen as a food for the sick into a food for the entire population. The leading role was played by the multinational Danone, which by the end of the period was not only leading the Spanish yogurt market with its Spanish subsidiary but also was the ninth-largest producer of ultra-processed foods in the world. Danone deployed very ambitious marketing campaigns with a deep impact on the population, emphasizing the health benefits associated with regular yogurt consumption. Alongside this nutritional element highlighted by advertising discourse, it is important to appreciate a sensory element that undoubtedly contributed to the take-off of the product as a mass food: its generous sugar content. Plain natural yogurt had moderate success, but its sugared version achieved greater dissemination. Although advertising frequently emphasized the natural character of the product, the latter gradually adopted features of what we now call ultra-processed foods. This did a lot to improve the sensory experience for consumers. This was also the angle from which Danone achieved great success with the launch of its fresh cheese Petit Suisse, with a presentation similar to that of yogurt, advertising focused on the child audience, and the addition of flavours and colourings that were traditionally not used in that niche (Castro, 2008; Lacasa, 1990; Langreo, 1995; Matallana, 1973; Wood et al., 2023).

For both cheese and yogurt, a final factor that contributed to making consumers more receptive was the increase in the variety of products available to them. With stronger production chains and more efficient commercial circuits, consumers began to have the possibility of buying different cheeses than those produced in their local area. The gradual liberalization of Spanish trade policy, first in the final stretch of the dictatorship and then during the country's process of accession to the European Economic Community, opened up some room for importers like Teodoro García Trabadelo to bring French, Dutch, and other European cheeses to Spanish stores and supermarkets. The activation of new life cycles for this type of cheese reinforced the effect that was already arising from the dynamics of the national market. As García Trabadelo (1980: 11) himself summarized, 'Variety attracts and increases consumption.' The same happened in the area of fresh desserts. In addition to plain natural yogurt and sugared natural yogurt, producers launched flavoured yogurts, the most popular of which was strawberry and yogurts with fruit pieces. Moreover, other desserts different from yogurt proliferated, quickly capturing the consumer's attention. Some replicated desserts with some domestic tradition behind them, such as flans and custards. Others offered something more novel, such as chocolate creams, shakes, or ice cream cakes. All of them were, in any case, what an editorial of the time called 'real treats' ('Ángulo', 1979: 3): ultra-processed products with a sugar content higher than that of other dairy foods.

All in all, there were still significant limits to the expansion of the consumption of dairy products. The variety of available cheeses was increasing, but even in the 1980s many consumers continued to trust only a few. Furthermore, consumer culture left fewer spaces for cheese than, for example, in France or Italy. Most consumers ate cheese for sandwiches and minor meals but not as a daily dessert after lunch or dinner, which was a niche dominated by fruit. Cheese also did not have a prominent gastronomic presence in the preparation of main courses. Yogurt consumption, on the other hand, was spreading, but the product remained somewhat uprooted and artificial for a certain fraction of the public. Even around 1990, as much as a third of Spanish households actually never bought any yogurt ('Ángulo', 1980; Arteaga, 1982; Nombela, 1984; 'Un mapa', 1983; Vázquez de Prada, 1991; Vivanco et al., 1976: ch. 20).

Be that as it may, the trend to incorporate more cheese, more yogurt, and more dairy desserts into the diet was quite widespread across the social spectrum. Although there was no trend towards social equalization comparable to that of milk, we cannot speak of the dairy products of this period as powerful status markers. They were just a modest complement that supported consumers' alignment with nutritional recommendations and made their dairy basket a bit more pleasant from a sensory point of view.

Conclusion: Coming together … for some time

The triumph of the mass dairy consumption model became possible once a congruent combination of changes occurred in various spheres. The macroeconomic and macrosocial environment facilitated a widespread and unprecedented increase in household income. Microeconomic developments were more favourable than in the years before 1965, and, under the leadership of an emerging liquid milk processing industry, affordable and reliable products were made available to consumers. Cultural perceptions of dairy as a food aligned with these developments, not only at the generic level of nutritional messages but also at the more specific level of consumer interest in the types of milk and dairy products available to them at any given time. It was primarily between 1965 and 1980 that favourable developments in these spheres combined, resulting in extraordinary and widespread growth in milk consumption. In combination with some simple milk-based products acting as supplements, the vast majority of Spaniards reached a nutritional situation by around 1990 that, in terms of dairy, could be considered satisfactory. It was a consumption pattern that allowed sufficient intake of the nutritional values most commonly associated with dairy, especially calcium, and did so across the social spectrum without significant status differences.

The dairy consumption pattern achieved by around 1990, however, was clearly an unstable endpoint. Already in the 1980s, trends had begun to emerge suggesting that the combination of factors that had supported mass consumption after 1965 was starting to break down. In a cultural environment where the traditional concern for malnutrition due to insufficient intake began to coexist with a new concern for malnutrition due to excessive intake, consumers' perception of milk began to change. In part because of this, and in part due to internal dynamics within the sector, the dairy industry was poised to radically renew consumers' choice space, offering them a much broader range of dairy products than at any time in the past. How could the pattern of dietary consumption be stable if, along the way, it had become connected to an economic system that, in the words of Schumpeter (1942: 102), was 'by nature a form or method of economic change and not only is but never can be stationary'? The long and tumultuous journey that had moved Spaniards away from their traditional bad diets was about to be quickly succeeded by an innovative journey … back to bad diets.

Part III

Sophisticated Deviation (1990–Present)

7

Upgrading games

'Innovation drives dairy consumption', said the Minister of Agriculture, Fisheries and Food Elena Espinosa in the presentation of a strategic report on the Spanish agri-food sector in 2004. 'The most innovative products,' she went on, 'take our consumers by storm. At least, the battle for consumption is being won' ('La innovación', 2004: 6–7). It is highly unlikely that Espinosa, a member of the Socialist Party, was aware that her allusion to a battle for dairy consumption was connecting her to a minister of Franco's dictatorship almost half a century earlier. Espinosa's battle was, however, very different from that of Ullastres. Its objective was not the massification of milk consumption, but rather that consumers engage in an upgrading of their dairy basket. This would involve substituting the nutritionally adequate basket that they already had around 1990 with another basket that was more sophisticated and entailed higher spending. Yet, as discussed in Chapter 3, the outcome of this second 'battle for dairy' was more dismal than that of the first. The upgrading of the dairy basket according to the money metric of consumer society (or, for that matter, food capitalism) did not translate into an upgrading according to the nutritional metric or the perspective of the good life. Dairy under-consumption returned, ultra-processed products proliferated, and surplus consumer spending was not directed towards relevant societal challenges.

Under-consumption in an era of surplus spending

The aggregate consumption of milk and dairy products decreased steadily, especially in the case of the product that had previously acted as the engine of the expansive previous model: liquid milk. Consumers increased their purchases of cheese, yogurt, and other dairy products, which together ended up absorbing more than two-thirds of their total dairy expenditure (Table 7.1). However, in

Table 7.1 Domestic Consumption of Milk and Dairy Products Per Person and Year

	1990		**2008**		**2019**	
	INE	**MAPA**	**INE**	**MAPA**	**INE**	**MAPA**
Consumption						
Liquid milk (L)	121.1	100.0	82.9	80.0	65.2	69.3
Canned milk (kg)	1.8	1.4	0.3	0.7	0.3	0.6
Cheese (kg)	5.7	5.1	6.9	7.7	6.5	7.8
Butter (kg)	0.3	0.1	0.4	0.2	0.4	0.3
Yogurt[a] (kg)	7.6	7.1	19.0	15.2	15.8	14.4
Other (kg)	1.6	3.3	8.3	10.5	6.4	12.6
Share of consumer spending on dairy (%)						
Liquid milk	54	50	35	34	28	27
Canned milk	6	3	1	3	1	2
Cheese	26	28	29	29	37	33
Butter	1	1	1	1	2	1
Yogurt[a]	11	11	24	20	23	18
Other	2	7	10	14	10	18
Total	100	100	100	100	100	100

Note: [a]Includes all fermented milks.
Sources: INE (1965–95, 2023a), MAPA (1988–91, 2023a).

physical terms, this did not compensate for the rapid decline in their milk intake. This is the immediate cause why our data in Chapter 3 revealed that consumers were moving out of the band defined by dietary references.

The return of dairy under-consumption has been a particularly acute problem in low-income households and young households (Table 7.2). Low-income households led the movement towards lower milk consumption, and their purchases of dairy products fell far short of compensating for it. High-income households, on the other hand, joined the reduction in milk consumption later and from the outset incorporated substantial quantities of cheese, yogurt, and other desserts. Young households, in turn, consistently showed lower milk consumption levels than households led by older individuals, and this gap widened over the period. Each new cohort consumed significantly less than the ageing cohort that disappeared for biological reasons. However, except for high-income households and the oldest households, the return of dairy under-consumption was a widespread trend affecting most Spanish households.

Table 7.2 Domestic Dairy Consumption Per Person and Year by Consumer Profiles

	Milk (litres)			Dairy products (kg)		
	1990	2008	2019	1990	2008	2019
Average	100.0	80.0	69.3	15.6	33.6	35.1
By social class						
Upper	94.1	94.2	77.9	17.4	41.2	39.4
Middle-upper	95.8	80.6	69.5	15.9	36.3	36.3
Middle-lower	103.5	80.3	70.4	15.4	33.1	35.6
Lower	101.8	68.7	62.5	15.2	25.6	30.8
By age[a]						
Less than 35	89.3	68.6	53.1	18.6	35.6	29.4
35 to 49	100.4	73.4	60.3	14.8	32.2	32.7
50 to 64	93.1	78.3	68.7	13.9	32.2	34.6
65 and more	121.0	105.3	96.9	18.2	36.7	44.0

Note: [a]Age of the household member in charge of purchasing food and drink.
Source: MAPA (1988–91, 2023a).

The diversification of the consumption pattern, with a growing emphasis on milk-based products, not only did not go far enough to prevent this problem but also generated others along the way. Nutritionally, what was still a basket full of simple foods in 1990 gradually turned into a basket increasingly populated by ultra-processed foods. It is not just that milk is a simpler processed product than cheese or, especially, most yogurts and fresh desserts. It is also the fact that, within each of these categories, there was an extraordinary expansion of the number of specific product varieties purchased by consumers, and this expansion was characterized by a plethora of increasingly complex dairy products.

Yogurts and fresh desserts, in particular, were presented in continuously renewed versions, characterized by their engineered nature. The basic types of yogurt were natural and simple transformations of it, such as flavoured yogurt and yogurt with pieces of fruit. While these varieties became more complex with new flavour and ingredient combinations, all kinds of fat-free yogurts and a new generation of 'functional' dairy products, ranging from fermented milk with probiotics like bifidus to fermented milk with plant sterols, were incorporated into the new consumption pattern. Somewhat replicating what had happened a generation earlier with milk, the increase in aggregate consumption of fermented milks hid the overlap of two very different product life cycles (Figure 7.1): that of the so-called 'classic' yogurts, expanding until the late 1990s, and that of the new

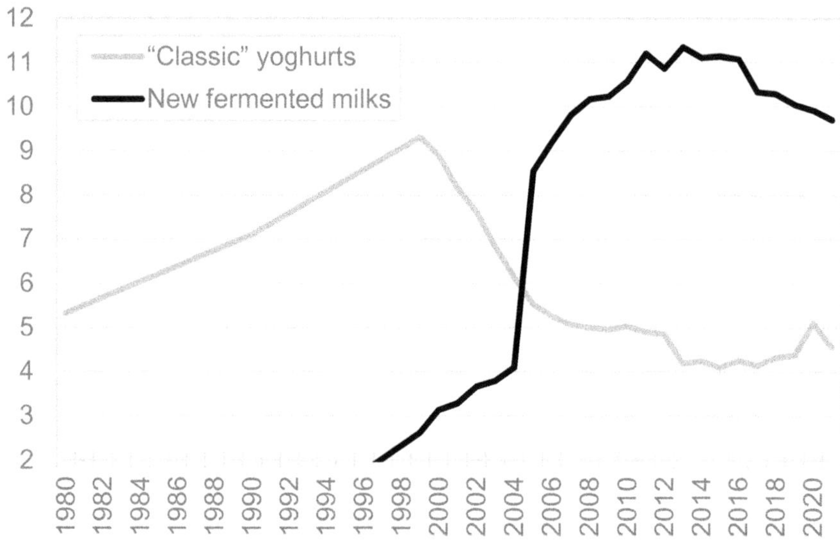

Figure 7.1 Consumption of fermented milks (kilograms per person and year), 1980–2021.
Source: MAPA (1988–91, 2023a). The 1980 figure is re-scaled back from INE (1965–95). See Appendix Table A17.

fermented milks, which took over from that point and reached its peak towards the Great Recession. Something similar happened with the continuous renewal of shakes, both milk and yogurt-based, or with the incorporation into the diet of increasing amounts of dairy desserts that had traditionally been homemade, such as flans and custards, or that had never been part of the diet, such as chocolate and cream. Even in the world of milk, the simplest processed product par excellence, there had been a renewal with the appearance and diffusion of milks enriched with minerals and vitamins, which before the Great Recession had already captured a quarter of the market ('Análisis', 2006: 116).

Of course, not all new varieties of dairy products appearing in the shopping basket were NOVA 4 foods, that is, ultra-processed. In the world of cheese, for example, such novelties coexisted with others that would be better categorized as plain processed foods. Until 1990, most consumers who ate cheese focused on hard-cured cheeses that, with some imprecision, were associated with the *Manchego* name and some other more or less local varieties. Soon various fresh, melted, and creamy cheeses became regular parts of the diet. In addition, differentiated products appeared among cured and semi-cured cheeses, from artisanal PDO cheeses that established a link with the traditional production practices of an area to industrial cheeses that made use of various combinations of types of milk. Consumers also started purchasing more substantial amounts of cheese varieties from France, the Netherlands, and other European countries. In turn, the formats of the consumed cheeses changed a lot, moving from voluminous pieces of several kilograms to slices, tubs, and wedges. Much of this diversification developed in the NOVA 2 region of plain processed foods.

However, the data are clear: the consumption of yogurt and the so-called 'other' dairy products, mostly ultra-processed foods, grew much faster than that of cheese and quickly began to absorb a proportion of consumer spending higher than that of the latter. Dairy products were contributing to the eventually controversial transition to a diet rich in ultra-processed foods. Moreover, some of them were displacing healthier foods: this was the case of refrigerated dairy products displacing fruit for dessert or shakes displacing milk for breakfast ('Crece', 2018; Langreo, 2003; López Plaza, 1995).

Both nutritional problems, the classic one of low intakes and the new one of ultra-processed foods, must be put into their economic context. Just as low-income households led the return of the classic problem of low intakes, high-income households were the ones that contributed the most to the emergence of the new problem of consumerism. This was due to their rapid shift from milk to cheese, yogurt, and various desserts. However, as the period progressed, even lower-status households ended up incorporating increasing amounts of dairy products into their diet, spending money beyond what would have been necessary to buy the basic, nutritionally adequate basket. As we saw in Chapter 3, only a very small fraction of this surplus spending was for consumption based on values and oriented towards societal challenges, such as organic milk or PDO cheese.

These were the underlying trends of the new consumption model, but we should recognize the importance of the Great Recession as a turning point in its trajectory. Before 2008, the contracting dynamics of physical consumption were not as pronounced. After all, milk consumption did not begin to decline until around the turn of the millennium. It is true that its eventual decline began to distance consumers, especially in low-income and middle-low-income households, from the zone defined by nutritional recommendations, but the consumption of cheese, yogurt, and other dairy products grew rapidly. The problem was more the diffusion of ultra-processed foods and the inefficient surplus spending in which more and more households, including eventually lower-status ones, were involved. After the Great Recession, this problem stabilized. The consumption of ultra-processed foods slowed down. The product life cycles that had unfolded so dynamically during the twenty years before the recession quickly entered a phase of maturity, if not decline. The case of yogurts and the rest of fermented milks, perhaps the great symbol of the sophistication of the consumption pattern that had taken place, is particularly eloquent. However, given that milk consumption continued to fall in all social strata and age groups, the stabilization of consumerism could only lead to a broader diffusion of aggregate dairy under-consumption. In what could be identified as the beginning of the end of the post-1990 consumption model, the Great Recession interrupted the upward wave of most milk-based products but did not return households to the type of essentially adequate dairy basket that was normal in 1990. The downward wave of milk consumption continued, and consumers fell increasingly short of nutritional recommendations.

'A variety that captivates'

A fundamental reason why the dairy basket of 1990 was not a stable situation was that stability threatened the interests of the processing industry that had been shaping up during the previous decades. This is the perspective from which we must consider the proliferation of an increasingly wide variety of dairy products in the market: what a promotional slogan of the National Federation of Dairy Industries (FENIL, *Federación Nacional de Industrias Lácteas*) aptly called 'a variety that captivates' ('Boletín', 2011a: 45). Before asking why consumers were interested in these new options, we must study why these options came to exist in the first place. Before asking why consumers acted as they did within their choice space, we must study why that choice space expanded so significantly.

The answer, in short, is that the industry created these products to soften the forces that were leading it towards a harsh structural adjustment. The exhaustion of the great expansive phase of consumption that had taken place in the previous decades could not fail to have consequences for the dairy industries. This alone probably would have been sufficient to provoke a transition in the sector from its previous phase of 'transformation' to one of 'rationalization', to use the terms of evolutionary economics. With demand decelerating, it was time for increased competition and the concentration of activity in a small number of highly productive and efficient companies. But this horizon of structural adjustment, already unsettling in itself, was outlined even more forcefully by parallel changes in the political economy of the chain (Collantes, 2019b).

Spain's accession to the European Economic Community in 1986 led to the dismantling of the network of milk centrals created by the Franco regime after 1952, as well as the associated market regulations. The deregulation of the production chain was not total, as farmers were integrated into the European dairy quota system, which, in an attempt to correct the overproduction caused by the Common Agricultural Policy, allocated a production volume to each farm. It was, however, a significant deregulation, which almost suddenly threw the milk centrals into an environment characterized by a kind of competitive tension to which they were not accustomed. Moreover, and in a way that affected not only the centrals but all other industries as well, retailing was displacing processing as the dominant link in the food chain. In contrast to the traditional fragmentation of the sector, in the final stretch of the twentieth century most dairy sales ended up concentrated in a small group of large supermarket and hypermarket chains (Figure 7.2). The culmination of this 'retailing revolution' gave supermarkets and hypermarkets unprecedented bargaining power, which they used forcefully to press down the prices they paid to their suppliers and, consequently, the latter's profit margins. Large retailers also developed a strategy to manufacture and promote their own brands, which gradually gained increasing market shares based on their lower prices. This left their suppliers in an even more subordinate position, with quality standards and profit margins

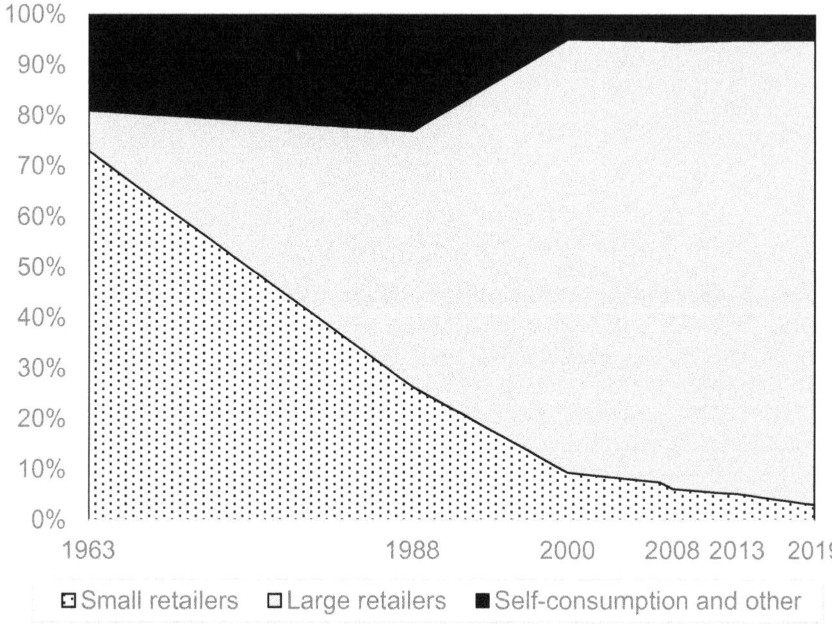

Figure 7.2 Retailer shares of the dairy market (%), 1963–2019.
Sources: Collantes (2016: 5), updated with MAPA (2023a). See Appendix Table A18.

closely controlled by supermarkets. If demand trends were already shaping a horizon of structural adjustment in the dairy industry, political deregulation and the rise of supermarkets ensured that a particularly harsh version of this adjustment was under way (Collantes, 2016; Langreo, 1995, 2005).

Even though there are some difficulties involved in the estimation, the available data on profit rates suggest a contrast between the significant profitability of investment in the dairy industry during the decades of mass consumption and the much lower profitability that has been obtained in the last three decades, when the added value of the dairy industry ceased to grow (Figure 7.3). In

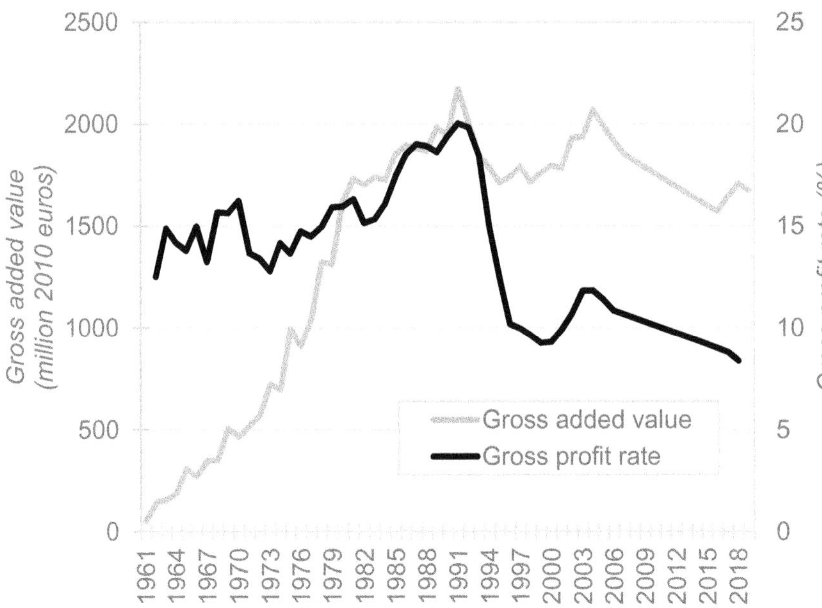

Figure 7.3 Added value[a] and profitability[b] in dairy processing, 1961–2019.
Sources: 1961–80: INE (2023d), old series; 1978–92: INE (2023d), new series; 1985–94: INE (2023e), 1986 baseline; 1995–2000: INE (2023e), 1995 baseline; 2000–2007: INE (2023e), 2000 baseline; 2015–18: INE (2023f), 'legal units' series; 2018–19: INE (2023f), 'statistical units' series; deflator: Prados de la la Escosura (2017), updated series, htpps://frdelpino.es. When two different sources overlap at any given year, it is their average that is retained. See Appendix Table A19.
Notes: [a](V – C), where V is output value and C is intermediate consumption (in 1961, when electricity costs are not available, we assume that the ratio of electricity to fuel costs was similar to the one that we can observe for 1962).
[b]Three-year moving average of [$S/(C + P)$], where S is the gross operating surplus, C is intermediate consumption, and P is personnel costs. For 1961–80, S is calculated as output value minus all costs (personnel, electricity, fuel, and raw materials) and C includes electricity, fuel, and raw materials.

the early 1990s, outside the small club formed by the three multinational corporations operating in the sector (Danone, Nestlé, and Kraft), the profit rate was below 1 per cent. By the end of that decade, the journal *Industrias Lácteas Españolas* expressed it emphatically: 'Industries are not what they used to be. There are fewer benefits now, and the landscape has complicated. Any time in the past was better' ('Tiempos', 1999: 9). Some estimated that the Spanish dairy industry had a significant excess of production capacity, perhaps around 50 per cent, compared to effective demand (Astarloa, 1986: 11; 'Panorama', 1992a: 65).

The response of the vanguard of Spain's dairy industry to these troubling pressures for its 'rationalization' was to project the beginning of a new phase of 'transformation' that would make structural adjustment unnecessary, or at least soften it. The project was to give birth to what we might call a 'Galbraith moment': inducing new needs among consumers to prevent them from being satisfied with the consumption basket they had already reached. Once the milk cycle was exhausted, continued business growth involved either expelling competitors from a declining market or, alternatively, initiating new product life cycles. Production shifted from milk to milk-based products, and within each of these categories, from traditional versions of products to more complex and sophisticated versions. As in Galbraith's world, the project consisted of rebuilding a scarcity-centred economy after it had died from success at the end of the previous period.

Both for its direct achievements and its demonstration effect on other companies, a key actor in defining this project was Danone, whose profit rate remained clearly above average (Langreo, 1995: ch. 5; 'Panorama', 1992a: 65). In a talk given in the early 1990s, one of the most visible faces of the company explained to his dairy industry colleagues that

> The economic development strategies of companies require a constant contribution of new products to the market that allows them to occupy new segments of consumption or expand existing ones. This effort has materialized in the Spanish market with the constant appearance of new fresh dairy products. (Mateos, 1991: 36)

International business organizations, such as the European Dairy Industry Association, and experts from companies in other countries conveyed similar messages to Spanish industrialists, emphasizing the importance of innovation, imagination in developing new products, the creation of added value, and qualitative competition. National experts with whom industrialists had more direct contact also made similar recommendations. A figure as respected as

Jaime Lamo de Espinosa, president of the Dairy Studies Foundation and former minister of Agriculture, Fisheries, and Food, warned them in a conference that 'to face the future, it is necessary to ... move towards products with higher added value since producing only milk and butter will not succeed in the medium and long term' ('La cuota láctea', 1993: 56). A widely circulated report among industrialists showed with statistical data that, in Spain, the profit rate was higher among companies oriented towards dairy products than among those oriented towards milk (Barili, 1988; 'Información', 1993; 'Panorama', 1992a).

Although we obviously cannot take it as precise evidence, the addition of new items to the statistics of the Food Consumption Panel gives us an idea of the magnitude of the change (Table 7.3). In 1987, when the first edition of the Panel was published, there were twenty items, some of which actually overlapped (for instance, types of milk by fat content overlapped with types of milk by processing method). Twenty years later, by the time the Great Recession erupted, supermarket shelves devoted to dairy products had become so heterogeneous that no less than thirty-four new items were considered necessary to add. As an anonymous writer pointed out in 2001 in the sector's most important professional magazine, 'If we guide ourselves by the number of novelties presented by dairy industries in recent times, we must say that the dairy sector is booming' ('Panorama', 2001a: 66).

It is true that, according to the data in Table 7.3, the change seems to have slowed down, and in the last decade, only a couple of items related to lactose-free milk and cheese have been added to the statistics.

Table 7.3 Dairy Rubrics in the Food Consumption Panel

	1987	**New rubrics**		
		1999	**2008**	**2019**
Liquid milk	Pasteurized Sterilized Raw Whole Skimmed Semi-skimmed		Fortified[d] Goat's milk	Lactose-free
Canned milk	Condensed Powdered Evaporated			

Table 7.3 (*Continued*)

	1987	New rubrics		
		1999	**2008**	**2019**
Butter	Butter	Packed Raw	Light	
Cheese	Fresh Cream Hard[b] Other	Semi-hard	Regular fresh Light fresh No-salt fresh Low-salt fresh Fortified[e] Tender Sheep Goat Edam Emmental/Gruyère Blue	Lactose-free
Yogurt[a]	Natural Flavoured Fruit bits	Other yogurts	With additives Skimmed Fortified Probiotics[f] Other ferment[g]	
Other	Milk shake Yogurt shake Other	Ice cream[c] Cream Curd	Shake with cereals Shake w/ additives Ice cream cake Custard *Crème caramel* Chocolate cream Catalan cream Creamy desserts	

Notes: [a]Includes all fermented milk.

[b]Includes semi-hard.

[c]Includes ice cream cake.

[d]With calcium, vitamins, bifidobacteria and fibre, royal jelly, linoleic acid, or 'other'.

[e]With calcium or vitamins.

[f]Milk fermented with bifidobacteria.

[g]Fermented milk other than yogurt or milk fermented with bifidobacteria.

Source: MAPA (1988–91, 2023a).

However, especially between 1990 and 2008, consumers' choice space expanded enormously. How did consumers behave within that expanded choice space? It is time to resume our analysis of purchasing power and response factors.

Soft budget constraints

Most consumers were subject to a soft budget constraint most of the time. Over the decades leading up to 1990, we had already seen this constraint soften, and the trend continued from 1990 onwards (Table 7.4). Both in the twenty years prior to the Great Recession and in the ten years following it, consumers' purchasing power for milk, cheese, yogurt, and other dairy products clearly increased. Although there were temporary interruptions, such as a brief upturn in prices in the early years of the new millennium and the impact of the Great Recession on household incomes, these were fleeting exceptions.

Table 7.4 Annual Compound Rates of Change (%)

	Short periods				**Long periods**	
	1990–2000	**2000–8**	**2008–13**	**2008–19**	**1990–2008**	**2008–19**
Income[a]	1.7	1.7	−3.8	2.1	1.7	−0.6
Price[b]						
Milk	−2.9	3.4	−5.5	−0.8	−0.1	−3.0
Cheese	−2.5	0.3	−2.7	0.1	−1.3	−1.2
Yogurt	−3.5	4.2	−4.4	−1.5	−0.1	−2.8
Other	−4.8	2.8	−3.2	−0.2	−1.5	−1.6
Purchasing power[c]						
Milk	4.6	−1.8	1.7	3.0	1.8	2.4
Cheese	4.2	1.3	−1.1	2.0	3.0	0.6
Yogurt	5.2	−2.5	0.6	3.6	1.8	2.2
Other	6.5	−1.1	−0.6	2.4	3.2	1.0

Notes: [a]Household income per consumption unit (2019 euros).
[b]Nominal price deflated by the general price index (2019 euros).
[c] $[r(Y) - r(P)]$, where r is annual compound rate of change, Y is income, and P is price.
Sources: Income 1990–2008: INE (2023e); income 2008–19: INE (2023g); nominal price: MAPA (2023a); deflator: INE (2023c).

Originally, the key was an increase in consumer income. Until the outbreak of the Great Recession, the growth of the Spanish economy raised household incomes in a widespread manner, without significantly accentuating inequality. While this growth was not as rapid, and the reduction in inequality not as pronounced as in the period 1950–75, it was sufficient to drive sustained improvement in purchasing power. However, the financial crisis between 2008 and 2013 led to a drastic deterioration in household incomes, particularly when considering the simultaneous increase in distributional inequality. The average data presented in Table 7.4, already sufficiently illustrative, tends to smooth out the impact suffered by most households. As of 2019, and despite six years of economic recovery, neither the average household nor any social stratum had reached an income level comparable to what they had enjoyed before the recession. The crisis triggered by Covid-19 in 2020 only pushed that horizon further away.

However, the tremendous economic and social turbulence unleashed by the recession did not have such lasting and substantial effects on dairy purchasing power because it was soon offset by reductions in the consumer price for these products. Except for a brief parenthesis in the years immediately prior to the recession, the relative price of milk and dairy products had been persistently falling, becoming an additional source of growth in consumer purchasing power. The data in Table 7.4 do not do justice to the magnitude of this price drop because, aggregated by product groups, it does not extract the effect of the sophistication that occurred within each group. The 'average' yogurt in 2019 is a more complex and higher-priced yogurt than the simple 'average' yogurt in 1990. Even underestimated in this way, the drop in relative prices over the last thirty years has been formidable. If we delve into the price transmission along the chain, we find that, as in the past, one of the pillars of price reduction was the persistent decrease in the price that farmers received for selling their raw milk to industries (Figure 7.4). However, this time there was also a noticeable downward contraction of the rest of the prices along the production chain. In fact, the gap between the price of milk sold by farmers and the price of milk purchased by consumers remained fairly stable throughout our period. This aligns with the supply-side picture we have painted in the previous section: the production chain was undergoing a severe process of structural adjustment, this process was driven by a small number of large supermarkets competing intensely with each other, and supermarkets transmitted that tension upstream towards industries and farmers. Although product innovations pulled the average price of dairy

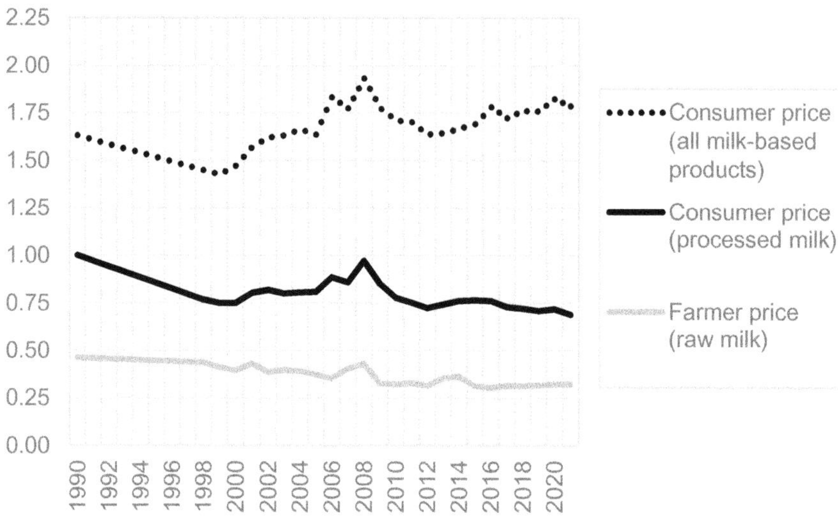

Figure 7.4 Farmer and consumer prices (constant 2013 euros), 1990–2021.
Sources: Consumer price: INE (1965–95, 2023a); farmer price: MAPA (2023b). See Appendix Table A20.

products upwards, the underlying trend towards reducing the price of each product individually weighed much more heavily.

This meant that, especially during critical moments like the Great Depression and its aftermath, consumers' purchasing power for dairy products could continue to increase without serious disruptions. During the upswing phase of the macroeconomic cycle, before 2008, the drop in relative prices already made a significant contribution to the improvement of household purchasing power. This was important at a time when, although real income was growing, it was by no means growing at the accelerated rate it had during the second half of Franco's dictatorship. However, it was mainly after 2008 that the drop in relative prices proved crucial to prevent the economic crisis from severely deteriorating consumers' purchasing power for milk and dairy products. While their real income deteriorated, the extent to which the relative prices of milk and dairy products fell even faster meant that the purchasing power for buying milk, cheese, or yogurt did not decline as much. By 2019, no status group had recovered its pre-crisis income level, but all of them, even the lower class (hit particularly hard by the recession), had a greater purchasing power to buy milk and dairy products.

At least in terms of dairy products, the budget constraint that consumers were facing did not significantly tighten and, in fact, tended to continue softening. From an economic perspective, a great diversity of possible paths for the evolution of consumption was therefore feasible.

Different responses for different products

The response factors reveal strong contrasts among different dairy products. The response factor for milk, which had already fallen slightly below zero in the 1980s, remained in negative territory, reaching an even greater magnitude (Table 7.5). Consumers were not interested in channelling their increased purchasing power towards buying more milk. Enriched milk did have a positive response factor, as a new product at the beginning of a reasonably successful life cycle, and the response factors for low-fat milk (semi-skimmed and skimmed) remained near zero. None of this could, by any means, compensate for the declining interest of consumers in whole milk, the product that had acted as the driving force behind the previous consumption model.

It is not that milk had become what an economist would call an inferior good. When the Great Recession erupted, and consumer income plummeted, they did not return to increased milk consumption. Income was not a key variable from a cross-sectional perspective either: it was not the upper classes that, having surpassed a certain income threshold, began to reduce their milk purchases.

Table 7.5 Response Factor of Milk Consumption

	1990–2008		2008–2019	
	MAPA	INE	MAPA	INE
Aggregate	−0.68	−1.13	−0.55	−0.97
By social class				
Upper	0.00		−0.66	
Middle-upper	−0.53		−0.56	
Middle-lower	−0.64		−0.50	
Lower	−1.18		−0.44	
By age				
Less than 35	−1.00		−1.17	
35 to 49	−0.84		−0.86	
50 to 64	−0.42		−0.56	
More than 64	−0.51		−0.23	

Sources: MAPA (1988–91, 2023a), INE (2023a); see Table 7.4.

It was actually the lower classes that, already in the 1990s, did so. The diffusion of the trend occurred from the bottom-up in the social ladder. The middle classes joined somewhat later and more moderately, and the upper classes only did so after the Great Recession. The disaggregated response factors by social status tell this story clearly. Rather than some kind of drastic change in their economic situation, what propelled the lower classes towards under-consumption was their negative orientation towards milk. And what later spread this issue upwards in the social pyramid was the diffusion of that attitude, rather than (again) the evolution of income levels or relative prices.

The response factors lead to a similar conclusion when disaggregated by age groups. Rather than the economic evolution of households, what made the difference were their very different orientations towards milk. The young cohorts at the end of the period had significantly higher purchasing power than their counterparts at the beginning of the period, but simply did not use that purchasing power to buy more milk. If we track the cohorts over time, we find that only those cohorts surpassing retirement age seemed to increase their response factors and orient positively towards milk. If the rest of the cohorts and age groups did not, it was not because their economic circumstances forced them to.

In summary, consumers were reverting to the under-consumption zone, but for different reasons than in the past. In the past, before the 1960s, low consumption was closely related to the severe budget constraints faced by most households in most regions of the country. Now, however, budget constraints were very soft, and the key issue was that increasingly broad segments of consumers, in all social strata and almost all age groups, showed no interest in maintaining a diet rich in milk. In the classic era of malnutrition, consumer interest could fluctuate, and indeed, we have studied its deterioration during the challenging period at the end of the 1950s and the beginning of the next. But not even at that time were we close to openly negative response factors as those found for the late twentieth century and up to the present.

Dairy products, of course, were another story. Their response factors were generally not only positive but extraordinarily high (Table 7.6). In the twenty years leading up to the Great Recession, consumers were more interested than in the immediate past in channelling their increased purchasing power towards the purchase of cheese and, especially, yogurt and all kinds of fresh dairy products. Consumers responded to the increase in their purchasing power much more than proportionally, producing response factors exceeding two, reminiscent of those obtained for milk during the initial stage of its life cycle in the decades

Table 7.6 Response Factor of the Consumption of Dairy Products

	1990–2008			2008–19		
	Cheese	Yogurt[a]	Other	Cheese	Yogurt[a]	Other
Aggregate						
MAPA	0.78	2.36	2.10	0.14	−0.21	1.75
INE	0.52	2.24	3.91	0.82	−1.48	n.a.[b]
By social class (MAPA)						
Upper	0.97	3.52	2.30	−1.16	−0.36	0.01
Middle-upper	0.83	2.51	2.07	−0.34	−0.29	0.87
Middle-lower	0.72	1.92	1.89	0.02	−0.09	2.11
Lower	0.29	1.72	1.65	3.11	−0.06	4.75

Notes: [a]Includes all fermented milks.

[b]Because the variation in income is almost exactly similar to the variation in relative price, the variation in purchasing power is almost exactly zero (0.0051) and the order of magnitude of the response factor (460.40) is disproportionate.

Sources: MAPA (1988–91, 2023a), INE (2023a); see Table 7.4.

before the Civil War. This comparison even underestimates the strength of the new life cycles that began to unfold in this area: in the case of fermented milks, for example, the response factor of traditional yogurts (natural, flavoured, and those containing pieces of fruit) evolved moderately, while that of bifidus and other novel versions of the product skyrocketed. We can observe something similar in the rest of the fresh dairy products: rather than the shakes, ice creams, or desserts that already existed in the market around 1990, what pulled up the response factor was consumers' interest in their new versions.

If consumers' distancing from milk seems to have motivations that transcend the economic, their reorientation towards milk-based products was closely linked to economic circumstances and social status. The Great Recession may not have severely affected consumers' purchasing power to buy dairy products, but it did mark a turning point in the reorientation of their attitudes and preferences. The response factor for cheese contracted. That of fermented milks, perhaps the product that best symbolized the pursuit of an alleged upgrade in consumption patterns, turned negative. Quite drastically, consumers decided to stop channelling their increased purchasing power towards buying so much cheese and freed up resources that they previously allocated to the purchase of yogurts and fermented milk to use them for other purposes. Only their interest in other fresh dairy products, mostly ultra-processed desserts, more or less intact survived the whirlwind of the Great Recession. (And, as we saw in Table 7.1, even this could be questionable according to one of the two available statistical sources.) When faced with unexpectedly unfavourable economic situations, the recession prompted consumers to reflect on their overall consumption pattern (not just dairy or food-related) and identify areas where cutting expenses could be feasible. Everything indicates that many of the dairy products that had aroused so much interest in the years before the recession were quickly identified as one of those dispensable areas.

The high-status groups led both trends, both the interest in dairy products before the Great Recession and the loss of interest in many of them during and after it. When, from the 1990s onwards, the space of choice for consumers began to expand with new dairy products, it was mainly the upper classes that showed greater interest. It is not that their purchasing power to buy these products grew more than that of the lower classes; in fact, the opposite was generally true. What differentiated them was their greater orientation towards channelling those increases in purchasing power towards the purchase of dairy products. The response factors were clearly ordered by socio-economic status. The lower classes made some room to buy milk-based products thanks to their rapid reduction in milk purchases, but clearly had other consumption priorities in mind. Over time, however, the middle classes and even the lower class showed more interest in the consumption of dairy products. In fact, although the response factor curves have a certain positive slope, it is not a very pronounced slope, at least in comparison with the generic differences between different products. In other words, there was a social gradient in the diffusion of new attitudes among consumers, but it was moderate and temporary.

To such an extent we find a sequence of demonstration by high-status groups and subsequent diffusion downwards in the social ladder that, when the Great Recession broke out, lower-class households distinguished themselves by continuing to incorporate larger quantities of dairy products into their diet. Despite their purchasing power declining, new dairy products had become a consumption goal that had to be pursued. While the response factors of the upper class and the middle classes began to decline, those of the lower class were surprisingly high. However, as we will see later, there are indications that over time, disinterest in dairy products also spread from top to bottom on the social scale.

These results must be interpreted with caution because the methodology used is more effective when applied to homogeneous products than, as in this case, to product groups characterized by variety and change over time. Between 1990 and 2008, the movement towards higher-priced dairy varieties than the original ones would imply an underestimation of their purchasing power and, consequently, a bias towards higher response factors. The opposite would be true for the period after 2008. However, an analysis of change in 'surplus spending' in response to changes in income, a synthetic measure of sophistication that is not subject to this problem, offers similar results (Table 7.7). The response of the upper classes was very elastic, increasing their surplus spending before the Great Recession and contracting it afterwards. The middle classes moved in the same direction but more moderately. And the lower class went from showing little interest in making surplus spending before the recession to continuing to do so after it, even though their income level was deteriorating.

Clearly, this exploration of response factors raises more questions than it answers. Its function has been to guide much of the subsequent chapters towards those questions. Why did consumers lose interest in milk? Why did they become interested in milk-based products, especially before the Great Recession? To explain the return of bad diets, both in its classic form of under-consumption and in its new form linked to ultra-processed foods and inefficient surplus spending, it is essential to understand consumer orientations. The choice space

Table 7.7 Response Factor of Surplus Spending to Changes in Income

	Average	**By social class**			
		Upper	**Middle-upper**	**Middle-lower**	**Lower**
1990–2008					
Income[a]	1.7	1.6	1.7	2.0	1.6
Surplus spending[b]	1.8	3.0	2.2	1.7	0.4
Response[c]	1.09	1.88	1.30	0.83	0.27
2008–19[d]					
Income[a]	−0.6	−0.6	−0.5	−0.6	−1.0
Surplus spending[b]	−0.3	−0.8	−0.4	−0.2	0.6
Response[c]	0.45	1.36	0.85	0.25	−0.56

Notes: [a]Annual compound rate of change in disposable income per consumption unit (2019 euros).

[b]Annual compound rate of change in the ratio of total spending on milk and dairy products to 'basic spending' as defined by the 1990 basket.

[c]*r* (*S*)/*r* (*Y*), where *r* is compound annual rate of change, and *S* and *Y* are, respectively, surplus spending and income as defined above.

[d]When interpreting the responsiveness factor for this period, it has to be kept in mind that income decreased and, therefore, a positive (negative) factor describes how much consumers decreased (increased) their surplus spending on dairy products.

Sources: Income 1990–2008: INE (2023e); income 2008–19: INE (2023g); deflator: INE (2023c); surplus spending: MAPA (1988–91, 2023a) as in Figure 3.9 (method 1).

was wide, and budget constraints were soft, so various paths of change in the diet were feasible. Why did consumers make those decisions and not others? These questions will occupy a significant part of our analysis in the next two chapters.

Conclusion: Another punctuated dynamic

Just as the massification of milk consumption was part of a broader improvement in living standards in Spain, the new dairy consumption model that triumphed from 1990 onwards is part of a more ambiguous picture. It is not only that bad diets have returned and have brought the nutritional problems typical of affluent societies with them. It is also that a new wave of consumer society left a bittersweet balance. The proliferation of new possibilities for consumers, from all kinds of electronic devices to the spread of tourism in exotic locations to the move towards larger and better-equipped homes, seemed far from ensuring significant improvements in the well-being of individuals, which seemed more closely related to the quality of social relations instead (Collantes, 2017b). What Avner Offer (2007) refers to as the 'challenge of affluence' had arrived in Spain.

The period was marked by the outbreak of the Great Recession, though. 'The consumer resorts to the basics', lamented the editorialist of *Industrias Lácteas Españolas* in 2010, as Spain became entangled in a particularly harsh version of the recession ('¿Se podrá?', 2010: 4). This simple phrase captures well the extent to which the dairy consumption model that had begun to take shape around 1990 had been relying on consumers engaging in what we have referred to as surplus spending. It also clearly reflects something that the results presented in this chapter show: the recession became a critical event that altered the trajectory of Spanish dairy consumption. That is why we will now conduct a separate analysis of the conjunctures before and after the recession.

8

A Galbraith moment (1990–2008)

When, in the 1960s, the International Dairy Federation began to perceive that milk consumption was starting to stagnate in some Western countries, its recommendation was clear:

> This trend must be combated by all means, including the commercialization of a new assortment of milk-based products and the presentation of dairy products in attractive packaging adapted to modern commercial conditions. ('El XVII Congreso', 1966: 179)

At that time, the context for Spanish industrialists, just beginning an extraordinary wave of mass consumption of milk, could not have been more different. However, by 1990, that point had been reached. Already during the 1980s, some signs had been observed that the wave of mass consumption was coming to an end, and a new consumption model was taking shape. This model reached its most characteristic version in the twenty years leading up to the outbreak of the Great Recession.

'Spain is doing well'

Except for a brief crisis in 1993/4, the Spanish economy grew rapidly in the twenty years leading up to the Great Recession. The driving sectors, closely linked, were residential construction and finance. Tourism and a wide range of services of all kinds, as well as a declining industrial sector, also played complementary roles. The economic upswing was primarily supported by domestic demand but benefited from the inflow of migrants and capital made possible by the Europeanization and globalization of the Spanish economy. Although not comparable to the growth during the dictatorship between 1950 and 1975, it was sufficient to ensure that the income of the average household continued to rise (Collantes, 2017b). Successive government leaders boasted about the country's macroeconomic record. If conservative José María Aznar popularized the expression 'Spain is doing well' in the late 1990s, a few years later socialist José Luis Rodríguez Zapatero proposed a vision in which the Spanish economy was triumphantly integrated in the 'Champions League of world economies', in which it was the one 'winning the most matches, scoring the most goals, and conceding the fewest' ('España', 1997; 'Zapatero', 2007).

These were also years in which a middle-class society was consolidated. While income distribution was more unequal than in other European countries, the country had been grappling with dangerous tendencies towards explosive unemployment rates since the industrial crisis of the 1970s. However, income distribution did not tend to polarize further during this period, and, except for the brief crisis of 1993/4, the unemployment rate tended to decrease, reaching a situation not far from full employment at the end of the upswing in 2007. Unlike in other countries, especially in the Anglo-Saxon world, where the deployment of the information revolution and the financialization of the economy were contributing to a resurgence of inequality, Spain's economic growth model was less oriented towards technological sectors and less intensive in human capital. Although this could pose problems for Spain's long-term growth potential, in the short term it favoured social cohesion by generating abundant employment opportunities for lower-status and lower-educated groups, as well as only moderate wage gaps with higher-status groups. The consolidation of a welfare state with significant expenditures on social protection, health, and education also contributed to preventing a resurgence of inequality (Collantes, 2017b).

The increase in household income paved the way for the start of a new wave of consumer society in Spain. Consumers were ready to incorporate a variety of novel goods, such as personal computers and mobile phones representing the information revolution, into their shopping baskets. The consumption of services that had previously been confined to higher-status social groups also spread more widely. Tourism, for example, became a widely experienced activity among Spaniards, whether within the country or, increasingly, to other countries and continents. Finally, there was also room to upgrade basic consumer goods. The spread of homeownership, which had already begun in the previous period, was completed, reinforced by the move to larger and better-equipped homes, especially in new residential areas emerging near major cities. In food consumption, all kinds of qualitative substitutions occurred. The sophistication of the dairy consumption pattern is a good example, but there could be many others: from extra virgin olive oil, organic peas, and PDO wine to croissants with chocolate chips, pre-cooked pizzas, and fast-food restaurant menus (Collantes, 2017b; Díaz Méndez and Gómez Benito, 2004; Germán, 2009; Maluquer de Motes, 2005).

In the case of dairy products, the income effect was amplified by a price effect. The complex production chain that had supported mass consumption during the previous period had no serious difficulties in supplying dairy products at increasingly lower prices. Farmers continued to specialize in milk production, relying on high-yield cows, intensive practices on their farms, refrigeration tanks, and advanced technological assistance (e.g. mechanical milking and mechanization for forage collection). Industries, in addition to guiding and supporting these changes in farming, continued to invest in improving their plants and production processes. Supermarkets benefited greatly from the information revolution, gaining efficiency in managing their processes and designing systems of supply chain management that would have been hardly viable just a few years earlier (Calcedo, 1996, 2004; Casado, 2005; Collantes, 2019b; Langreo, 1995, 2005; López and Cebrián, 2005).

Consumer prices were also pressured downwards by severe forces of structural adjustment. Competitive tension among supermarkets was strong, and they transmitted it upwards along the production chain. Whether through the open market or within their own value chains, supermarkets exerted increasing pressure on the price perceived by their suppliers. Both processing and farming were increasingly reduced to a small fraction of high-productivity units capable of surviving this 'rationalization' dynamic. In the processing industry, the elimination of the milk centrals network, and of the local market regulations that went with it, intensified the forces that tended towards national business concentration. The further deepening of the European process of economic integration, with the consequent increase in capital movements across national borders, took this logic to an international scale, especially with the growing involvement of French business groups. By the turn of the millennium, 60 per cent of the liquid milk market was in the hands of four large companies: the Asturian Capsa, the Andalusian Puleva Food, the Castilian-and-Leonese Pascual, and the French Lactalis (Langreo, 1995, 2003).

In the case of farming, structural adjustment was further accelerated by the definitive incorporation of farmers into the European Union's milk quota system. In its negotiation for access, Spain had not been able to secure a milk quota equivalent to its production volume, which deteriorated the expectations of numerous farmers. Despite successive governments maximizing the possibility of benefiting from a transitional period after the 1986 accession, and despite reasonable suspicion that the circulation of milk outside the quota was deliberately allowed, political dynamics clearly pointed towards a harsh version of structural adjustment. The more than two hundred thousand dairy farmers in Spain at the end of the 1980s had been reduced to just over thirty-seven thousand on the eve of the Great Recession (Calcedo, 2004; Langreo, 1995, 2004).

It is true that, in the years immediately before the recession, the production chain faced an unexpected tightening of global agricultural markets as a result of the extraordinary demand surge from China and other emerging economies, the impact of biofuel promotion on grain supply for human consumption, and the extension of financial speculation to the global food system (von Braun, 2011). The rising prices of basic grains in the international market affected the cost structure of Spanish dairy farmers because, in their process of technical intensification, they had increasingly relied on industrial feed. In the short term, before other actors had the opportunity to reallocate resources and restructure networks, this caused an unexpected surge in the prices perceived by farmers, which was transmitted downwards along the chain to consumers. It was nevertheless a temporary episode whose magnitude should not be overestimated: by 2008, all dairy products still had relative prices that, after all, were lower than they had been in 1990.

In summary, between 1990 and 2008, consumers' purchasing power to buy dairy products improved clearly. Why did they use it in the way they did? For example, why did they abandon the consumption of milk?

New views on milk

The social image of milk deteriorated as the lipid hypothesis, according to which an excessive intake of saturated fats increases the risk of cardiovascular diseases, became widespread. Not unrelated to this, in a society that had already reached a point roughly comparable to what Malassis (1997) terms the society of 'average satiety', concerns began to emerge regarding the impact of excessive fat intake on physical appearance, particularly on body weight and waist length. These trends had started to manifest during the 1980s and were now becoming stronger (Díaz Méndez and González, 2008).

The diffusion of the lipid hypothesis originated in the scientific community, from where it transferred to the media and, in a more decentralized manner, to physicians in daily contact with their patients. Public administrations tended to endorse this shift in the perception of milk and took some direct actions to promote it. However, it is fair to acknowledge that their abandonment of the 'gospel of milk' assumed a much lower profile than their previous adherence to it. The lipid hypothesis also spread, however, with the help of those who ostensibly opposed it: the dairy industry. Industrialists did not miss the opportunity to present themselves as victims of a campaign against their interests and to question the scientific validity of the lipid hypothesis. To provide an example among many, Puleva's director of research and development argued vehemently that

> The alleged connection between cholesterol intake and the development of coronary disease in humans is currently disapproved by the scientific community, and it is necessary to convey to consumers worldwide the fallacy of that theory and the risks associated with low consumption of milk and dairy products. (Gil, 1992: 21)

Nevertheless, none of this deterred each of them individually from redirecting their business strategy towards the production of low-fat or skimmed milks. This implied an implicit acceptance of the lipid hypothesis or, at the very least, an acknowledgement of the need to accommodate the fact that a growing segment of consumers believed in it. The advertising accompanying the launch of skimmed milk then became a powerful agent in disseminating both the lipid hypothesis and the idea that thinness, especially in females, was associated with the consumption of skimmed dairy (Díaz Méndez and González, 2008).

Whole milk, which had been at the core of the previous consumption model and whose health virtues had been extensively praised, had become a dubious food in the era of 'negative nutrition'. This shift in perceptions had a significant impact because traditional milk marketing had focused almost exclusively on health. The dissemination of a positive image of milk had never been based on the possibility that it might be tasty and enjoyable. In fact, the technical changes endorsed by the industry, supermarkets, and consumers themselves before 1990 did little to prevent the sensory experience of drinking milk from deteriorating. UHT milk, increasingly dominant in the Spanish market, was undoubtedly the variety that provided the least pleasure to the consumer. When the winds of negative nutrition began to blow through the meat industry, a significant counterweight was the fact that most consumers enjoyed eating meat, and doing so was not just a matter of aligning with nutritional recommendations and obtaining proteins. Milk, and even more so UHT milk, did not enjoy such a counterweight. Consequently, the effect of the transformation of nutritional perceptions was drastic (Barreiro et al., 2001; Mendelson, 2008: 55–9).

The limited sensory appeal of milk may also have contributed to its gradual disappearance from secondary niches. The main niche for milk was certainly breakfast, but its consumption could also extend to snacks such as afternoon tea or even as a final complement to dinner. In each of these segments, alternatives began to appear that, beyond nutritional aspects, consumers could find truly gratifying. Some of these alternatives could belong to the dairy world itself, as in the cases (which will be studied later) of yogurts and other desserts and snacks. Others came from the unrelated worlds of soft drinks, meat (such as sausages and other processed meats), or industrial pastries (ANSOAP, 2010; Contreras and Gracia, 2008; '*Lactobacillus*', 1998; 'Noticias', 1987: 72; 'Panorama', 2003a: 55).

The social image of milk deteriorated even further as an increasingly large proportion of the population began to identify as lactose intolerant. Although the statistical basis for measuring this medical condition is improvable, it seems that intolerance was somewhat more prevalent in Spain than in other European countries. There was a small but significant segment of the population that could experience some difficulties digesting milk. Increasingly, doctors themselves began to reconceptualize intolerance as a biological condition, rather than the dubious pretext for deviant behaviour with which it had been equated in the past. Many of the intolerant individuals also began to self-diagnose as such (Patterson, 2000).

The deterioration of the social image of milk was completed with the emergence, admittedly still very embryonic, of more philosophical objections to its consumption. Concerns about animal welfare and the implications of intensive livestock farming were generating small circles of adherence to vegetarianism, some of which renounced the consumption of milk. After all, what other species besides humans continued to insist on drinking milk after the biological period of lactation? And, if this were not suspicious enough, was there any other species that stole that milk from another? Although vegetarianism had a small statistical impact, its discursive impact might have been somewhat greater, contributing to the portrayal of the traditional pro-milk narrative as a debatable vestige of the mental maps that had dominated the twentieth-century West.

These cultural changes sprouted with particular intensity among younger populations. Older populations carried tastes and habits forged during the previous period and could not change them as flexibly. Moreover, many of them were developing dental problems that increased the appeal of drinkable foods such as milk (Mataix, 2005). Their advanced age favoured, on the other hand, closer monitoring of their nutritional health by medical professionals. Even if these professionals were supporters of the lipid hypothesis, they could find reasons to recommend regular and sustained consumption of low-fat or skimmed milk to, for example, mitigate the osteoporosis problems that commonly appeared in the late stage of life. In contrast, the consumption pattern of the younger population quickly diverged from nutritional recommendations.

The deterioration of the social image of milk was quite striking in all status groups. Lower-status groups were the ones that, in a more precocious and determined manner, began to cut back on their milk purchases, probably because they were the ones who, in the midst of the deterioration of the social image of the product, more quickly identified milk as a discretionary expense that could be redirected towards the pursuit of other acquisition goals. Higher-status groups had more economic leeway to incorporate these new dairy products into their diet, but for lower classes, buying less milk freed up valuable resources to avoid being completely left out of, for example, the transition to the new kinds of dairy products that (as we will see) were beginning to appear.

The industry tried to respond to this deterioration in the social image of milk by launching new versions of the product that addressed at least some of the reasons why consumers were abandoning it. Already in the 1980s, skimmed and semi-skimmed milk had been launched, and their life cycles continued to unfold between 1990 and 2008 with special support from female consumers (Comunidad de Madrid, 2001, 2008; Durá, 2008). The major product innovation of the period was, however, enriched milk. This was generally skimmed milk that included additional doses of calcium, vitamins, or other potential nutritional values in its composition. The engineering of milk actually became one of the spearheads of the trend towards so-called 'functional foods' in Spain.

The leading company in this niche was Puleva, which mobilized a considerable volume of economic and human resources for the research and development of new products, as well as their subsequent marketing to consumers. In 1992, Puleva launched a skimmed milk enriched with vitamins A and D, to which it later added extra doses of calcium. Because the absorption of calcium by the body depends on these vitamins, which are naturally present in milk's fat, Puleva's enriched milks allowed consumers to ingest more calcium and less fat, and yet avoid any deterioration of their ability to retain calcium in their bodies. Just six years later, Puleva's food engineering would cross an important boundary: from enrichment with components naturally present in milk, it moved to enrichment with ingredients extracted from other foods. If the idea that unsaturated fats, such as those present in olive oil or some types of fish, were beneficial to health was gaining ground, why not remove the naturally present saturated fat from milk and replace it with unsaturated fat? The result was enriched milk with omega-3 fatty acids extracted from fish. As Puleva vice president Guillermo Mesonero-Romanos (1998: 68) argued, the focus had to be on

> the development of new design products that are capable of meeting emerging dietary needs primarily associated with the age and lifestyle of … individuals who are concerned about health, viewed from a preventive standpoint.

Puleva supported the launch of these designer milks through ambitious marketing campaigns that included conventional advertising in the media, animation at points of sale, promotion activities aimed at health professionals, and the collaboration of celebrity physicians as opinion leaders. The underlying idea was to restore the battered slogan 'Milk is health' ('Campaña', 1995; Langreo, 2003; 'Panorama', 1992b, 2001b; 'Puleva', 2008).

Consumers received these product innovations with some enthusiasm. Thanks to the pull of higher-status groups, the life cycles of low-fat milks, and, above all, enriched milks, were able to take off. With their high level of education, these groups were probably more sensitive to the lipid hypothesis and more prone to reforming their habits and reduce saturated fat intake. With their higher purchasing power, upper-middle-class and upper-class individuals also showed greater interest in enriched milks, which, for a slightly higher price than conventional milk, promised additional health benefits. On the other hand, older cohorts found in the new milks a good way to reconcile their need for calcium to combat osteoporosis with their fear that excessive saturated fat intake would make them more prone to cardiovascular diseases. The doctors who attended to them on a daily basis contributed significantly to this perception.

However, the new life cycles of low-fat and enriched milks did not compensate for the fact that the life cycle of whole milk had entered a terminal phase. There was a transfer of certain consumer groups, especially those of higher status, those of advanced age, and women, from whole milk to the new milks. But there were also consumers who either abandoned milk in any of its forms altogether or substantially reduced their consumption. This suggests that the lipid hypothesis, while starting the deterioration of the social image of milk, was just one of the factors involved. The sensory experience of consuming the new milks, all processed using the UHT system, continued to be unstimulating. On the other hand, the new milks also did not solve the problem for those who had such unpleasant consumption experiences that they self-diagnosed as lactose intolerant.

In the years immediately preceding the Great Recession, some companies tried a different strategy to launch new product life cycles: introducing organic milk to the market. Its marketing had, as always, a health component, emphasizing the advantages that could arise from a more natural diet, away from the worst excesses of food Fordism. Organic milk, produced using extensive methods and without resorting to industrial inputs, could also be better for the environment, thus appealing to a certain social responsibility on the part of consumers. However, the key issue remained health and, especially, food safety. In the aftermath of the scandal of 'mad cows' and bovine spongiform encephalopathy that erupted in 2000, consumer confidence in the long chain of industrial food was teetering, and some might decide to pay a price premium, sometimes as high as 100 per cent, to leave behind conventional milk and be able to consume more reliable organic milk ('Barcelona', 2002; 'Panorama', 2003b).

However, the general interest of consumers in organic milk was minimal. There remains a doubt as to whether this interest would have been greater if a larger number of companies, including the leading processors, had developed organic milk lines, and had launched the multi-million-euro advertising campaigns that were earmarked for the promotion of enriched milks. Or if supermarket chains had bet more strongly on organic milk, giving it a more extensive and visible space on their shelves. The case of organic milk before 2008 shows us the importance of the paths not taken by the consumption model. It is true that it was a more expensive product than conventional milk, but it is equally true that, both in this field and in others in the dairy world, consumers were enthusiastically embracing the purchase of 'high value-added' foods to achieve some sort of 'upgrading'. Upgrading could have taken place in the direction of organic instead of functional milk. The first key decisions in this regard were made by dairy industries and supermarket chains, and only later by consumers, who found themselves with a choice space in which, while there was a small niche for organic milk, it was primarily enriched milks that stood out. Neither the distrust of conventional production nor social responsibility values were so widespread as to prevail over the business narrative that emphasized the benefits that each consumer could obtain for their own private health.

Positioning new dairy foods

The sequence we have presented for the world of milk was replicated on an expanded scale in the world of milk-based products. Between 1990 and 2008, the forefront of the dairy industry, in an attempt to mitigate the most severe effects of the ongoing structural adjustment, enthusiastically oriented itself towards product innovation. Their R&D departments designed a wide range of novelties, ranging from new varieties of existing foods, now with slightly different ingredient combinations, to truly innovative products that cannot be said to have existed until then. Their marketing departments developed ambitious communication strategies aimed at presenting the new products and proposing to consumers a narrative that made them interesting. Initially defined by a small number of leading industries, as the period progressed they were eventually joined by other industries and supermarkets with their own brands. If by 1990, the top ten of the Spanish dairy industry was populated mostly by companies strongly specialized in milk production, by 2008 more diversified business groups prevailed (Table 8.1).

Even companies like Pascual, which had initially expressed their intention to consolidate their prominent position in the liquid milk market, ended up embracing the diversification strategy. In words that at an earlier stage would

Table 8.1 Major Orientations among Top Ten Dairy Processors According to Sales (Ranking Position in Brackets)[a]

	1989[b]	**2001**	**2008**
Only milk	Pascual (5) CLAS (6) Uniasa[c] (7) ILAS (8)	Puleva[c] (4) ILAS (9) Celta (10)	Puleva[c] (4) Celta (9)
Only cheese	Larsa (4)	Kraft (6)	TGT (3)
Only yogurt or 'other'	Danone (1) Nestlé (2) Delasa (9)	Nestlé (1) Danone (2)	Danone (1) Iparlat (10)
Two or more products	LESA (3) Clesa (10)	CAPSA (3) Pascual (5) Clesa (7)	CAPSA (2) Lactalis (5) Pascual (6) ILAS[d] (7) Clesa (8)

Notes: [a]Major orientation towards 'Only milk' means that the processor is in the top ten for milk but not for other products, and so on.

[b]Placed in categories based on Langreo (1995).

[c]It is important to note that Uniasa-Puleva's permanence in the 'Only milk' category conceals the fact that the company strongly reoriented towards fortified milk (see main text).

[d]Since ILAS does not appear in any of the product-level top ten lists, it has been placed in the 'two or more' category.

Acronyms: CLAS: Central Lechera Asturiana; ILAS: Industrias Lácteas Asturianas; LESA: Lactaria Española S.A.; CAPSA: Corporación Alimentaria Peñasanta S.A. (formerly CLAS); TGT: Teodoro García Trabadelo.

The company that appears in the table as Uniasa (1989) was later renamed Puleva.

Sources: 1989: Dun and Bradstreet (1989); 2001 and 2008: Mercasa (2003, 2010).

have seemed reserved for Danone executives, their general manager could be heard assuring, 'We work permanently on the development of new products' (Moreno, 1984; 'Panorama', 2001a: 71). Another company originally specialized on the milk market, Central Lechera Asturiana, provides us with a vivid description of what diversification meant for consumer options (Table 8.2). The result of this wave of creativity was that, when shopping in 2008, consumers

Table 8.2 Products Sold by Central Lechera Asturiana

	1992	New products by 2008
Liquid milk	Whole, semi-skimmed, skimmed	Fortified: calcium (NaturCalcio Growth, Mummies, Plenitude; Plus whole, semi-skimmed, skimmed), fibre (BioFibra, NaturFibra with or without cereals), royal jelly (whole, semi-skimmed, skimmed, NaturJalea with royal jelly), 'growth' (Superman Energy and Growth, Energy Growth)
Canned milk	Powder milk (whole, skimmed)	
Cheese	Cheese blocks	Fresh cheese (white, skimmed Naturlínea, NaturCol), cheese portions (natural, light, premium), and fortified Superman little cheeses
Butter	Conventional	Light, Mediterranean, easy-to-spread, small portions, with flavours (strawberry, garlic, and fine herbs)
Yogurt[a]	Natural, strawberry, raspberry, wild fruits, fruit salad with cereals	NaturActiva with added fruits (royal jelly, valerian and peach, soy and cranberries, green tea and lemon, soy with kiwi and apple, soy with red fruits, strawberry and mint, pineapple and green tea), Vegetánea with added vegetables (strawberry-carrot-tomato, apple-cucumber-leek, plum-beet-spinach), NaturCol (with vegetal sterols), low-fat NaturLínea (liquid, cream, multi-fruit cream), fibre-rich NaturFibra (skimmed, red fruits, liquid with kiwi and apple), BioActiva with probiotics (hazel, red fruits), creamy (strawberry with cream, banana-chocolate, apple pie, caramel), skimmed (edulcorated, pineapple), kefir (conventional, with lychee and green tea), Superman (fortified for children)
Other	Milk shakes (cocoa, vanilla, strawberry) and liquid cream	Superman milk shake (fortified for children), milk with tea (green, white, red), cream sauce (blue cheese, pepper, carbonara, sea-style, light), rice with milk, 0% flan, hazel cream, chocolate mousse with cream

Note: [a]Includes all fermented milks.

Sources: Central Lechera Asturiana (1992), 'Panorama' (2008a: 202).

could choose from a much greater variety of dairy products than consumers in 1990.

The leading company in the Spanish dairy industry, especially when it came to product innovations, was Danone, the French multinational that was persistently among the ten largest producers of ultra-processed foods in the world throughout the whole period. Danone's business model, focused on fresh desserts, had always been based on product innovation. Yogurt, in particular, was initially a little-known product for most Spaniards, and much of Danone's success in the Spanish market in the decades before 1990 had consisted precisely in making the product known and arousing interest among an increasingly broad range of consumers. In the twenty years leading up to the Great Recession, Danone was able to give this strategy an extraordinary scale and depth, launching a huge number of new product life cycles. Some of them were only minor adaptations of existing desserts, such as the gradual introduction of skimmed versions of the various yogurts in the company's catalogue. In other cases, innovation aimed to develop new ingredient combinations that offered new flavours to those consumers who might be experiencing some monotony with traditional yogurts. In many others, finally, innovation was more radical. Danone thus launched an increasingly wide range of high-tech, functional foods whose health benefits could be presented as superior to those of conventional dairy desserts (Castro, 2008; Wood et al., 2023).

The three major milestones of this strategy were the Danone brands Bio, Actimel, and Danacol. All three of them were fermented milk of one kind or another. Bio products, which the company launched in 1988 and was forced to rename as Activia in 2006 (after the European Commission had prohibited using this term for non-organic foods), were fermented with bifidus and facilitated digestion. Actimel products, launched in 1995, were fermented with lactobacilli and Danone claimed that they made the immune system stronger. Danacol products, finally, included plant sterols and were introduced to the market in 2005 with a communication campaign that emphasized its ability to reduce cholesterol levels in the blood. These radical innovations, in turn, were subsequently subjected to incremental adaptations that allowed Danone to market many functional foods with distinct flavours and formats (Castro, 2008; 'Danone', 2005; '*Lactobacillus*', 1998: 45; 'Panorama', 1988, 2004, 2005a, 2005c).

Health was at the centre of the narrative that Danone built to interest consumers in its new products. To achieve this, the company established effective partnerships with the world of sports, incorporating famous footballers, basketball players, and tennis players into its advertising. It also obtained the status of official sponsor of the 1992 Barcelona Olympics, with the declared aim of 'capitalizing on the spirit of the Olympic Games for Danone' ('Lactonoticias' 1991a: 7). It also aligned itself with emerging initiatives that took shape in its own city, Barcelona, around the promotion of the Mediterranean diet as an asset in terms of both public health and cultural heritage. Even though the decalogue of the Mediterranean diet that resulted from these initiatives clearly pointed out the need to promote minimally processed foods, mentions of cheese, yogurt, and fresh foods in general were apparently enough to make Danone's alignment credible ('El Senado', 2002: 119).

In a society where concerns about dietary excesses were widespread, the line between health claims and those that were more related to the promotion of physical attractiveness could be very thin. Danone's advertising not only combined both types of claims but repeatedly established connections between the consumption of its desserts and the improvement of physical appearance. In its 2006 television commercial for the Vitalínea skimmed yogurt, for example, the beneficial properties of the product were mentioned, but the centre of the story was elsewhere: in the way a young, thin female consumer could, thanks to her interest in the product, get to establish some personal relationship with one of the great sex symbols of the time, James Bond's Pierce Brosnan. Other slogans from Danone at the time included 'I like to seduce', 'Being below has its advantages', and others that, like 'You'll lick your fingers' and 'Natural pleasure can be drunk', were presented in overtly sexualized contexts (Danone, 2006).

Alongside health and physical attractiveness, the other major axis of innovative activity in the dairy industry was what we will call consumer convenience: the development of foods that, while not terribly different from existing ones, allowed consumers to save preparation time or improve household logistics. A wide range of dairy desserts fell within this line of innovation: custards, puddings, creams that had a certain tradition of homemade preparation and now proliferated ready to consume on supermarket shelves. They did so in an increasingly diverse range of flavours and ingredient combinations. The motivation to save time was commonly intertwined with the motivation to break away from monotony and try new foods.

The world of cheese provides further illustration. Even before 1990, the main cheese companies, generally smaller than those in the worlds of yogurt or milk, were engaged in standardization processes to make their product more reliable for consumers, but now consumer convenience took on a broader meaning. Largely under the influence of supermarkets that perceived this as one of the major limiting factors for consumers' cheese purchases, the main cheese companies began to address the issue of format. Cheese makers retained production lines for traditional large and heavy pieces but increasingly developed other lines aimed at producing formats that consumers found more convenient. Cheeses began to be presented in smaller pieces, and later also in slices and sliced wedges. Another expanding line during the period, grated cheese, can also be seen as a service food that allowed the consumer to save time (Canut, 1991; Sanz, 2002).

These convenience-oriented innovations were difficult to separate from innovations aimed at offering consumers a greater variety of cheeses. Throughout the 1990s, with Spain fully integrated into the European Union, supermarket shelves began to offer a much greater variety of cheeses from other countries. The main exporters to the Spanish market were France and the Netherlands, both of which had notable production surpluses and a powerful promotion machinery that aimed to have an impact not just on final consumers but also on supermarkets and restaurants. These were slightly different varieties of cheese than traditional Spanish ones and, above all, quickly became associated with new culinary uses. In cases such as the mozzarella-type cheese used on pizzas (a meal that had no previous tradition in Spain), the convenience of the format was linked to the novelty of the food for which the product was used (García Trabadelo, 2002; 'Panorama', 2005b; Viñas, 1993).

Another key motive for the product innovations developed during these years was consumer gratification. The most obvious case was ice cream. Following in the footsteps of other dairy products, ice cream manufacturers did not give up trying to build an image of a healthy food, but their success in this area was small. What truly inspired innovations was the desire to offer consumers a sensorially pleasurable experience. The business project here was to expand the market for home consumption, which by 1990 was quite small because the market was heavily concentrated on occasional consumption outside the home during the summer. Ice cream manufacturers developed a strategy based on causing a permanent revolution in the consumers' choice space. Production lines were thoroughly renewed each year, and the life cycle of most ice creams was short. Except for the rare case of ice creams that for some reason became very popular, one ice cream was quickly replaced by another. This somewhat frenetic rotation was expected to keep alive the interest of a consumer whose motivation was understood to be closely linked to the impulse to obtain pleasure and, therefore, was thought to be in great need of being awakened time and time again (Bonmatí, 1990, 1992; Cano, 1993; Roig, 2005).

It is important to appreciate that gratification was also a hidden card of many other launches in the dairy industry during this period. Returning to the paradigmatic case, Danone could fill the story accompanying the launch of its new products with all kinds of health claims, but it also attached great importance to sensory pleasure. While its functional projects like Bio and Actimel were doing well, the company sought to incorporate the hedonistic consumer through products such as Greek-style yogurt and yogurt cream. In the words of the yogurt cream developer, 'We realized that we needed to target those consumers who avoided consuming yogurts due to their taste. We have worked intensively to address this factor, [resulting in] a yogurt with a smoother and creamier texture' ('Panorama', 1998a: 51). Some of the ultra-processed dairy products were indeed promoted exclusively from the perspective of gratification, such as 'Danone custard, ready to please'. Along the way, the fact that many of the product innovations were sugar-rich ultra-processed foods was obscured: the term 'ultra-processed' had not even been coined, and regarding sugar, studies on consumer reading of food labelling reflected that their main concern was fat, not sugar. The way was clear for Danone to position, for example, its Chocolate Cup as a healthy food because of its alleged contribution to children's growth and bone health ('Empresas', 1997; 'Lactonoticias', 1996; 'Panorama', 1998a, 1998b, 2008b).

When, beyond specific companies and products, we observe the underlying dynamics of the dairy consumption model during this period, the contrast between the poor sensory experience consumers obtained when drinking milk and the sweetness they could enjoy when eating carefully designed yogurts and other dairy desserts is striking. Also in the case of another cornerstone of this consumption model, cheese, studies showed that the main variable involved in consumer purchase was flavour ('Panorama', 2005b; 'Reordenación', 1992).

We conclude this journey through product innovations by mentioning that, as in the case of milk, novelties oriented towards differentiated territorial quality or organic production were also developed. An increasingly dense network of small producers and associations bet on presenting consumers with PDO cheeses, the most important of which were (in terms of market share) *Manchego*, from Castile-La Mancha, and *Mahón*, from the Balearic Islands. Their price was higher than that of conventional cheeses, but in return, compliance with demanding quality standards was guaranteed, in line with the artisanal traditions of each region. There were also business ventures, generally on a small scale, for organic cheeses and yogurts. However, the capacity of these actors and their networks to implement ambitious marketing strategies was very limited. Any comparison with the advertising investments made by Danone, Pascual, or other giants in the dairy industry would be out of place.

Dairy consumerism

The intertwined motives of health, gratification, and convenience prevailed among consumers, who showed interest in diversifying and sophisticating their dairy basket. Market studies of the time reveal that dairy products were among the foods that generated the most trust among consumers. As seen in the previous chapter, the response factors for cheese consumption, fermented milks, and other dairy products were clearly positive. Some voices even claimed that cheese was 'in vogue' or that yogurt, whose growth had surpassed the optimistic forecasts made by experts at the beginning of the period, had acquired the advantageous status of a 'healthy treat' ('El consumidor', 2004: 89; 'Nuevas innovaciones', 1995: 55; Vázquez de Prada, 1992: 24, 2004: 30).

This favourable disposition towards dairy products was particularly evident among higher-status groups. The upper class, first and foremost, possessed an educational and cultural level that facilitated the reception of nutritional messages associated with dairy products. Functional dairy products, in particular, were complex foods whose marketing was more effective the greater the consumer's familiarity with a constellation of concepts including cholesterol, active principles, plant sterols, intestinal flora, or the immune system. Similar to the early stages of the historical nutritional transition, when concepts such as proteins or vitamins were necessary to explain the health benefits of dietary changes, consumers with higher educational and cultural levels were better prepared to understand health claims from companies like Danone and take them seriously.

A higher income level could also favour receptivity to novelties and, in general, orientation towards various dairy products. After all, milk-based products represented a more expensive way to access the generic benefits of dairy products than milk. In cases like functional dairy products, an additional health benefit could be expected from them, and it seems clear that this extra had characteristics of a 'superior good': its potential demand would be considerably higher among high-income groups than among low-income groups that likely had other (not just dietary) consumption objectives to pursue. The absence of pending battles in other areas was helpful in entering the new battle for dairy. An increasing fraction of high-status groups was also experiencing the time pressures typical of households with two income earners. Many of these households had a high income level but were time-poor in terms of organizing their domestic life. This made them avid consumers of prepared dishes of all kinds. In the specific case of the dairy world, this included custards, puddings, and other desserts traditionally made at home, as well as cheese in various formats (grated, powdered, sliced) that could be used to prepare sandwiches, pizzas, or other fast meals.

Certainly, the line between saving time to consume existing foods and seeking slightly different versions of those foods was thin, and crossing it led to the realm of pleasure as an additional motivation for the consumption of dairy products. High-status groups were more interested than others in products like shakes and home-consumed ice creams. Rather than relatively expensive ways to access the health benefits of dairy, these products were seen more as a promise of gratification that, for reasons different from functional dairy, also had characteristics of a 'superior good'. Having a higher income level and a more comfortable economic situation made these households more prone to indulge in such pleasures. Similar considerations could be made about the orientation of high-status groups towards differentiated quality foods, such as PDO cheese. The producers and merchants in this network were aware that their target audience was a high-income consumer, but one also open to familiarizing themselves with a 'gourmet' culture that they knew was absent in most households in the country (Palacios, 1996; Tutusaus, 2004). Focusing on the most important case, that of *Manchego* cheese, its producers were aware that 'it is not a cheese for mass consumption. Its price and delicacy make it suitable for certain social strata to which it is destined' (García Arroyo, 1992: 39). They admitted that 'it is normal for a person who decides to buy a *Manchego* Cheese with Designation of Origin to have a basic knowledge of the world of cheeses' (Altares, 1994: 27).

These attitudes and orientations towards dairy products spread especially among high-status groups, but the middle classes also participated in them very early on. In the 1990s, the middle classes already had positive and high response factors, reflecting a favourable predisposition to channel their increases in purchasing power towards buying more cheese, yogurt, or ice cream. Although this predisposition did not reach the intensity of high-status groups, it would be a mistake to think that the middle classes were left out and that milk-based products became severe status markers. Even if in a more moderate way, the nutritional messages associated with the new dairy products were also reaching the middle classes. These households were also increasingly experiencing time pressures due to the incorporation of more women into the labour market and, due to their economic position, had a certain capacity to regularly grant themselves gratifications. A fraction of the middle class also began to be willing to pay a price premium for PDO cheeses ('Los consumidores', 2003; Moscoso, 1997).

It is true that the lowest class, the quartile of the lowest socio-economic status, took a bit longer to adopt these new orientations. Nevertheless, their response factors were remarkably high. During the 1990s, lower-status groups basically used the resources freed up by their cuts in milk purchases to finance higher purchases of milk-based products. This aligns with what was happening in other countries where the later incorporation of the lower class into the new consumption model was accompanied by a rapid liquidation of some elements of the previous model (Fine et al., 1996). By the time the Great Recession hit in 2008, the interest of the lower class in dairy products had already led them to make surplus spending, which, although moderate compared to that of the upper class or even the middle classes, still reflected their desire to participate in the new battle for dairy. Like the other status groups, the lower class was no longer satisfied with securing their basic consumption basket from the beginning of the period. Also in their case, variable combinations of health claims, convenience, and the search for gratification were gradually redirecting the basket towards dairy products.

The diffusion of these new orientations was surprisingly rapid across different demographic groups. Initially, Danone, to return to the most influential company, focused mainly on young consumers, attributing to them a particularly developed capacity to appreciate its new proposals. However, elderly populations embraced these lines of innovation with notable enthusiasm, especially for breakfast and snacks: these were tasty and digestible foods that posed no chewing problems and required no preparation work (Aranceta, 2005; Farré, 1995; Robles, 2002).

The most striking difference was actually not between social strata or generations, but between different dairy products. The dairy products whose consumption increased most strongly were those that the industry classified as 'high value-added products', which were the subject of ambitious marketing campaigns and were chosen by supermarkets to occupy relevant spaces on their shelves. Danone's products were, once again, paradigmatic in this sense. The investment in R&D and advertising behind the launch of each new product cycle by Danone was extraordinary. In 2005, this investment amounted to 56 million euros, compared to the meagre 47 million that corresponded to Spain's entire cheese subsector taken as a whole ('Panorama', 2005c: 107; 'Variedad', 2004: 27). Danone also secured a good position on supermarket shelves, not only because many of its products were innovations that initially could not be found in the catalogues of other companies but also because the company had managed to consolidate a leading brand image among consumers, allowing it to maintain significant market shares even in the later stages of the life cycles of its products.

By the end of the period, its market share not only rose to an extraordinary 80 per cent in the functional milk-based foods segment but also reached almost 50 per cent for the entire fresh desserts category. When Danone's competitors organized tastings to refine the development of their new products, they found that consumers overwhelmingly preferred the taste of Danone desserts. Market surveys repeatedly revealed that Danone was the most highly valued brand by Spanish consumers, not only within the dairy or food sector but for the entire consumer goods sector ('El consumo de yogur', 2004: 38; Fernández-Albalat y Méndez, 2004; 'Panorama', 1999c: 57, 2005d: 41).

Obviously, not all business ventures were successful. A particularly notorious failure was Pascual's project of launching yogurts fermented after pasteurization. Although consumers could have appreciated their logistical advantages on paper, as they did not require refrigeration like conventional yogurts, in practice these yogurts were found unattractive. In previous decades, Pascual had done a lot to disassociate milk's image from that of a fresh product and have consumers accept the UHT alternative, but it could not achieve the same success in transforming the social image of yogurt. One significant reason is that, unlike in previous decades (when the pasteurized milk market was fragmented in the territorial areas of milk centrals), this involved fighting against a giant business that, like Danone, had extensive financial and discursive resources to maintain the social image of yogurt firmly linked to the cold chain. The situation is reminiscent of what happened in 1960 when Ullastres admitted that, in the eyes of consumers, powdered milk was not the same as liquid milk, and that this path would not lead to the long-awaited massification ('Nuevos frentes', 2002: 7).

Even though there was no magic recipe to guide consumers towards new dairy products, corporate structures clearly conditioned the final outcome. Neither PDO cheeses nor organic yogurts, to give two examples, were the subject of advertising campaigns that, in magnitude and quality, could be compared to those of Danone or other giants in the Spanish dairy industry. At the beginning of the period, the deputy director general of Food Promotion at the Ministry of Agriculture, Fisheries, and Food, José Antonio Rocha, doubted that there were many people in the ministry who could name the seven cheeses with designation of origin at that time and joked that 'maybe not even I myself' ('El sector lácteo', 1991: 18). Prospective surveys indeed showed that half of consumers could not name a single PDO cheese, or if they did, they confused them with industrial cheeses from multinational companies like Nestlé and Kraft. By the end of the period, this proportion had dropped to 20 per cent, but most consumers could only name three of what were then almost thirty Spanish PDO cheeses ('Panorama', 2005b; 'Sólo el 40%', 1997).

Supermarkets also did not strongly endorse this line. Armed with increasingly precise mechanisms to analyse and predict demand trends (including the use of information derived from their customers' loyalty cards), supermarkets quickly concluded that consumers would be much more interested in sophisticating their dairy consumption basket in other different ways. Taking into account the inequality of forces between the marketing apparatuses of one product and another, this was probably a correct conclusion but also to some extent a self-fulfilling prophecy: because supermarkets left little shelf space for quality differentiated cheeses and tended to get rid of specialized cheese counters and sellers, the product did not have the chance to compete on equal terms with functional dairy, prepared desserts, or even conventional cheese ('I Edición', 2006; Sanz, 1992).

If we adopt the perspective of 2008 and look back twenty years, it is clear that the surplus spending that consumers made during this period could have been directed towards differentiated quality or organic dairy products. It is also clear, of course, that they could have made no surplus spending, considering their 'dairy problem' resolved with the basic basket reached around 1990. That these alternative paths were not followed is a testament to the success of the business project that the dairy industry and supermarkets designed at a time of rationalization and structural adjustment. It is also a testament, as we will examine carefully in the final chapter of the book, to the absence of public policies that kept corporate strategies aligned with the general interest.

Conclusion: 'Anticipating consumer needs and preferences'

In the two decades leading up to the Great Recession, a confluence of circumstances destabilized the adequate pattern of dairy consumption that had been established around 1990. The strategies employed by companies involved in the production and distribution of dairy products served as the starting point, envisioning a sort of 'Galbraith moment' wherein consumers purchasing new, more expensive, and complex dairy items would help alleviate some of the tensions and issues affecting the business community. Through ambitious communication and marketing campaigns, industries successfully piqued consumer interest in products they were initially unfamiliar with and did not miss. Danone's president, Javier Robles, could assert, 'We are facing a dynamic sector that constantly meets the increasing demands of consumers', yet this supposed demand had been entirely inspired by the producers themselves. As rightly pointed out by an industry observer when the company launched its first bifidus, 'Danone scored a point by anticipating consumer needs and preferences' ('Diversificar', 1988: 7; Robles, 2002: 15).

However, the forging of the new consumption model required a favourable combination of this entrepreneurial project of creative destruction with developments occurring in other domains. Alongside shifts in consumer culture, a crucial factor was the relatively rapid, as well as reasonably inclusive, growth of the Spanish economy during these years. The significance of these factors would be starkly illustrated with the onset of the Great Recession in 2008.

9

Turbulence (2008–present)

Commenting on the post-1929 economic crisis, Schumpeter (1939: 370) asserts that 'The depression acted as an efficiency expert.' There is something in the way Spanish consumers altered their behaviour regarding dairy that resonates with this. The Great Recession was a critical event that, through various channels, marked the history of the post-1990 model of dairy consumption. In the twenty years leading up to its outbreak, a combination of developments had steered the Spanish pattern of dairy consumption along a path of dubious value. The recession would propel this model into an uncertain phase of turbulence, dismantling the combination of factors that had been sustaining what we have referred to as the Galbraith moment. On the other hand, however, the legacy of the Galbraith moment persists to this day and the prospects for the return of good diets are unpromising.

'We all thought we were rich'

The outbreak of the Great Recession deteriorated the economic position of most Spanish households. The burst of financial and real estate bubbles drastically halted economic growth, causing contractionary effects across various sectors and making Spain one of the economies worst affected by the crisis. Unemployment soared again, reaching at its worst moment a rate exceeding 25 per cent of the active population. Largely due to this, income distribution became more unequal. Spain remained a middle-class society, but it faced the threat of increasing inequality in opportunities and positions. The country still had a welfare state capable of cushioning some of these impacts, but the extraordinary crisis in public finances that occurred after 2008, combined with the controversial political handling of the recession by the European Union, forced leaders to make cuts in social spending. The blow was particularly harsh among the lower classes but also affected the middle and upper classes (Maluquer de Motes, 2014).

From 2014, the Spanish economy emerged from the recession, but the situation of many households took time to improve significantly. The constraints imposed by belonging to the eurozone forced a kind of 'internal devaluation' based on wage moderation. Unemployment decreased, but at a slower pace than it had increased during the crisis. The deep impact of the Great Recession was still clearly visible by 2019, after six years of economic recovery had not allowed any social stratum to restore the income level they had attained before the recession, just before the Covid crisis once again pushed that horizon further away. After 2008, in summary, Spanish household economies have been immersed in trouble, which sharply contrasts with the trends of the two decades before the recession (Castro-Valdivia and de-Prado-Herrera, 2023).

It is important to note, however, that none of this led to the return of hard budget constraints to the world of dairy. Throughout the entire period after 2008, the price of milk and dairy products continued to decline rapidly. The cheapening of milk and dairy products mitigated the impact of falling income during the recession and, after it, drove a rapid recovery in consumers' purchasing power for dairy products. Unlike the overall purchasing power at the macroeconomic level, dairy purchasing power did rise: by 2019, it was clearly higher than in 2008.

Some of this price decline, especially in the toughest years of the recession, had cyclical causes, especially the easing of tensions that had affected global food markets in 2007–8 and had been transmitted to the Spanish dairy chain through the price of animal feed. Viewed from a broader time perspective, the persistent decline in dairy prices must be seen, in any case, as a continuation of the trends from the previous period, that is, as a result of the relative ease of production in the dairy chain. The productive potential of farmers, in particular, continued to expand vigorously. Farms were becoming larger and had an increasingly wide range of technological supports, from the traditional genetic selection of cows to automatic systems for milking and feeding animals. On the other hand, farmers were involved in a tough structural adjustment, through which production was increasingly concentrated in a small number of high-tech, professionalized farms. In just nine years, between 2007 and 2016, the thirty-seven thousand dairy farms in the country were reduced to less than twenty thousand (INE, 2023h). As in previous periods, the productivity gains of farmers were rapidly transferred down the production chain through low prices for raw milk, and this was crucial for a steady decline in consumer prices.

This relative ease of production was not only a matter of technological potential but also of efficiency. Supermarkets and hypermarkets continued to play a central role as coordinators of the rest of the actors in the chain, particularly the industries. Considering that the market shares of large retailers already exceeded 90 per cent for milk and most dairy products, any ambitious industrial strategy involved placing products on their shelves. This gave supermarkets an overwhelming power in their relationships with industries. A few industries could aspire to place their brands on the shelves, but more and more ended up integrating into the systems of supply chain management by means of which supermarkets developed brands of their own. In any case, supermarkets intensified their price pressure on industries, which in turn was transmitted to the pressure that industries applied to farmers. The growing concentration of business in a few supermarkets might suggest images of competition restriction, collusion agreements, and extraordinary profits in the worst sense of the term, but the truth was that these supermarkets competed fiercely with each other. Their profit margins were very low, and indeed, one of their main competitive strategies was to identify pockets of inefficiency throughout the chain that could be corrected to achieve reductions in consumer prices. '[Until] 2008,' explained the director of dairy purchasing at the country's leading retailer, the Mercadona supermarket chain, 'we all thought we were rich and, therefore, we despised the cent. From that year on, we have had to strive to have more efficient products and save costs' ('Boletín', 2010a: 48). On the other hand, the simple fact that supermarkets succeeded in redirecting more and more consumers towards their own brands tended to push down the average price in our statistics (Collantes, 2016).

In other words, even more acutely than in the previous period, the dairy chain was in a phase of 'rationalization' in which, under the leadership of dominant supermarkets, strong pressures for a reduction in consumer prices for dairy products were unleashed. However, there was a significant qualitative difference from the previous period. During the twenty years before the Great Recession, the vanguard of the dairy industry had responded to supermarket pressure by trying to initiate a new phase of 'transformation' that would protect its profit margins and allow them to avoid the kind of severe structural adjustment that farmers were going through. The focus of that strategy had been the development of numerous product innovations, all of them characterized by their high added value from a business perspective. However, in the years of the Great Recession and beyond, the balance of power shifted so clearly towards supermarkets that not even this strategy, if developed successfully, was feasible anymore. The efficient supply chain strategies that supermarkets implemented allowed them to produce in an ever shorter period of time their own versions of the new products that the industry had launched. The time during which a branded company could hope to reap the extraordinary profits of its success in a market of monopolistic competition became increasingly shorter. The time supermarkets needed to redirect competition in such niches towards the price variable was getting shorter. This put all dairy industries in a difficult position, even those that had been able to maintain a certain branded image that supermarkets could not ignore in their purchasing and shelf positioning decisions. Now, however, even the great innovation giant, Danone, found itself in an existential crisis. Supermarkets like Mercadona no longer received its new products with as much enthusiasm and could even withdraw them from shelves after a short period, confident in their own brand's ability to occupy those niches ('La decisión', 2009; Langreo and García-Azcárate, 2021; Rosado, 2015).

Thus, supermarket hegemony ceased to be a stimulus for product innovation and ended up being pointed out by industries as a discouraging element for it. Even shortly before the Great Recession had started, the president of the National Federation of Dairy Industries, Roberto Moré (2006: 63), had wondered, 'How can we protect the dairy industry from imitators and especially from the competition of private labels that, without investing or risking one single euro, enjoy all the positive evolutions of the market the next day?' Why spend several million euros developing and advertising new products if supermarkets were going to quickly produce their own replicas at a lower price and with the best shelf positions? Why work towards a 'Galbraith moment' if any success in 'transformation' would be quickly redirected to 'rationalization' mode?

It is not that product innovation suddenly stopped, but it certainly slowed down. The atmosphere in the sector had changed substantially:

> Most of the processing industry … had in its DNA the … battle to increase sales … Lately, the feeling is the opposite. It seems that industries, executives, have decided to look back. They change position in their chairs and, instead of dedicating themselves to selling, they are becoming obsessed with buying … You have to save on electricity, on R&D, you have to save on personnel and, especially, on the purchase of raw materials. ('Mirar', 2015: 4)

Even Danone, the quintessential brand-based leader, eventually entered 'rationalization' mode in 2014, striving to identify pockets of inefficiency that would allow for some extra cost-cutting. This new atmosphere had a first-rate consequence for the evolution of the dairy consumption model: the space for consumer choice, which had expanded spectacularly during the twenty years before the recession, became more stable. Novelties continued to appear, especially in relation to environmental sustainability and animal welfare, as well as improvements in textures or changes in added sugar content, but the contours of the choice space remained basically the same as they had been established before 2008 (Bandrés, 2020; González de los Reyes-Gavilán, 2015; 'Precios', 2014).

Cracks in dairy consumerism

While the return of budget constraints did not directly impact the world of dairy, where relative prices were persistently declining, its indirect influence on consumer preferences proved crucial. The interest consumers had previously shown in milk-based foods, especially the new generation of such products, began to wane. The response factor of cheese consumption dropped to nearly zero, as consumers were hesitant to channel their increased purchasing power towards buying more cheese. The shift was even more pronounced in the area of fermented milks. The flagship of the new dairy consumption model entered negative territory: akin to their behaviour with milk in preceding years, consumers reduced their purchases of yogurt and other fermented milks, showing little interest in leveraging the opportunity presented by growing purchasing power. The intriguing deterioration of response factors in dairy products did not occur immediately after 2008, when most consumers claimed to be 'returning to basics' ('El 81% de los españoles', 2012: 23) but primarily during the post-recession period starting in 2014.

Why did the consumption wave led by dairy products deflate? Before delving into the impact of the recession and its aftermath, it is essential to recognize that one of the catalysts of the surge significantly decelerated: product innovation. The overwhelming dominance of supermarkets' 'rationalization' in the dairy chain from 2008 led to far fewer product cycles. As consumers ceased to be so exposed to the impact of product innovations, as well as to the costly advertising campaigns that went with them, consumer culture became less dynamic.

Within this more stable choice space, the return of budget constraints prompted most households to identify expenses that could be considered dispensable. At a time when the Spanish political debate was overshadowed by the delicate issue of budget cuts to restore fiscal balance, most households also faced a reflection on how to cut their private spending to accommodate the deterioration that was taking place in their income levels. And this inadequately expresses the magnitude of the adjustment that numerous households affected by unemployment had to consider. For them, the issue was not only the decline in their income levels (partly mitigated by social protection subsidies) but also the uncertainty and difficulty in projecting future scenarios. Many of the dairy products that had played a leading role in the pre-recession surge were identified as one of those cuttable, and within the complications always associated with the term, superfluous expenses:

> Customers have decided to buy cheap. Just four months ago, they were attentive to their health and chose functional products, while now they go to self-discount and do not hesitate to take the cheapest in the store. ('El tirón', 2008: 16)

It was the higher-status groups that initiated change. They were the ones who had originally embraced incorporating larger quantities of dairy products into their diet. Now, it was they who most clearly reoriented themselves in the opposite direction. Despite the recession having a more moderate impact on their household economy, high-status groups quickly reduced their purchases of cheese and fermented milks. Here, one cannot help but perceive a certain relativism regarding many health claims that, in many cases disproportionately, had been made about the new generation of dairy products. A well-known dairy industry consultant dared to state that consumers were facing a 'range of products that, in a large number of cases, we are almost certain are nothing more than pure placebos of little utility and no health benefits' (Ramírez, 2013: 10). Certainly, by the end of the period, consumers claimed that their primary motivation for eating yogurt, mostly as a dinner dessert, was pleasure, with health being a distant secondary motivation. By then, consumer perceptions had been substantially influenced by the growing focus of nutritional discourse on excessive sugar intake, prompting yogurt producers, for the first time, to launch defensive communication campaigns similar to those long undertaken by milk producers ('II encuentro', 2019; 'La realidad', 2018; López et al., 2020; Ortí, 2019).

It is true that as we descended social strata, more consumers had pending issues. When the recession erupted, they were engaged in an emulation process that, with some delay, had ended up orienting them towards dairy products, and not even the severity of the recession prompted them to reorient. It was only later, paradoxically when the worst of the crisis had already passed, that the lower class showed some signs of reorientation, especially for fermented milks (López et al., 2020; Ortí, 2019). The sensitivity of surplus spending to variations in the income of different groups vividly illustrates this social gradient in consumer reorientation. As the recession erupted, the upper class contracted its surplus spending, while the middle class and, to an even greater extent, the lower class continued to expand it despite their real income levels falling. It was only during the post-recession period, after 2013, that the middle and lower classes began to cut surplus spending, paradoxically just when their economic situation was starting to improve. Nevertheless, the lower class, whose consumption of cheese and fermented milks remained considerably lower than that of other social groups, made more modest cuts. Conditioned by the fact that substantial differences persisted by 2008 in the presence of dairy products in the diets of different social groups, the reorientation of consumers towards less enthusiastic attitudes about dairy products spread from top to bottom in the social pyramid.

If the most dynamic niches of the previous period were beginning to run out, others that had maintained a more secondary character failed to replace them. At a time of growing environmental awareness, organic dairy products emerged as a possible alternative to the type of surplus spending consumers had been making on ultra-processed foods, but none of the leading companies in the chain, whether in the industrial or retail phase, strongly embraced such a strategy. Even less so for differentiated quality dairy products; products like PDO cheese represented, like few others, the 'superior' food market that the recession was momentously destroying. The leading supermarket chain, Mercadona, for example, could almost completely do away with such products on its shelves and, with great success, focus on offering a limited range of conventional dairy products at increasingly lower prices. If times had become challenging for Danone, what would not happen to that network of artisanal cheese producers that had always struggled to connect with the country's mass consumers? ('La importancia', 2010).

The only pillar of the 'Galbraith moment' that remained intact was the heterogeneous category composed of ultra-processed desserts, ice creams, and shakes. Here, a livelier pace of product innovation was maintained. In the case of ice creams, for example, it was common for market-dominating multinational corporations, such as Nestlé, to thoroughly renew their catalogue every year, with the declared goal of preventing consumers from losing interest. Also, it is crucial to bear in mind that, unlike many of the fermented milks that had been introduced to the market with the healthy codes of functional food, these products had always based their appeal on the pleasure one derived from consuming them. In times of economic recession, gratification could become more important than ever. Again, the lower class was the most enthusiastic in orientation towards these ultra-processed products. There was also a social gradient here, with this enthusiasm moderating as we ascended the social pyramid. By 2019, unlike the situation with other dairy products, the middle class was already on par with the upper class, and the lower class was not far behind. Lower-status groups were immersed in an emulation mission they were not going to easily abandon, especially if it involved foods that, despite their unhealthy nature, offered cheap gratification at a time when other avenues of gratification (from summer tourism to gatherings with friends in restaurants and bars) were under intense domestic scrutiny as possible cuttable expenses ('Un segmento', 2016).

There were some corrections, though. The life cycle of some ultra-processed products (especially fermented milks) entered a mature phase, and consumers at least stopped diverting as many resources to excessive spending of dubious impact on their quality of life. There were no signs of a reorientation of surplus spending towards more beneficial purposes, but, echoing Mercadona's proposed 'return to simplicity' ('Boletín', 2010a: 48), the expansive trend had at least stabilized. The situation was very different regarding the other element of bad diets from the previous period: dairy under-consumption. Consumers continued to cut their milk purchases rapidly, and for the reasons we have just examined, dairy products were farther than ever from being able to compensate for this trend.

The shrinking of milk

As the consumer culture surrounding dairy products became less dynamic, that of milk consumption continued to disintegrate. An anonymous columnist from *Industrias Lácteas Españolas* expressed with admirable clarity the limited influence of economic variables on the decline in consumption:

> The reduced consumption of regular liquid milk, which is actually become cheaper and cheaper, does not seem attributable to the economic crisis. Selling fewer yogurts with blueberries or Greek-style is understandable, but in the case of milk in cartons it has different underlying reasons. ('Dentro del laberinto', 2014: 7)

Cultural dynamics that had begun to manifest in the preceding period, especially from the late 1990s onwards, continued their course.

The lipid hypothesis, which had initiated the decline in milk consumption, remained firmly entrenched among consumers. Scientifically, anomalies were accumulating that questioned or, at the very least, suggested alternative hypotheses to interpret the evidence. Works of popular science were also suggesting that the demonization of saturated fats had gone too far, emphasizing the impact of added sugars instead (Pollan, 2008; Popkin, 2009). However, this potential paradigm shift in 'negative nutrition' was still in its infancy. The majority of the medical profession, responsible for monitoring consumer health on a daily basis, continued to firmly adhere to the lipid hypothesis. Additionally, beyond health considerations, the abandonment of whole milk was also linked to the desire of an increasingly large segment of consumers to maintain an attractive physical appearance and avoid potential effects of fats on body weight. Lastly, social tolerance towards lactose intolerance continued to increase. Although quantifying such a biological condition is challenging, estimates of intolerant population increased from 15 per cent at the beginning of the period to a range of 30–50 per cent by its end ('Fenil', 2009: 23; 'Intolerancia', 2019; Ortega, 2020: 12). Whether a generous portion of those self-defining as intolerant did so based on a self-diagnosis deemed unreliable by some nutritionists was a secondary issue: the main issue was that several population segments, especially among younger generations, were abandoning milk consumption.

In theory, any of these issues, considered in isolation, could be circumvented by consuming other types of milk. However, as discussed in the previous chapter, none of the new product cycles introduced by the dairy industry managed to compensate for the collapse occurring in the whole milk sector. This trend persisted during the Great Recession and its aftermath. Skimmed milk allowed for a consumption aligned with the lipid hypothesis and supposedly conducive to weight control, but its taste and texture were largely unappealing. Semi-skimmed milk ended up dominating a market in clear contraction, serving as a compromise solution that, nevertheless, garnered little enthusiasm among consumers. The fact that these low-fat milks could be transformed into functional foods through enrichment processes with calcium and vitamins did not alter the fundamental reality that, especially for younger populations, milk had ceased to be an attractive food: its health claims were seen as debatable, and its consumption provided little pleasure, if not physical discomfort.

The industry attempted to respond to these trends by launching new types of milk that could retain some of the consumers who were inclined to abandon it. For those who were lactose intolerant or felt so, lactose-free milk appeared (Pérez de Lema, 2018). The fact that this new product cycle was far from compensating for the exhaustion of more traditional cycles underscored how complex the reasons for consumers abandoning milk were.

For those with issues regarding taste, the industry resurrected pasteurization from oblivion. This had been a path not taken during the massification and standardization period of 1965–90, when a combination of industry interests, supermarkets, and consumers themselves had favoured the triumph of UHT processing. This had resulted in less tasty milk, while pasteurized milk was almost off the market by the time the Great Recession started. The return of pasteurized milk began at a local scale as farmers and cooperatives from different parts of the country installed vending machines in urban marketplaces. They aimed to reach an alternative consumer dissatisfied with UHT milk and likely with industrial food in general. The moderate success of some of these initiatives in local markets was enough to inspire industries and supermarkets. Promising better taste, and sometimes also making health claims (based on the lesser impact of pasteurization on naturally present vitamins in milk), pasteurized milk returned to the shelves and occupied a small niche in mainstream circuits. However, none of this substantially altered consumer trends. The logistical advantages that UHT milk offered, which could be purchased in bulk on a weekly or bi-weekly basis, remained unassailable. In a way, they felt even more widespread than in the 1965–90 period, given that female activity rates (and the resulting time pressure on households with two income earners) were now higher. Moreover, the pasteurized milk found on the shelves did not present a taste advantage over UHT milk as clear as before. In an attempt to return to a less perishable product and one more convenient in terms of both business and household logistics, the industries leading the pasteurized milk revival had opted for the so-called 'high pasteurization' processing system. This was more aggressive than traditional pasteurization and allowed industries to offer consumers a milk that, instead of expiring in three or four days, could remain in good condition in their refrigerator for ten or twelve days. Along the way, however, most of the distinctive taste that had marked the return of pasteurized milk through local farmers' vending machines a few years earlier was lost. A small segment of consumers showed enough interest in the product to keep it moderately present on the shelves, but no life cycle opened that was sufficient to compensate for the collapse of traditional life cycles ('Boletín', 2010b, 2011b; 'Empresas', 2010; 'Panorama', 2009).

Similar events unfolded concerning organic milk and milk produced under animal welfare conditions. The former had emerged on a very small scale a few years before the recession, partly in response to food safety concerns sparked by the so-called 'mad cow disease', and now it became produced by a larger number of companies. The latter, on the other hand, developed during our period, especially once the economic crisis began to ease, and the income level of most households began to rise again. These new types of milk were able to generate some interest among an emerging consumer profile dissatisfied with conventional industrial food. 'Increasingly,' explained an executive from the French company Lactalis, with a strong presence in Spain, 'consumers want products to be as natural as possible, without artificial elements, originating from sustainable raw materials and respectful of the planet' ('Potenciar', 2021: 23). For this consumer profile, it was a matter of transitioning to a healthier diet that could also be considered responsible in terms of respecting future generations and the animals from which the milk was obtained.

However, this was a minority profile. In a way, something similar happened as in the case of pasteurized milk: these were high-end products, priced higher than conventional milk, and thus the initial response from high-income households would be crucial. Although it was certainly in these types of households that pasteurized and organic milk achieved some degree of presence, it was also in these households where it became most evident that the new life cycles were not gaining enough traction to compensate for the decline in the consumption of conventional milks. Higher-status households had joined the decline in milk consumption that started in the late 1990s, albeit later than others, but by our period, they were firmly oriented in that direction. While in the world of dairy products behaviours tended to diffuse from the top-down in the social pyramid, in the world of milk, it tended to be the opposite. Under these conditions, it was unlikely that higher-status groups would indicate a path through which the incorporation of new types of milk could compensate for the abandonment of conventional ones. Even less feasible was it for lower-status groups, for whom price was more of an obstacle and for whom converging on the (more rewarding) area of the consumption of dairy products seemed to be more imperative.

In addition, a consumer profile began to emerge whose objections could not even be addressed by launching new types of milk, as these were much more generic objections to milk as a food. Consumers were exposed to a cacophony of arguments and counterarguments among which it was not uncommon for some voices, sometimes with a considerable public profile, to point out that milk consumption was implicated in the prevalence of certain diseases or that it was essentially unnatural, as evidenced by the fact that humans are the only mammals that consume milk after weaning. Although these were often strident arguments, categorized by the industry as that 'anonymous dissident, generally offensive and generally false, offered to [the consumer] on the internet and forwarded by a friend, family member or acquaintance' ('Serpientes', 2017: 6), the overall tone of demystifying the role of milk in the diet undoubtedly permeated consumer culture, which, on the other hand, had begun to question the status of scientific messages and the power associated with them more than in the past ('Crónica', 2012a; 'Desmontados', 2010; 'Día', 2016; Díaz Méndez and Gómez Benito, 2010; 'Esfuerzo', 2016). Doctors themselves, who had already tempered their enthusiasm by redirecting consumers towards low-fat milks, now could even convey relativistic attitudes. In a way that would have been unthinkable in the era of massification, some of them could be heard assuring readers of one of the country's leading newspapers that 'In the Anglo-Saxon world, dairy is very important, but we prefer the Mediterranean diet, of which milk is not an essential element' (Díaz, 2011).

The final blow was the capture of a notable portion of the consumer profile potentially interested in organic milk by the plant-based beverage industry. The production of soy-based milk substitutes had begun in Spain in the years before the recession but now reached a more significant scale. It was soon accompanied by new options, such as oat-based beverages. The rise of the plant-based beverage market was supported by lactose-intolerant consumers but especially by consumers uncomfortable with intensive livestock farming. Modern milk farming was viewed by this consumer profile as the nexus of various interconnected problems, from the deterioration of nutritional health in affluent societies to global-scale climate change, through threats to animal welfare. By severing any connection between consumers and intensive livestock farming, plant-based beverages offered a more holistic solution to these concerns than lactose-free milk, organic milk, or animal welfare milk. It would be an exaggeration to position plant-based beverages as the central cause of the decline in milk consumption. This decline began earlier and was caused by the variety of factors we have been studying since the previous chapter. Nevertheless, it is undeniable that the onset of the plant-based beverage life cycle contributed to the ongoing decomposition of the milk life cycle (ANSOAP, 2010; Gozzer, 2015).

By the end of the period, consumer culture had plummeted to the extent that, according to a study, 70 per cent of those reducing their overall consumption were not even aware of doing so. Breakfast remained the most common consumption time, but even in this segment, an increasing number of consumers were forsaking milk in favour of more gratifying ultra-processed products, such as shakes and yogurts ('Crece', 2018: 11; 'Día', 2018: 10–11; 'IV Encuentro', 2022: 16).

Covid time

Up to this point, our analysis and narrative have finished in 2019. This approach has allowed us to adopt a broad perspective on the period post-1990, particularly focusing on the critical event that shaped it: the Great Recession. We have refrained from extending the analysis beyond 2019 to avoid distortions arising from the peculiar circumstances that surrounded Spanish society in 2020. The Covid-19 pandemic was poised to emerge as a new critical event, which, even more abruptly than the Great Recession, generated multifaceted impacts. Initially, the fight against the pandemic led Spain, like other European countries, into a severe economic contraction. With a GDP decline exceeding 10 per cent, the income of numerous households was significantly reduced. The complementary social protection measures implemented, including temporary employment regulations, substantially mitigated the blow. Nonetheless, it is evident that, at a time when the average household had not yet fully recovered its pre-recession income level, a new crisis ensued that inevitably influenced consumption decisions. In the realm of food consumption, the pandemic also induced more direct impacts. For a few months, lockdown measures compelled a massive shift in food consumption patterns, redirecting consumption from restaurants and bars back to households. Even after the relaxation of stringent restrictions, notable constraints on food and beverage consumption outside the home persisted (Castro-Valdivia and de-Prado-Herrera, 2023).

Although out-of-home dairy consumption had always had a minor share in total consumption, our data cannot help reveal some discontinuity in 2020. Under the peculiar circumstances we have just described, the proportion of surplus spending by consumers reached its historical peak. The consumption of dairy products experienced robust growth, even in the case of products like fermented milk, which appeared to be in decline. In part, this simply reflects the inclusion in our household consumption data of expenditures that, under normal conditions, would have occurred in bars and restaurants. However, it also reflects how lockdowns and restrictions prompted consumers to intensify their focus on foods that provided some gratification, including yogurts and shakes. At a time when social interaction was minimized, and psychological well-being was under threat, the role of food as a source of pleasure was accentuated.

In normal conditions, surplus spending had been stagnant for nearly a decade, but now it experienced a brief final surge. The 'Galbraith moment' that took shape before the recession and had been dormant for years briefly resurrected ('En 8 de cada 10 hogares', 2020; 'Panel', 2021).

Events post-2020 indicate the continuation of the turbulent phase that the dairy consumption model entered after the Great Recession. The long-term perspective reveals a production chain with fewer (and less striking) product innovations than in the 1990s and 2000s. It also depicts a less dynamic consumer culture, with more and more consumers not only omitting milk from their daily diet but also showing less interest than in the past in channelling their income increments towards the purchase of dairy products. The absence of substantial public policies in the area of food consumption (a topic we will deal with in the concluding part of this book) also contributes to shaping a horizon where the dynamics of the last decade may persist. Nevertheless, we also perceive elements that, over time, could lead to the rise of a new model of dairy consumption. The business project remains centred on inviting consumers to consider new ways of upgrading their basket. As explained by Tomás Pascual (2018: 19), son and successor of the founder of one of the country's major dairy companies:

> When discussing the dairy sector, I like to use the term revitalization. Together, we must revitalize the market: energize demand and revalue the product by reinforcing the concept of quality and incorporating value-added products tailored to consumer needs.

This general approach could materialize in diverse possibilities such as organic nutrition, a new generation of functional dairy products, heritage foods with differential quality, new ultra-processed items that captivate consumers through pleasure and gratification, or a realignment with nutritionists' recommendations through a return to a diet based on simple foods.

All these possibilities are economically feasible. Today, with no less than thirty years of perspective since we attained a reasonably good dairy consumption pattern, we can perceive to what extent consumers would have saved money had they remained on the 'Keynes situation'. We can also perceive to what extent their surplus spending could have been directed towards a widespread substitution of conventional milk with organic milk. At the time of its launch in the early millennium, organic milk had a much higher price than conventional milk, and its mass adoption would have compelled consumers to incur significantly higher expenses than those they were incurring, both in absolute terms and as a percentage of their income (Figures 9.1 and 9.2). These were the times when,

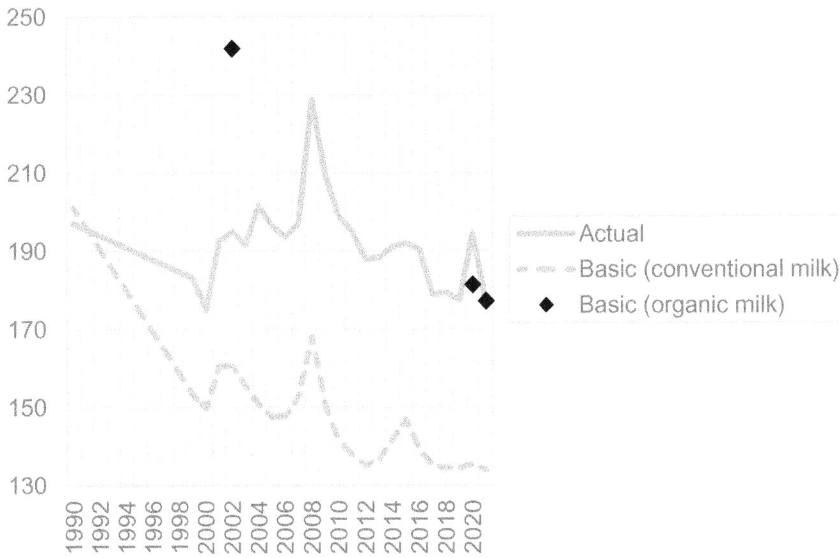

Figure 9.1 Per capita consumer spending in dairy products (constant 2019 euros), 1990–2021.
Sources: MAPA (1988–91, 2023a), 'Barcelona' (2002: 76), INE (2023c). 'Basic (organic milk)': modified 1990 dairy basket, with organic instead of conventional milk; the figure for 2002 is approximative. See Appendix Table A21.

in the words of one of the most prominent leaders in the Spanish dairy industry, the founder of Industrias Lácteas Asturianas Francisco Rodríguez (2008: 15), 'only the very wealthy can ultimately afford to feel ecological'. In the twenty years since then, however, not only have we witnessed a reduction in this price premium, but there has also been a decline in the relative price of all milks. Today, we have reached a point where the average consumer can afford to buy an improved version of the 1990 dairy basket, with conventional milk replaced by organic milk. We know this 'organic upgrading' could be afforded because the required expenditure would be very similar, even slightly lower now, than what consumers effectively spend today on their dairy basket redirected towards high-price ultra-processed items.

As evidenced by the history of our ventures along the 'Galbraith path', the 'Mazzucato path' is also feasible. The notion that most consumers cannot afford it (Paarlberg, 2021; Popkin, 2009) has become outdated. The question is whether the outcome of the historical crossroads we find ourselves in will correct the problems that have permeated the consumption model that took shape in the 1990s and has yet to be replaced by another.

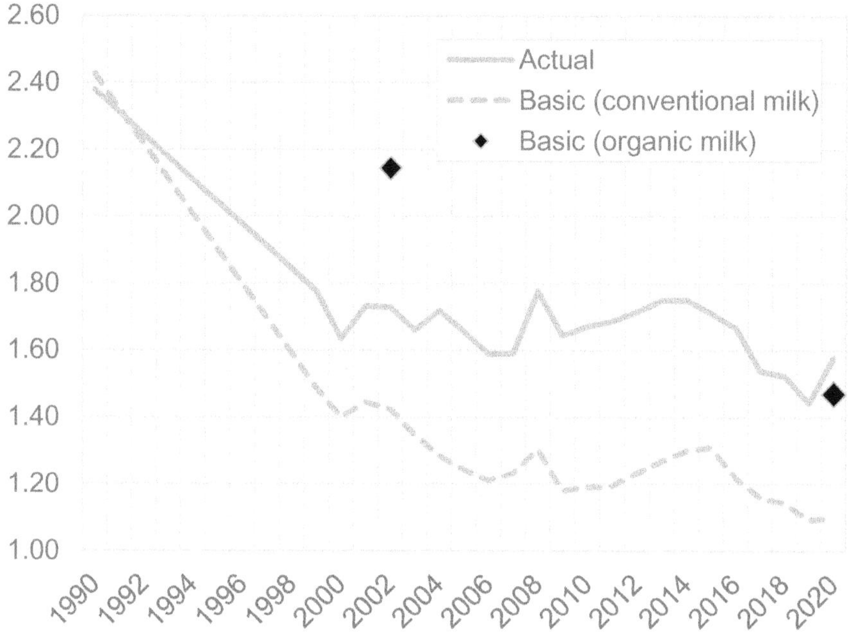

Figure 9.2 Share of consumer income required to purchase three alternative dairy baskets (%), 1990–2020.
Sources: Spending on dairy: Figure 9.1; income: INE (2023e, 2023g). See Appendix Table A22.

Conclusion: 'Returning to basics'?

The dairy consumption model that took shape in the 1990s was plunged into turbulence following the outbreak of the Great Recession, and these disruptions have persisted to the present day. Some of the components that had combined to foster its ascent began to fall or, at the very least, weaken. In the business sphere, trends of rationalization and structural adjustment increasingly dominated over industries' attempts to overcome them through product innovation. For household economies, the soft budget constraints that prevailed before the recession became more stringent, inducing a careful redefinition of priorities and objectives. Along the way, consumers ceased to exhibit such a favourable orientation towards dairy products that had been acting as a driving force for the consumption model. It is true that some other foundations of this model remained more or less intact. The development of the production chain continued to enable substantial reductions in relative prices, mitigating the impact of the recession on household income levels. Consumers continued to show some interest in certain dairy products, and it cannot be claimed that industries completely abandoned the pursuit of product innovations to keep this interest alive. The relative sophistication of the dairy consumption basket continued its course as consumers increasingly trimmed their milk purchases.

Whether we consider that this dairy consumption model has a significant future ahead or has already begun to collapse (an issue that, in our opinion, is challenging to ascertain with the available evidence), what is clear at this point is that this model has not embodied either what we referred to in Chapter 2 as the 'Keynes situation' or the 'Mazzucato path'. The fact that we have witnessed a certain dissolution of the 'Galbraith moment' in recent years does not mean that we have ceased to be within the terrain defined by that path during the twenty years prior to the recession. Despite most consumers claiming to be 'returning to basics' ('El 81% de los españoles', 2012: 23), this occurred within certain ranges and brands, but not in the sense of reverting to the nutritionally and socio-economically adequate dairy consumption basket of 1990.

Part IV

Conclusion

10

What can we learn from this case study?

'To let the murder out and to start my final thesis,' wrote Schumpeter (1951: 154) in a draft on the historical analysis of business cycles that he was not able to fully revise before his death, 'what is really required is a large collection of industrial and locational monographs all drawn up according to the same plan.' According to Schumpeter (1951: 155),

> The most serious shortcoming of modern business cycle studies is that nobody seems to understand or even to care precisely how industries and individual firms rise and fall and how their rise and fall affects the aggregates and what we call loosely 'general business conditions'.

While we would not make such categorical statements about the shortcomings of dietary change studies, we have certainly embraced the perspective of a small case study with the intention of advancing the state of the art along less-trodden yet, in our view, necessary paths. Now is the time to resurface and highlight how our 'commodity monograph', to paraphrase Schumpeter, contributes to the broader issue of the rise and fall of good diets in Spain and the Western world.

Creative destructions

In this book, we have interpreted the dietary problems of affluent societies as part of a longer-term sequence that includes the eradication of classical malnutrition. That is why we have talked about a rise and fall of good diets. However, this does not imply that, as suggested by some researchers (González de Molina et al., 2020; Otter, 2020; Pollan, 2008; Pujol and Cussó, 2014), today's bad diets fall within a sort of 'great acceleration' condensing events between the mid-twentieth century and the present. On the contrary, the case of milk and dairy products in Spain illustrates the need to continue taking seriously Grigg's

(1999: 11) assertion that after the post-Second World War decades there was a 'fundamental break with the past'. In line with Malassis (1997), we have found evidence of two distinct models of dairy consumption, the first one going from 1950 to approximately 1990 and the second one from 1990 to the present. This is a periodization that was common in the 1990s and early 2000s, when it was vindicated not only by geographers like Grigg or heterodox economists like Malassis but also by mainstream economists like Popkin (1993), sociologists like Friedmann and McMichael (1989), and historians like Montanari (1993), Levenstein (2003), and Oddy (2003). Whether the argument was presented in terms of consumption models, nutritional transitions, or dietary regimes, the point was to emphasize two distinct stages. Our case study strongly supports this argument.

By exploring a single product group in detail, we have been able to better identify the nature of the rupture. Along our journey, we found elements of the 'behavioral change' that Popkin attributes to consumers after the nutritional transition, such as a moderation in total dairy intake and an increasing substitution of traditional whole dairy products with lower-fat alternatives. We also found illustrations of the 'quality turn' described by neo-Marxist sociologists and geographers, which would eventually create a contrast between 'food from somewhere' and 'food from nowhere' exemplified by organic milk and PDO cheese compared to their conventional counterparts. We have also found the kind of 'qualitative substitutions' discussed by Malassis: a substitution of milk with increasingly sophisticated milk-based products. We have even proposed a new indicator, 'surplus spending' (the spending required for consumers to go beyond the basic basket), which, in our opinion, captures this vector of change more precisely than Malassis does. And yet, with its emphasis on new additions to the diet, this perspective overlooks the trajectory of foods that were already part of it.

Our perspective on successive food consumption models is more in line then with Schumpeter's concept of 'creative destruction', which he coined to study a different (albeit not unrelated) topic: the business cycles that his modern followers have called 'long waves' or 'techno-economic paradigms'. The first dairy consumption model was a creative destruction in which different product life cycles coexisted. The core of the model was the mass consumption of processed milk. However, it is essential to appreciate that the rise of this product life cycle coexisted with the exhaustion of the life cycle that had dominated the consumption pattern until then: raw milk. Consumers did not merely substitute raw milk with processed milk. Instead, the emergence and spread of processed milk expanded the market, allowing the product to reach new social groups and territories and become massive.

Similarly, the dairy consumption model that succeeded, especially during the 1990s and much of the following decade, was not limited to the deployment of vigorous life cycles of various types of cheeses, yogurts, and various desserts. It was also a process of creative destruction that dismantled the dairy consumption pattern that had come to prevail around 1990: a pattern composed of simple foods such as processed milk and a limited range of basic dairy products. The life cycles of these products, especially that of processed milk, eventually collapsed. Consumers did not merely replace old dairy products with new ones. On the contrary, the consumption of increasingly complex dairy products did not compensate for the decline in milk consumption.

This is not a purely descriptive issue; it also influences our view of the implications of dietary change. It has become a common argument that our societies have transitioned from hunger to obesity. Malnutrition due to scarcity has transformed into malnutrition due to excess. Our study shows, indeed, a case among many possible of a society where, until the mid-twentieth century, most people were undernourished. At the beginning of our story, milk consumption was excessively low, contributing to nutritional deficiencies in proteins, vitamins, and especially calcium. The massification of milk that took place under the first consumption model helped mitigate these deficiencies and aligned the dairy consumption pattern with nutritional recommendations. However, this was not a stable situation. The second consumption model set in motion a dynamic that would eventually bring malnutrition back. Consistent with conventional wisdom, this was partly due to the generalization of a diet increasingly rich in ultra-processed foods, one of the most problematic vectors of recent dietary change. However, alongside this problem of excess, the return of bad diets was also the return of literally the same under-consumption problem that had become solved around 1990. The collapse of the life cycle of milk and the inability of new life cycles to compensate for it in nutritional terms led much of the Spanish population to a diet that, once again, did not guarantee the recommended intake of calcium. We can better understand these fluctuations in the nutritional adequacy of diets by viewing successive consumption models in terms of creative destructions rather than as simple adjustments in a particular direction.

The most striking rupture between one model and another is the deterioration in the nutritional efficiency of consumer behaviour. In traditional societies marked by hunger and scarcity, consumers were highly efficient: they had little room for error and allocated their resources in a way that provided them with a level of nutritional health that was fairly close to the best possible given the magnitude of those resources. The fact that nutritional health was deficient in most cases reflected the precariousness of their resources rather than a misuse of them. In our case study, the dynamics of the first consumption model largely adhered to this pattern. Consumers used their increased purchasing power to buy more milk and improve their diet, and they did so in a way that could hardly have absorbed fewer resources. Perhaps they could have foregone processed milk, relying on raw milk, which was cheaper. However, under the problematic conditions in which raw milk reached most consumers, it also posed greater health risks. Therefore, it is only a slight oversimplification to label the spending consumers made around 1990 as 'basic'. After 1990, however, consumers, increasingly oriented towards complex and relatively expensive dairy products, started to make 'surplus' spending that went beyond that basic pattern. It is evident that, from a strictly nutritional standpoint, this represented a deterioration in their efficiency. The return of bad diets does not reflect a lack of resources allocated to nutrition but rather an unproductive use of those resources. The evidence presented in this book shows that, at least in our case study, this was true for all strata of consumers, not just those in the upper or upper-middle class.

Of course, this nutritional inefficiency must be read in broader socio-economic terms. The problem with the consumption model that emerged in the late twentieth century is not only that the spectre of poor nutrition has reappeared but also that the magnitude of surplus spending conveys a strong sense of missed opportunity. In our case, the 1990 consumption pattern was nutritionally adequate but could have been improved from other perspectives. It would not have been a bad outcome for consumers to have felt comfortable in what we have referred to as a 'Keynes situation': satisfied with what they had achieved, they would have considered their 'dairy problem' solved and they would have stabilized their consumption pattern. However, it is also true that this nutritionally adequate pattern was based on foods whose production and marketing generated a notable environmental impact, from the methane emissions of cows in increasingly intensive farms to the carbon dioxide emissions of the fleets of trucks transporting raw milk to factories and processed milk to supermarkets, not to mention the demanding material requirements of packaging. Considering that organic dairy products were more expensive than their conventional counterparts, some mobilization of consumer surplus spending was essential to make any attempt to transform the food chain in sustainable ways. What has been said for a possible 'organic upgrading' of the basic basket would be valid for a possible 'quality turn' towards foods produced on small scale using semi-artisanal techniques and local knowledge. These changes could exemplify a 'Mazzucato path' where entrepreneurial innovation and consumer surplus spending are directed towards relevant societal challenges.

In current debates, it is sometimes argued that this type of 'Mazzucato path' is essentially unfeasible because most consumers cannot afford it. In our case study, however, the evidence shows a substantial volume of surplus spending that consumers from all social strata could have directed towards such purposes. The problem is not a lack of capacity to go beyond basic spending but a deviation of surplus spending towards socially irrelevant purposes. Especially until the outbreak of the Great Recession, surplus spending fuelled progress along the kind of 'Galbraith path' that has often been criticized not only from the perspective of nutrition but, more broadly, from the perspective of consumer society and the good life.

Our case also illustrates the specific features that these problems take on in Southern Europe. In the historical strongholds of the now-praised Mediterranean diet, the contrast between the two dietary consumption models has been particularly abrupt. The gap between the actual consumption pattern and the recommendations of nutritionists has been particularly disheartening because, in this case, the recommendations did not revolve around some type of abstract ideal but around a diet that was the country's own until well into the twentieth century. Nevertheless, the case of dairy products in Spain introduces a significant nuance. Not all historical versions of the Mediterranean diet were equally healthy. In Spain's case, the prevailing diet until the 1960s had virtues but also flaws: low dairy consumption, for example, led to widespread calcium deficiency. Spain's later incorporation into the paradox of eating in affluent societies was not a 'fall from grace' concerning a long and venerable tradition but rather a brief interlude within the mass agro-industrial consumption model. The problem is not why a society that already had a healthy traditional diet abandoned it and succumbed to excess and imbalance. Instead, the issue is why a society that needed to improve its traditional diet was unable to, once that improvement was achieved, remain in the zone recommended by nutritionists, preventing new dietary changes from pulling it out of that zone and from absorbing economic resources that could have been more profitably devoted to other purposes.

Processed milk and the mass consumption model

The triumph of the mass consumption model in Spain and the West after the Second World War has often been explained through arguments that may be unfair to label as monocausal but have certainly tended to focus almost exclusively on one of the social subsystems involved in dietary change. As we saw in Chapter 1, in both Spanish and international studies we can find a developmental narrative focused on macroeconomic changes, a microeconomic perspective focused on food chain dynamics, and a cultural approach stressing changes in consumer orientations. Our study on the massification of milk consumption in Spain from approximately 1950 to 1990 reveals the limitations of these explanations and, instead, emphasizes the combination of relatively autonomous changes in different subsystems.

There is no doubt that, as developmental explanations suggest, the macroeconomic and social changes of the post-war decades favoured the transformation of diets. These were years of extraordinary growth in the disposable income of most households, and its distribution became somewhat more equitable. This created room for a powerful wave of consumer society development, first in the United States and later in Western Europe. Spain was not unaffected by these trends, creating a highly favourable context for the massification of milk consumption among diverse social groups and regions of the country. However, these changes were not sufficient to guarantee the transformation of diets. In our case, the increase in disposable income could exert its influence because it combined with scientific messages emphasizing the health benefits of milk consumption, political levers amplifying the dissemination of these messages, and an enhanced receptivity on the part of consumers as a result of urbanization and educational progress. Even so, it was not until the mid-1960s, fifteen years after household income had begun to grow rapidly, that the definitive shift towards mass consumption occurred. It was only around the mid-1960s that a fairly dense network of liquid milk processors consolidated, and only then did consumers regain interest in dairy products.

On the other hand, our case study does not support any attempt at substituting developmental explanations with purely microeconomic approaches to food chain dynamics. Neo-Marxist sociologists, ecological economists, and agricultural historians have in different ways contributed to a narrative suggesting that the transformation of diets in the decades after the Second World War is little more than a direct result of parallel changes on the supply side: the shaping of a 'food regime' dominated by large processing companies, or the socio-metabolic transition towards an industrialized and environmentally unsustainable food system. In our case, these changes, materialized in the emergence of a liquid milk processing industry, undoubtedly form part of the explanation. However, their channel of influence is different from that emphasized by this narrative. The industrialization of the dairy chain made possible reductions in consumer prices that made milk more affordable, but this effect took time to materialize and was substantially smaller than the effect derived from the increase in disposable income. Macroeconomic change was more critical than change in the food system in smoothing the budget constraint faced by households. In contrast, dairy industrialization was fundamental in bringing to the market a standardized product that consumers could consider reliable. At least in our case study, the triumph of the industrial diet did not rely heavily on a Fordist logic of low prices, capable of attracting consumers and driving pre-existing organic production circuits out of the market. Industrial milk was actually at all times more expensive than raw milk, which, until well into this period, continued to be distributed in numerous cities and towns in the country. Its strength lay more in its capacity to seduce consumers who wanted to enjoy the health benefits of milk without becoming entangled in the issues of fraud and reliability that had been clouding the raw milk market. Although sociologists and geographers have spoken of a 'quality turn' whereby a vanguard of consumers today distance themselves from Fordist eating, the previous triumph of the industrial diet was also based on a certain notion of quality (as standardization and reliability), and not just on the quantitative power of economies of scale.

Our perspective, therefore, emphasizes the congruent combination of changes in different spheres, especially the macroeconomic, microeconomic, and cultural. This aligns with the approach proposed by Louis Malassis, but with a difference worth noting. For Malassis, the post-war consumption model remains a 'stage' (the third in a sequence of four) that begins around 1950 and ends around 1980. According to him, this stage is explained by the convergence of changes in demand capacity, supply capacity, and the cultural environment. However, precisely because the elements involved are relatively autonomous from each other, their convergence is by no means stable, nor can it be taken for granted. What we find is more of a punctuated dynamic in which periods of dietary change that best illustrate the essence of food consumption models alternate with more turbulent periods in which some subsystems have not yet evolved in the necessary direction, and others have ceased to do so at all. In our case study, the phase that best corresponds to the essence of the post-war consumption model was short-lived: the extraordinary growth of processed milk consumption that took place between 1965 and 1980. Before and after this phase, however, there were mismatches between different social subsystems, resulting in turbulence where the decline of one wave of change blended with the beginning of the next. Between 1950 and 1965, the raw milk cycle was depleting before the processed milk cycle had unfolded intensively. In the 1980s, on the other hand, the latter cycle began to show signs of exhaustion, and a new cycle based on dairy products began to take shape. Only from the 1990s onwards, however, would the necessary combination reoccur to turn such a cycle into the driver of a new food consumption model.

Dairy products and the sophisticated deviation

The triumph of a successor consumption model cannot be adequately explained in purely cultural terms. In our case, this triumph was based on favourable macroeconomic conditions, which, until the outbreak of the Great Recession, allowed most households to transition to a world of softer and softer budget constraints. This was important for consumers to purchase increasing quantities of the new and expensive dairy products that companies were launching. Additionally, socio-economic change also influenced the reorientation of consumer preferences: the avant-garde of sophistication was among high-status groups, while the middle classes participated more moderately, and lower-status groups took longer to join. The recession clearly illuminated the role played by macroeconomic factors and the way in which many researchers, especially those focused on consumer culture, had neglected them during the capitalist *belle époque* that followed the fall of the Berlin Wall.

This does not mean that we can rely on a purely developmental framework. If the wave of dietary change progressed in tandem with socio-economic change, this was because simultaneously there was a reorientation of consumer preferences. And this reorientation cannot be explained exclusively (or even mainly) in developmental terms. To begin with, the very choice space on which consumers were called to express preferences was radically expanded by the diversification and innovation strategies of dairy industries. The starting point for explaining the new consumption model must actually be placed in the dynamics and tensions of the business subsystem, and not so much in a set of consumer needs waiting to be satisfied. In turn, the success of this 'Galbraith moment' in Spain's dairy chain depended on the renewal it induced in consumer culture, as increasingly broader segments of the population became interested in new products, whether for health-related reasons (the then-emerging 'functional foods') or for sensory gratification and time-saving. Significant support here came from the orientation of scientific and technological efforts, sometimes with public support, towards these ends. However, as we have seen in this book, renewing consumer culture was not something that companies could aspire to control fully. Rather, and in line with the institutionalist view of convention theory, a certain convergence of interpretative frameworks among different social groups and organizations involved in the process was necessary. Once again, the combination of dynamics in relatively autonomous subsystems is key to explaining the return of bad diets.

This is also true for the more purely nutritional aspect of the problem. Although we have chosen not to place much emphasis on it, it is true that Spanish dairy consumption fell below nutritional recommendations, and this would be poorly explained in developmental terms. The significant decline in liquid milk consumption in the last quarter-century is not because, for some reason, this product has become what mainstream economists call an inferior good: the kind of food that, as income levels increase, is replaced by better-regarded alternatives. In our case, the abandonment of milk was not led by the upper classes but by lower-status groups. Moreover, when the later outbreak of the Great Recession provided a kind of natural experiment on how the shopping basket would change if income levels were lower, consumers did not backtrack to consume more milk. Simply put, consumers gradually but relentlessly lost interest in the product. In a stage of less unanimous scientific messages about the virtues of milk, it was mainly the younger generations that led the spread of a consumer culture increasingly oriented towards gratification and more sensitive to issues such as lactose intolerance.

In summary, and as was the case with the previous consumption model, our study confirms the importance of developmental reasoning but highlights the need to adopt a more inclusive view where other variables also play a role. The study's relationship with the neo-Marxist view of food regimes is, however, more tense. We have found that social class does matter: it mattered in the classical era of the nutritional transition, a point that no one has questioned, and it still matters in the consumption model of recent decades, a point that neo-Marxist researchers have strongly stressed in an academic conversation that has sometimes ignored it. Our point of disagreement is not about the importance of social class but about the reason for its importance. In no way have we found low-status groups forced to buy 'food from nowhere'. Nor have we found high-status groups diverting their surplus spending towards 'food from somewhere', except for marginal niches like PDO cheese. In fact, it is not even clear that the upper classes have managed to avoid the dangers of bad eating habits to a greater extent than the lower classes: they did delay and moderate their abandonment of milk, but they also shifted towards ultra-processed foods more precociously and intensively. This aligns with an intuition suggested to Otero (2018) by his data and which, if thoroughly explored in the future, could redirect the neo-Marxist narrative towards a view more similar to what we are proposing here: what Otero calls 'luxury foods', consumed by high-status groups, does not necessarily equate to what McMichael calls 'food from somewhere', characterized by superior nutritional quality.

Both high-status and low-status households had reasonable economic possibilities to eat well: in fact, not only high-status groups but also low-status groups made surplus spending to try to go beyond the basic dairy basket. Our calculations on shopping baskets, budget constraints, and surplus spending clearly show that, even for low-status groups, another type of diet was possible. In fact, if low-status groups had retained the dairy basket they had reached around 1990, not only would they have achieved better nutritional health, but they would have also spent less money than they eventually ended up spending on dairy products. This is obviously true for high-status groups as well, but it is worth emphasizing the fact that it is such a general result that it even holds for low-status groups. The problem was not, at least in this case, that the only way to eat cheaply was to eat poorly. Far from our intention is to isolate responsibility in individuals who made these decisions: after all, and as we have examined in detail in this book, they made decisions subject to structural influences. But it is important to clarify that these influences, far from being limited to the economic sphere, were to a large extent derived from the participation of a broad majority of consumers in a shared food culture. Just as some dimensions of this culture have been identified as a buffer against the worst consequences of recent dietary change in places like Southern Europe, we should appreciate that other dimensions of it can simultaneously play an opposite role.

On the other hand, although our approach aligns with Malassis's emphasis on a combination of factors, it is again necessary to underscore the jagged nature of the history of this food consumption model. Rather than a Malassis-type 'stage', we are again facing a wave of change unfolding according to a punctuated dynamic. The contours began to take shape in the 1980s, the wave entered its most forceful phase between 1990 and 2008, and after the Great Recession, it began to deflate. This last point seems especially important because the different conceptualizations available about this consumption model originated in the

1990s, and it is not clear how the Great Recession should fit into the narrative. Some have suggested that the recession was a turning point because it forced consumers to face a more severe budget constraint, which, in turn, could have led them to select cheaper foods and, in general, to give greater weight to price as a purchase criterion. In our case study, we have found reasons to see a turning point in the Great Recession, but they were basically different. Although the recession seriously deteriorated household budgets throughout the social pyramid, it also accentuated the trend of the Spanish dairy chain towards 'rationalization', competition, and, ultimately, supplying dairy products at increasingly lower prices. A decade after the recession erupted, most households had not yet recovered their pre-crisis income levels, but, as the relative price of milk and dairy products had persistently fallen, they had more than recovered their purchasing power to buy milk and dairy products. Additionally, although many households surely now cared more about prices, there was no major restructuring of the dairy basket as a result: there was no return back to milk and the share of ultra-processed foods in the dairy basket actually increased. Although surplus spending stopped growing, it maintained the remarkable magnitude that it had reached during the years before the recession.

The main impact of the recession unfolded rather in the area of consumer culture. The pressure that household budgets came under motivated a noticeable reorientation: consumers were no longer as willing to channel any increases in purchasing power (which would mainly happen from 2014 onwards) towards the purchase of dairy products, especially yogurts and cheese. Additionally, the recession had another important indirect effect. It intensified the 'rationalizing' tensions within the production chain, and, as these tensions were largely coordinated by supermarkets as the dominant node, it reduced the viability of the product innovation strategies that industries had been implementing in the previous years. This substantially slowed down the expansion of the consumer choice space and prevented the emergence of as many new product cycles capable of sustaining consumer interest.

Finally, a passive protagonist in the history of the food consumption model of recent decades may be worth noting: politics. Unlike its predecessor, the Spanish dairy consumption model after 1990 was not influenced by a strong political vision of what the population's diet should be. Once classical malnutrition was eradicated, a view largely informed by the notion of consumer sovereignty prevailed, slightly supplemented with secondary and ineffective actions to address new versions of poor eating habits. There was a depoliticization of food consumption, and this amplified the impact of those business and cultural dynamics that would lead to the return of bad diets. There may be reasons, therefore, to include the 'market turn' of Western capitalism in the final stretch of the twentieth century (Offer, 2017) within the combination of factors that made the triumph of this controversial consumption model possible.

History, co-evolution, and dietary change

The rise and fall of good diets prompt us to reflect through the lens of history, implying an embrace of disequilibrium and change as normal states within the system. Throughout this book, we have endeavoured to address this challenge using a neo-Schumpeterian approach, considering a complex system composed of relatively autonomous subsystems. Consequently, the system evolves following a punctuated dynamic, wherein successive paradigms alternate with periods of transition and turbulence. Central to this approach has been the recognition of the power of combination. Paraphrasing the programmatic neo-Schumpeterian text by Chris Freeman (2019), we have emphasized the necessity to link history, co-evolution, and dietary change.

We have explained the creative destruction embodied by each food consumption model by combining developments in various social subsystems. In our case, the rise of successive food consumption models resulted from a combination of favourable developments in the macroeconomy, the dairy chain, and consumer culture. These subsystems, while maintaining diverse connections with one another, were also linked through various channels to areas such as politics, science, and social structure. Said connections were particularly evident during the two periods that best exemplify the essence of our two models of dairy consumption: 1965–80 for the first and 1990–2008 for the second. The heyday of the mass consumption model of milk in 1965–80 was made possible by a combination of changes, including generally rapid economic growth, a shift to a less unequal distribution of income between rich and poor households, the take-off of a national industry capable of supplying processed milk at affordable prices, the importance given by nutritional science to milk consumption, the state's dissemination of this 'gospel of milk', and consumers eventually accepting the advantages of processed milk. The peak of its successor model between 1990 and 2008, in turn, rested on a newly favourable macroeconomic and social environment, a marked reorientation of the dairy industry towards product innovations, the productive chain's ability to generate reductions in the relative prices of dairy products, new scientific views on the role of dairy in human nutrition, and a renewal of consumer culture that favoured dairy products.

It was the historically contingent combination of these diverse factors, rather than any of them in isolation, that led to the rise of both dairy consumption models. Both paths of dietary change demonstrated a certain capacity for persistence over time, largely because the different subsystems involved held connections and mutually influenced each other. The industrialization of the dairy chain under the first consumption model, for example, was a business trend heavily influenced by the changing political dynamics of Franco's dictatorship and the early democratic governments. At the same time, it can only be understood in the context of the extraordinary improvement occurring in the situation of most household economies in the country and the dissemination of pro-milk scientific and political messages among increasingly broader layers of the population. Once set in motion, however, dairy industrialization contributed to reinforcing all these dynamics, playing its small part in Spain's macroeconomic success, urging politicians to promote demand, funding the dissemination of pro-milk scientific messages, or deploying advertising campaigns aimed at transforming consumer culture.

Similar interactions were found under the second of our dairy consumption models. Continuing with the example, the industry's reorientation towards product innovations was favoured by an economic and social environment of prosperity, as well as tensions unleashed by the deregulation of the political economy of milk in Spain, the triumph of 'negative nutrition' in the field of nutritional science, and the erosion of milk consumer culture. And the implementation of these business strategies, in turn, reinforced at least some of these dynamics, contributing to economic prosperity, increasing competitive tension within the dairy chain, promoting the spread of new nutritional messages, and reshaping consumer culture through significant advertising investments.

However, although the subsystems were interconnected, they were also relatively autonomous from each other. Hence, it was feasible for their trajectories to decouple, giving rise to periods of turbulence during which the prevailing food consumption model began to blur. In fact, empirically, a substantial part of our time frame has been covered by such periods. Several of the drivers of mass milk consumption were already at work before 1965, but a processing industry capable of offering standardized milk at affordable prices across all regions of the country had not yet emerged. This, combined with consumer disinterest in some possible alternatives to incorporate more dairy into their diet (such as powdered milk or cheese), delayed the triumph of the mass consumption model until the mid-1960s. Another period of turbulence was the 1980s, when some pillars of this consumption model began to decouple. The growing diffusion of the lipid hypothesis and a certain reorientation of consumer culture towards cheese, yogurts, and other dairy desserts were, in fact, shaping what would be the triumph of a new model in the next decade. Finally, this second model also seems to have entered a turbulent phase after the outbreak of the Great Recession, which, through various channels, eroded some of its foundations: it deteriorated household economies, heightened social inequality, halted the industry's orientation towards product innovations, and prompted a reconsideration of priorities by consumers.

The case study developed here suggests, therefore, that explaining dietary change involves combining variables from different social subsystems. This contrasts with a historiography whose conceptual frameworks have often focused on a single subsystem, thus favouring the fragmentation of empirical research. With its emphasis on the articulation of variables and perspectives, the neo-Schumpeterian approach used in this book can be seen as a theoretical proposal to revitalize the intellectual tradition that connects the Annales school of the Braudel era with Malassis's agri-food economics. Whatever its limitations so far, we believe that this tradition best represents the need to seriously consider the power of combination in the study of dietary change.

Taking seriously the power of combination, however, forces us to identify at least one clear shortcoming of our study: its focus on a single group of products. Other studies may offer different lessons. An ongoing investigation into meat consumption in Spain from 1950 to 1990 suggests not only similarities but also differences (Delgado, 2023b). There was a movement towards mass consumption, as in the case of milk. But the role played by falling consumer prices, made possible by impressive technological change in the meat chain, seems to have been greater than in the case of milk, whereas changes in consumer culture seem to have been less drastic. All in all, the most appropriate scale of analysis is actually that of the entire diet. In purely nutritional terms, recommended consumption of a particular food is merely a reference that makes full sense only when considered in conjunction with others. In socio-economic terms, decisions that consumers make about a particular food can have important links to decisions they make about others. We have investigated those interactions that have taken place within the world of dairy (between milk and milk-based products, for example), but it is clearly worthwhile to do the same for interactions of greater scope (between dairy and meat or cereals, for example). Throughout the book, we have sought to emphasize the connections of our case with the more general question of dietary change in Spain and other developed countries, but a larger-scale analysis focused on the entire diet will be required to confirm the conclusions.

It would also be very beneficial to delve into international comparisons. Neither the West nor the Global North nor the other similar labels used throughout the book are homogeneous blocs. Although their countries have shared similar trajectories, we also find appreciable contrasts between them. A significant obstacle in the path of this type of comparative and integrated history is the nature of the sources necessary to write it. Many international comparisons rely on indirect estimates of food consumption provided by international organizations such as Faostat, which do not offer information for different consumer profiles and do not disaggregate much by product types. Specific sources from each country do provide this information, but these are generally not digitized, let alone standardized for international use. This is also the case with crucial explanatory variables, such as consumer prices for different foods. On the other hand, exploiting the kind of qualitative material that illuminates aspects such as consumer culture and business strategy requires familiarity with the sources and languages of other countries.

These obstacles can be overcome through international collaboration, but it will be all the more fruitful when informed by a shared theoretical framework. As Simon Kuznets (1951: 156) argued in his response to Schumpeter's plea for a 'large collection of industrial and locational monographs all drawn up according to the same plan', which has been presented at the start of this chapter, '[the] crux of the difficulty here … is partly in the availability of data and partly in the feasibility of establishing "the same plan" so that the results can be expected to be cumulative rather than discrete'.

Conclusion: Dietary change and the history of capitalism

According to Carlo Cipolla (1977: 368), 'the historical process does not consist of solving a well-defined set of problems; in the historical process, the very solution to one problem creates other problems'. This is precisely the sense in which our interpretation of bad diets in today's affluent societies is a historical interpretation. In addition to adopting a long-term perspective to situate the present time, we have demonstrated to what extent the dynamics of dietary change in recent decades have been conditioned by a prior dynamic aimed at eradicating classical malnutrition. The element that connects the two food consumption models we have studied in this book – the mass consumption model of the post-war decades and its successor born in the late twentieth century – is the history of capitalism. During the first of these waves, capitalism revealed itself as a significant force in eradicating malnutrition: the formation of a dynamic and reliable processing industry was a fundamental change in improving the nutrition of Spaniards. This is a good angle to interpret many other transformations in agriculture and the food system in the West between the late nineteenth century and the decades following the Second World War, a vector of change that is crucial to understanding how Europeans and North Americans achieved good nutritional health. On the other hand, the dynamics of creative destruction that are intrinsic to capitalism eventually turned against nutritional health at a later moment. For consumers, it might not have been a bad idea to consider their 'diet problem' solved (echoing Cipolla), but such an approach would have fatally wounded the interests of business groups formed in the previous stage. Once integrated into the capitalist circuit, food consumption could only be engulfed in a whirlwind of instability and disequilibrium. It was not possible to erase history: affluence posed its challenge.

This leads us to a political message that we develop in the next chapter. The challenge of affluence requires active public policies that mitigate the destabilizing inertia of capitalism on diets or, in those cases where we are already late, redirect these effects in the right direction. We need to politicize food consumption.

11

How to promote good diets?

Thomas Piketty (2013: 643, 646) points out that, although the 'aim of research in social sciences is not to produce preconceived mathematical certainties that replace public, democratic, and plural debate ... [Social science] researchers, like all intellectuals and especially all citizens, must participate in public debate'. So far, in this book we have paid little attention to the public debate. In order to clarify our journey from general questions to our case study and back to those questions, we have focused on the purely academic dimension of the debate. However, our study would not be complete if we did not also position it in the public debate, if only to provide some insights into its implications.

From non-agenda to agenda

In his renowned essay 'The end of laissez-faire', John Maynard Keynes (1926) borrows from Jeremy Bentham the distinction between Agenda and Non-Agenda, that is, between matters falling within the government's purview and those that do not. For Keynes, writing in the tumultuous interwar period, it was necessary to include in the Agenda a range of economic and social issues that had traditionally been considered Non-Agenda. Our historical analysis suggests that food consumption, often conceptualized as an area of individual freedom in which the government should not intervene, is one such issue. When bad diets are widespread, it cannot be assumed that, more or less spontaneously, economic and social change will lead to an appropriate food consumption pattern. It also suggests that achieving such a pattern is by no means a stable situation. On the contrary, public policies are needed to align dietary changes in the right direction and, once an appropriate consumption pattern is achieved, to ensure its preservation.

Public policies played a significant role in the nutritional transitions that took place in today's developed countries between the mid-nineteenth century and the decades after the Second World War. The case of the mass consumption of milk in Spain between 1950 and 1990 is just one among many. Especially during the Franco dictatorship, the state openly supported a diet rich in dairy products. This was part of the nutritional social contract that was closely tied to the regime's search for legitimacy. To this end, the state implemented not only measures on the supply side (whose effectiveness would require a separate analysis) but also (and this is what interests us now) measures aimed at guiding consumers towards increased dairy consumption. Some of these measures, such as promotional activities carried out within the framework of the International Milk Day or the school milk programme, were specific. Others, such as those developed within the EDALNU programme for food and nutritional education, were part of a more general policy to guide consumers towards healthier diets. Obviously, none of this alone could have led to the mass consumption of milk. Favourable conditions were also needed in other subsystems, and even then, we have documented to what extent it was one thing to influence consumers' generic preferences and quite another to influence their preferences for specific foods. However, in conjunction with parallel developments in these spheres, politics made its contribution.

A fundamental mistake, however, was not realizing that the nutritionally appropriate situation reached at the end of this wave of consumption was far from stable. In this, again, our small case study reflects a more general problem: developed societies embarked on the nutritional transition, leaving behind a long history of widespread malnutrition, but almost without interruption further dietary changes caused new malnutrition problems. Why did consumers not consider their 'diet problem' solved retaining an appropriate diet and redirecting their energies to other purposes? In the case of dairy consumption in Spain, the shopping basket achieved by 1990 was nutritionally adequate but could not be stable because that would have been disastrous for one of the subsystems involved in dietary change: the microeconomic subsystem. Of course, there were other disruptions that also explain the shift to a different consumption model from the 1990s onwards, for example (as we have studied), the consolidation of 'negative nutrition' as the new dominant scientific paradigm. But let us now retain the fact that a stagnation in dairy consumption, a scenario that began to take shape in the 1980s, blocked the growth prospects of dairy industries and associated farmers. The post-1990 consumption model was based on the extraordinary expansion of the choice space caused by the response of the dairy industry to this problematic horizon of structural adjustment: product innovations. This, in turn, contributed to a profound renewal of consumer culture and a wave of creative destruction of diets. Certainly, the rise of the new consumption model was due to a combination of causes, as we have summarized in the previous chapter. But it is important to appreciate that, in the absence of public policies oriented towards preserving the nutritionally adequate situation reached by 1990, the spontaneous dynamics of other subsystems, especially the microeconomic subsystem, could only lead to the destabilization of the consumption pattern.

It is clear that, in our case, such public policies were not implemented. It is true that there were initiatives to spread the virtues of the Mediterranean diet and encourage consumers to turn towards it, such as the 'Foods of Spain' (*Alimentos de España*) campaigns promoted by the Ministry of Agriculture, Fisheries, and Food from 1987 onwards. There were also initiatives to combat obesity: the NAOS strategy of the Ministry of Health and Consumption, implemented in 2005, sought to promote public-private collaboration to encourage healthy lifestyles, within which diet played a key role (Langreo and García Azcárate, 2021). In 2019, the Ministry of Health again launched a specific initiative aimed at reducing added sugars in processed foods ('II encuentro', 2019). We could also mention the public support granted to various projects shaping a 'superior' food market in socially progressive directions, from organic to PDO foods. However, as much as the state did not withdraw to a position of radical neutrality, it cannot be said that it implemented vigorous policies to promote good diets.

As a reference for comparison, advertising campaigns by food industries received much more financial support. Through these campaigns, industries created and disseminated their own discourse about what constituted a proper diet. In the world of dairy products, to return to our case study, any of the campaigns by major companies to launch their new desserts would have a much greater influence on consumer orientations than the parallel campaigns promoted by the state. In 1990/91, while the Ministry of Agriculture invested 300 million pesetas in its 'Foods of Spain' campaign, of which PDO cheeses were only one item, Pascual invested 5,471 million in advertising, and Danone 3,450 ('Lactonoticias', 1991b: 8, 1991c: 310). In 1997/8, while the publicly funded campaign to promote the consumption of milk mobilized 226 million pesetas, Danone's advertising investment amounted to no less than 10,370 million ('La Comisión', 1997; 'Panorama', 1998a: 51). How could the studies of the time not find that the main source of information for consumers on food-related issues was corporate advertising, followed by family, with the administration in a distant last place ('Nuevas tendencias', 2002: 36)?

It might even be worth examining the role of public policies in favouring, rather than hindering, some of the changes that have destabilized the diet. Frequently, policymakers encouraged industries to address their difficulties by diversifying their productions. In 2012, the director general of Food Industry at the Ministry of Agriculture and the Environment, Fernando Burgaz, summed up well the type of guidance that entrepreneurs had been receiving from successive governments since at least the late 1980s:

> The data we have shows that while the consumption of basic milk is decreasing in our country, there is a significant increase in other types of dairy products such as enriched milks, cheeses, and other foods that incorporate milk into their composition. Therefore, everything that is done to add value is going to be important for farmers to increase their production and for the industry to obtain greater benefits. ('El consumo de productos lácteos', 2012: 7)

Consistent with this, public funding lines were kept open to support entrepreneurial efforts towards product innovation. Public universities and research institutions often collaborated with companies in tasks ranging from providing scientific evidence for advertising to working side by side in the development of new products ('Actualidad', 2000; 'El aumento', 1994; 'Panorama', 1999a, 1999b). But, although this public-private collaboration might suggest images close to Mariana Mazzucato's (2013) entrepreneurial state, the state did not play a prominent guiding role. It supported companies' innovative ideas but did not tend to direct them towards relevant societal missions. In Burgaz's terms, from which consumers were conspicuously absent, 'everything that is done to add value' was positive. In the terms of this book, the state contributed to the project of creating a 'superior' food market where consumers would make surplus spending, but it did not worry about whether that surplus spending was oriented towards challenges such as environmental sustainability or the preservation of food heritage, much less whether the surplus spending could be actually working against the nutritional health of Spaniards. This guiding role would have clearly fallen to the state, not to companies involved in a tough process of structural adjustment, competitive 'rationalization', and search for new markets.

Public policies are necessary to guide the type of 'creative destruction' that improves our diets, as well as to block the type of creative destruction that makes them worse. This is a political premise that was evident for much of the twentieth century, especially during the heyday of 'coordinated capitalism' in the decades after the Second World War. That it is now necessary to explicitly reclaim it is a good testament to the ability of the 'market turn' and its associated ideology of consumer sovereignty to reform the terms of the public debate in the late twentieth century (Offer and Söderberg, 2016; Olsen, 2019). The rise of the post-1980 food consumption model occurred in parallel with this general political reorientation, and although the peak of so-called neoliberalism seems to be behind us in a post-Great Recession and post-Covid world, its legacy in this area undoubtedly lingers on.

From individuals to structures

The default position, as has been consolidating among Western governments since the late decades of the twentieth century, is that public policies should merely ensure that consumers have the best possible information to make their decisions. The academic foundation of this approach is rooted in neoclassical economics' conceptualization of information as a potential source of 'market failure'. In its latest academic iteration, this body of argumentation incorporates insights from behavioural economics to advocate for the role that redesigning the 'food environment' through low-profile regulations (e.g. on portion sizes) can play in aiding consumers to make better decisions without restricting their sovereignty (Etilé, 2011; Just, 2011). As a matter of fact, the entire 'informational turn' in food consumption policies, as Xaq Frohlich (2023) terms it, has been intimately linked to the rise of neoliberalism since the 1970s.

Researchers aligned with social democracy tend to be sceptical of an agenda solely focused on information and argue instead for more ambitious measures to reshape individual choices. In terms of the Nuffield ladder of public interventions for promoting healthy diets (Willet et al., 2019), these researchers advocate for climbing a few steps and implementing fiscal measures that, through taxes and subsidies, alter the incentive structure that consumers face (Popkin, 2009). The argumentative logic here is also neoclassical, drawing from the tradition of welfare economics associated with Arthur Pigou: as some food consumptions are above socially desirable levels and others below, the state should implement fiscal measures to realign each consumption with its desirable level.

Alongside these individual, choice-centred perspectives, a final group of voices emphasizes the economic structures underlying bad diets. If the logic of food capitalism has brought us here, the way out would be a restructuring of the food system according to the alternative principles of agroecology, food sovereignty, short circuits, and 'food from somewhere' (Otero, 2024; Rivas and Cussó, 2023). Instead of policies specifically directed at food consumption, a holistic approach would be needed, integrating dietary issues into a broader left-wing agenda that transcends individual consumer choices.

Any of these three political agendas seems promising or, so to speak, superior to the Non-Agenda alternative. Informational policies, for example, can play a role in promoting good diets. In Spain, there have been clear improvements in the quality of information on food labels, which for years have included systematic quantitative data on nutritional composition, allowing consumers to assess variables such as saturated fats or sugars in each food. The Nutriscore labelling system, classifying foods into five categories from healthiest to least healthy, is currently being implemented. It is evident that there is room for improvement in this field, though. The adoption of Nutriscore is currently voluntary for companies, while its impact would undoubtedly be greater if its adoption became mandatory. It is also unclear whether Nutriscore is the definitive tool. Various drawbacks in its algorithm have been identified, from the relative nature of its ratings depending on the food group (making cross-group comparisons misleading) to the complete absence of any criteria related to the degree of food processing. A good solution may be to complement Nutriscore with information about the category each food occupies in the NOVA scale, the most accepted instrument for distinguishing natural and minimally processed foods from ultra-processed foods (Monteiro et al., 2019).

On the other hand, our case aligns with those voices suggesting that, beyond information, it is necessary to climb the Nuffield ladder. In the world of Spanish dairy, there is reason to support the introduction of subsidies and taxes that reform the incentive structure that consumers face. As we have extensively analysed, the rise of successive models of food consumption has been supported by combinations of various factors, and it is by no means reasonable to conclude that the lack of information among consumers has been the prime mover. For example, it is highly doubtful that consumers shifted towards a diet richer in low-nutrient, ultra-processed dairy products, such as manufactured ice cream, simply because they lacked adequate information.

Therefore, public policies must alter the incentives that influence consumers' decision-making, tightening the budget constraints on less healthy foods and easing those affecting foods that are part of a good diet. First and foremost, it is necessary to ensure that consumers have access to a basic basket; in our case, the currently low value-added tax on basic dairy products such as milk should be maintained. Once access to a nutritionally adequate food basket is facilitated, a second set of measures can be deployed to significantly differentiate the tax pressure on the rest of the foods. Ultra-processed foods should be subject to much higher tax pressure to discourage their consumption. Moreover, considering that this consumption has a significant social gradient, with higher levels as household status increases, taxing it lacks the regressive implications usually attributed to imposing taxes on food consumption (Etilé, 2011). Conversely, foods embodying a progressive vision of dietary change, such as organic foods or those classified as cultural heritage, from organic yogurts to cheese with geographical indications, should be subject to more moderate tax pressure. In other words, after access to a basic basket has been guaranteed, the goal is for taxation to help redirect consumers' surplus spending in socially beneficial directions.

However, despite our advocacy for these Pigouvian corrections, we are sceptical about the centrality they sometimes acquire in the debate. Ours is more of an *ex ante* defence, based on a matter of principle, than an *ex post* defence based on the supposed ability of these fiscal measures to alter the underlying trends in consumption. In the case of dairy consumption in Spain, especially the post-1990 consumption model, it seems evident that the levels and trends of the response factors have been more decisive than any particular movement in budget constraints. This somewhat aligns with those who have questioned whether fiscal measures alone can bring about truly relevant changes in consumption trends (Etilé, 2011: 733–4).

The clash between advocates of the upper (fiscal) and lower (informational) steps of the Nuffield ladder is significant but distracts attention from the fact that this ladder, originating in the field of biomedical ethics, does not capture well the collective dimension of food consumption. It is necessary to shift the focus from individual choices to the social structures in which these choices are embedded. This is a step we take alongside those who argue that the diet question should be subsumed into the overarching question of the food system. In fact, our data do not support one of the main criticisms often raised against them: that their agroecological utopia would be difficult to generalize and would significantly increase the costs for consumers (Paarlberg, 2021; Popkin, 2009). The data we have presented in this book show that, at least in our study case, a Mazzucato-style path has ended up being economically as plausible as the Galbraith path that Spanish consumers have actually followed.

However, the idea of encompassing the diet question in a holistic agenda for transforming the food system seems unsatisfactory for other reasons. As we have emphasized numerous times throughout this book, it is by no means obvious that we can understand dietary change as a direct consequence of food chain dynamics. The industrialization of the dairy chain was a key element in the massification of milk consumption, but by no means did it operate alone. Similarly, and despite finding it convenient to talk about a 'Galbraith moment' between 1990 and 2008, the shift in business strategy towards product innovation and diversification was not the only driver of the new model of consumption. The rise and fall of successive consumption models are closely related not only to the political economy of the food system but also to other relatively autonomous developments in spheres such as macroeconomic history and cultural history. And if we cannot collapse the analysis of diet into the analysis of the food system, it is highly doubtful that we can follow that strategy when identifying effective policies against bad diets, let alone wait for a multi-level systemic transition that (however sympathetic we may be about it) remains an uncertain and, at best, lengthy process. On the other hand, although we find it pertinent to shift the focus from individual choice to what Otero (2024) calls 'structural conditioning', our data do not make it evident that, in the era of the return of bad diets, this conditioning has been primarily economic.

The key issue, in our opinion, lies in a theoretical observation made by Albert Hirschman (1985). Hirschman is sceptical of the traditional neoclassical solution when it comes to correcting consumption patterns, that is, reforming the incentive structure to align individual choices, based on tastes which are taken to be exogenous, with social optimality. Instead, Hirschman reminds us of the much more effective role that consumer values and 'changes in the civic spirit' can play. Some voices have recently insisted that the shift towards better diets will only be truly feasible if it is based on individuals' values and beliefs (de Schutter, 2017; Gracia-Arnaiz, 2017). Our own case study has repeatedly shown the influence of this type of cultural conditioning, highlighting a crucial area for active public policies.

These policies must be, first and foremost, policies of food education. When the lower steps of the Nuffield ladder talk about providing information, they overlook the fact that, as important as having quality information is having the cognitive tools to interpret it properly (Biltekoff, 2012). Few would actually argue that consumers in recent decades have had much more nutritional information than at any time in the past. It is crucial to interpret this information correctly, and nutritional education is fundamental in that respect.

Our case study has provided some examples. With new scientific messages, but above all with the interpretation made by dairy industries, consumers frowned upon saturated fats but were enthusiastic about ultra-processed functional foods. The information provided by advertising was not necessarily false. Was it not true that Danone's successful Actimel improved the body's defences and reduced the incidence and duration of diarrhoea? Of course it was, but according to the fine print of the information provided by the company, the beneficial effect consisted of hospitalized children with acute diarrhoea recovering more quickly if they took Actimel, reducing their recovery time from 2.4 days in the control group to 1.4 days, and that adults could reduce their probability of experiencing diarrhoea during travels ('*Lactobacillus*', 1998: 45–6). That a product with such marginal health claims could become a mass consumer good speaks highly of Danone's marketing department but much worse of the public sector's role in providing citizens with nutritional education.

The 'yogurt war' waged by two giants of the Spanish dairy industry, Danone and Pascual, in the late 1990s opened an interesting crack in the generally compact discourse of the industry. Pascual, fighting to market its milks fermented after pasteurization as yogurts (something that required legal changes vehemently opposed by Danone), went so far as to declare:

> Regarding the alleged preventive and curative benefits of yogurt, which have recently been boasted about with manifest frivolity and for clearly commercial purposes, Leche Pascual … wishes to join the increasingly numerous group of scientists, researchers, and nutrition experts denouncing manipulative and pseudo-scientific practices to increase sales of certain products. The Pascual Group will never be an accomplice to advertising claims that present yogurt as a miracle product, taking advantage of the deficient training and information of many consumers on health and nutrition issues. ('Postura', 1999: 36)

When Spain was plunged into the Covid pandemic, and the bar of rigour had to be consequently raised, the Spanish Academy of Nutrition and Dietetics and the General Council of Official Colleges of Dietitians-Nutritionists considered it proven that the consumption of fermented dairy products, even with probiotic or prebiotic supplements, did not improve defences, let alone prevent infection (Pérez de Lema, 2020). Along the way, and as we know, dairy and calcium intake had fallen below recommendations, while consumers spent more money on dairy than was necessary for a healthy and sufficient basket.

The state must combat the confusion that often arises from the circulation of decontextualized nutritional information. One line of action in this regard may involve exercising greater control over companies' advertising messages to polish their more strident edges (Levenstein, 2003: 255; Popkin, 2009: 166–7). But, above all, it is necessary to equip consumers with the educational foundations needed to interpret information competently. We should not force ourselves to accept consumers becoming mere recipients of necessarily fragmented Nutriscore colour signals. However much we improve the nutritional information available to consumers for each individual food, it is essential to improve their nutritional education to enable them to wisely combine different foods within a balanced and healthy diet. No front-of-package labelling on individual foods can perform that task for us.

And yet, this notion of nutritional education, so necessary to go beyond the mere reception of information, falls short. It is not only necessary to provide a cognitive framework in which information is processed appropriately but also a cultural framework in which that processing takes on valuable meaning. In an echo of Mariana Mazzucato's (2013, 2018, 2021) ideas about the entrepreneurial state, we believe that the role of the public sector in promoting good diets should not be limited to the somewhat gloomy task of correcting market failures, in this case providing better information or imposing Pigouvian taxes. The orientation towards education should open the door for the public sector to actively engage in the vibrant task of cultivating a food culture based on two major values: the nutritional adequacy of diets and the orientation of any possible surplus spending towards relevant societal challenges.

Public policies must actively promote the formation of consumer networks that, on a local scale, can exert a demonstration effect on increasingly large segments of the population. Their practices, based on principles such as sufficiency and the directionality of surplus spending, should be typified, publicized, and extolled. Their institutional forms, in conjunction with existing forms of consumer interest representation (e.g. consumer organizations), should be enhanced and incorporated into the political debate at all scales, from local to European. Only in this way will efforts to improve consumer information, reform the incentive structure, or even promote better nutritional education develop in fertile ground.

Institutional reform

A successful implementation of public policies aimed at promoting good diets requires a profound transformation of the institutional architecture. In the case of Spain, the role of what originally was the Ministry of Health and Consumption, later the Ministry of Consumption, and currently is the Ministry of Social

Rights, Consumption, and Agenda 2030, should be strengthened, whereas the role of the Ministry of Agriculture, Fisheries and Food should be deflated. This would make the ideal of 'food democracy', where elected politicians work for the public interest rather than being captured by interest groups (de Schutter, 2017), more feasible. The Ministry of Consumption is the public agency responsible for developing actions in the areas of nutritional information, food education, and grassroots consumer culture. More active policies in these fields by the Ministry of Consumption would complement the type of fiscal measures we have mentioned, which fall under the jurisdiction of the Ministry of Finance and Public Administration.

In contrast, the Ministry of Agriculture, Fisheries, and Food presents, as in other countries facing similar challenges (Kjaernes and Doving, 2009; Levenstein, 2003; Nestle, 2000), a historically poor record regarding nutritional information measures and the development of a new food culture. Under successive democratic governments of different political orientations, this Ministry has focused on defending the interests of producers, with a particular emphasis on farmers and the processing industries to which these sell their raw materials. The broader interest underlying our proposals, that is, achieving an adequate basic diet and directing surplus spending towards socially progressive goals, has had a decidedly marginal role in the actions of successive ministerial teams. At best, these objectives have been pursued (or, more accurately, mobilized) when they were seen as convergent with the interests of specific producers. In the dairy sector, for example, the support that the Ministry has granted to organic production or PDO cheese (support that, in any case, is modest when compared to its investments in other areas or to the magnitude of private investments in the sector) fits well with our view of surplus spending directed towards societal challenges. However, it is evident that the Ministry has lacked a genuine policy on food consumption, even though it would have fallen within its area of competence.

The Ministry received food-related responsibilities in 1981. This consolidated an institutional architecture that, more informally, had been taking shape during the dictatorship and under which food industry representatives tended to be recognized as interlocutors of the Ministry of Agriculture. In our case, it is clear that processed milk industries, especially the concessionaires of milk centrals in major cities, were progressively incorporated into such dialogue. Not by chance, we find repeated indications of the extent to which dairy industry representatives and interest groups (such as the National Federation of Dairy Industries) understood that the Ministry 'has always been our home' (Rodríguez, 2017: 44;

also 'Decimocuartas Jornadas', 1996: 8). What role was consumption supposed to play within this vision?

Clearly, policies related to consumption had as their main objective to improve the demand conditions in which farmers and industrialists had to develop their activities (Díaz Méndez and Gómez Benito, 2010). However, it is not possible to imagine a more unfortunate historical moment than the 1980s for food consumption policies to definitively fall under the Ministry of Agriculture. By then, Spain had completed the 'classic' nutritional transition and faced a horizon where the danger was the emergence of the modern type of malnutrition that had begun to appear in the affluent societies of Western Europe and North America. Until that moment, and the case of dairy illustrates it very well, it had not been very difficult to unite the interests of producers and the fight against malnutrition. After all, if the goal was to popularize the consumption of milk and eradicate calcium deficiency in the diet, the growth of farming and processing was clearly an essential part of the solution. However, this convergence of interests was about to collapse as a suitable dairy basket became widespread among consumers of various strata. A hypothetical stabilization of that basket, which would have been positive in nutritional terms, went against business interests. Already in the 1980s, with decelerated milk demand, pressures began to emerge for a structural adjustment that led those companies with more capabilities for innovation to project the transition to a different and (as we have argued) problematic consumption model.

During this period of turbulence, in which the dissolution of one consumption model overlapped with the emergence of the next, the Ministry's main concern was undoubtedly to support farmers and industrialists so that they could adapt to an uncertain and uneasy scenario, which, on the other hand, neither the Ministry nor the other key actors in successive governments (engaged in a process of European integration that demanded the dismantling of much of the 'coordinated capitalism' of previous periods) were willing to question. The Ministry repeatedly encouraged industrialists to use their imagination to develop new products that could interest consumers and diversify their activities into higher value-added niches. At no time do we find a concern for stabilizing the dairy basket at the healthy point it had reached by 1990 or an interest in directing consumer surplus spending towards relevant societal missions. Disconnected from the public health agenda that the Ministry of Health and Consumption and its dependent agencies (such as the Spanish Agency for Food Safety and Nutrition) were beginning to promote, the concern was to support producers at an undoubtedly difficult time for them (Díaz Méndez and Gómez Benito, 2010).

This bias was reproduced on numerous occasions in the subsequent years and up to the most immediate present. At the beginning of the new millennium, when the new consumption model was at its prime, ministers of Health and Consumption, such as Elena Salgado, could lament that 'the diet of our children has gradually moved away from the so-called Mediterranean diet, which we all praise for its goodness, but which seems that we consume less and less' ('El consumidor', 2004: 88). But what was the reaction of the ministers of Agriculture to the documented deterioration of the Spanish diet? Regardless of their affiliation with one or the other of the two major political parties, Agriculture ministers, such as Miguel Arias Cañete (conservative) or Elena Espinosa (socialist), did not hesitate to use a revealing plural to ensure that 'we are giving consumers the products they demand' or to celebrate, in the specific case of dairy, that 'the battle of consumption is being won' (Arias, 2001: 83; 'La innovación', 2004: 6–7).

Consumers were actually left out of the Agriculture minister's focus. Symptomatically, when in 2012 Arias Cañete tried to re-establish some public-private coordination in the dairy chain, his declared objective was 'a great agreement that brings together large retailers, processors, farmers, agricultural organizations, and cooperatives' ('El protocolo', 2012: 10), but not consumers. The final result of these efforts materialized three years later in a Support Plan for the Spanish Dairy Sector in which only two points out of a total of nineteen referred to consumption, and, characteristically, they referred to promotional campaigns and school milk programmes, that is, the usual role assigned to consumers as instrumental pieces for the success of producers' plans. If Adam Smith (1776: 644) famously stated that 'consumption is the sole end and purpose of all production, and the interest of the producer ought to be attended to only so far as it may be necessary for promoting that of the consumer', the Ministry of Agriculture has been reversing the terms for decades.

Even as late as 2020, the socialist Minister of Agriculture Luis Planas could celebrate that more and more people were willing to pay more for higher value-added products, in his opinion the best proof that the consumer 'takes care of himself and takes care of his diet' ('Consumo', 2020: 10). Planas engaged in a notable controversy with the Minister of Consumption Alberto Garzón when the latter, in a way that few nutritionists could find problematic, suggested that Spaniards should moderate their consumption of meat. At the time of writing these lines, the introduction of stricter regulations on food marketing in the National Strategic Plan for the Reduction of Childhood Obesity is blocked by

Planas's insistence on endorsing self-regulation by the business community (Medina, 2023). Self-regulation, however, has not prevented the current code from being violated in up to 90 per cent of cases (Sánchez Perona, 2022: 40–2). In the case of dairy products, self-regulation has served to rectify advertising messages that went against the interests of rival companies, but, by its very nature, it has been ineffective in addressing issues such as children's exposure to promotional campaigns encouraging increased consumption of shakes and other ultra-processed foods ('Actualidad', 2006: 28; 'Boletín', 2011c: 37; 'Crónica', 2012b: 28).

The Ministry of Agriculture is not only not part of the solution but is, in fact, part of the problem. Although we do not intend to conduct a political science analysis of the determinants of these trends, it seems clear that the problem does not lie with the specific individuals occupying the position of minister of Agriculture or other important positions within the ministry. Nor does it seem to lie in their political colour, as these biases have been as common among left-oriented governments as in right-oriented ones. The fundamental problem is one of institutional architecture. The Ministry of Agriculture responds preferentially to the political demands of a small but well-articulated group of producers who, from various positions in the food chain, are able to define short-term interests and build a narrative according to which the continuity of their livelihood is at stake. In comparison to this, the type of general interest that has guided our analysis, based on the notion of an adequate basic diet and the orientation of surplus spending towards relevant societal challenges, is a terribly diffuse and long-term kind of interest. Those who defend it are always at risk of being portrayed as arrogant individuals who have nothing better to think about while, in the real world, thousands of farmers and industrialists struggle to keep their businesses afloat and contribute to the country's prosperity. Political scientists explain that, in such asymmetric situations, one can expect political dynamics to continue postponing diffuse interests (Sheingate, 2000).

The only significant counterbalance that has set limits to this dynamic has been the determination of the Ministry of Economy to fight collusion practices among food industries. This became evident, in particular, with the clash between this ministry and the Ministry of Agriculture when the National Competition Commission, under the former's jurisdiction, fined practically all major dairy industries (including Danone, Nestlé, Lactalis, Capsa, Puleva, and Pascual) for collusive agreements to control the price of raw milk and prevent farmers from shifting from one company to another between 2003 and 2011. Isabel Díaz Tejerina, the conservative minister of Agriculture, expressed concern about the negative impact that the fine could have on the functioning of the dairy chain and the livelihoods of those involved in it, but the vision of Minister of Economy Luis Guindos, who argued the need to protect the consumer from artificially elevated prices, prevailed ('Exagerada sanción', 2015: 4; 'Multa', 2015: 21–2). The fact that this time Agriculture had to yield to a more powerful ministry should not distract us from the fact that the general interest that Economy was defending was narrowly defined in terms of food prices. The promotion of good diets, in both the nutritional and the socio-economic sense, has thus remained relegated to the marginal space reserved for diffuse interests. Only 'political entrepreneurs' who decide to mobilize this agenda, identifying clashes between the general interest and vested interests, and seeking to capitalize on them in electoral terms, can change this unpromising situation. As history shows, this a risky project, but not essentially an unviable one (Sheingate, 2000).

A politics of consumption

The policies related to food consumption should not only aim to promote health but also address what Avner Offer (2007) refers to as the 'challenge of affluence'. Food consumption is a clear, though not unique, case illustrating the danger that a potential disconnection between economic change and social well-being poses for developed societies. From this perspective, the ambition of a Ministry of Consumption should extend beyond its traditional functions, such as protecting consumer rights against corporate abuses, investigating fraud, or improving consumer information. It should also be responsible for shaping consumption patterns that, in addition to addressing relevant societal challenges (such as climate change or the preservation of cultural heritage), promote the cultivation of the 'good life'.

The history of capitalism teaches us that public policies are crucial for aligning economic growth with the good life. The early stages of industrialization, from the late eighteenth century to the mid-nineteenth century, provide an illustration of how the absence of adequate public policies can lead to a dissociation between economic change and social well-being. For the first time in history, European economies achieved sustained growth, but the living standards of most people remained mediocre. One fundamental reason why a more reliable connection between economic change and social well-being began to take shape around 1870 is that, in different ways according to national political cultures, public policies specifically oriented towards this goal were implemented. From pro-equality regulations in the labour market to urban planning policies to increased public spending on health, education, and social protection, the political sphere was crucial in ensuring that capitalism's extraordinary potential allowed for widespread improvements in living standards in the decades leading up to the First World War and during most of the short twentieth century, especially after 1945.

As argued throughout this book, the link between economic change and social well-being faces new and dangerous threats today. In recent decades, a new dissociation has been taking shape, and the fall of good diets is just one of its most visible facets. What is needed to address these threats is, in some cases, a revitalization of policies that played an important role in overcoming the dissociation of the nineteenth century. For example, pro-equality policies, as was the case for much of the twentieth century, should continue to correct the (probably natural) tendency of capitalism to concentrate the fruits of growth in a few hands (Piketty, 2013). In other cases, such as environmental sustainability, it is necessary to recall the importance that the 'entrepreneurial state' had in the past in guiding scientific research in beneficial directions and creating markets where useful entrepreneurial innovations flourished to address relevant societal missions (Mazzucato, 2013, 2021). But we should be aware that, along with these problems related to the production and distribution of wealth, affluent societies face the historically unprecedented problem of using that wealth wisely.

Therefore, they need a politics of consumption that goes beyond the traditional realm of information and rights protection. They should also have a greater fiscal content to correct the less favourable biases in the existing incentive structure. Above all, they must promote the rise of a less consumerist culture. In an increasingly wide space of choice, consumer culture becomes crucial, and this book has provided many examples of this. The other side of what Matthias Schmelzer (2016) calls the 'hegemony of growth' is the 'hegemony of consumerism': the adherence of large segments of the population to a lifestyle based on intense cycles of 'getting and spending'. Within these cycles, the definition of increasingly ambitious and sophisticated consumption goals is fuelled by the persistence of long working hours. Some have seen in recent decades a kind of new 'industrious revolution' in which, as happened in the prologue to modern economic development, the call for new consumption goals stimulates an intensification of the household's labour input, for example, through a more permanent incorporation of women into the workforce (de Vries, 2008). However, and beyond the debate on the merits and problems of early modern Europe's industrious revolution, there are accumulating reasons to question what Joseph Stiglitz (2008) has called 'excessive consumerism'. As a promoter of subjective well-being, consumption, once so decisive in alleviating life's most basic hardships, seems to have entered into diminishing returns (Offer, 2007). As a promoter of well-being in a more objective sense, it has been argued that, beyond a certain threshold of basic satisfaction, the pursuit of more income and more consumption may hinder, rather than help, people's access to some components of the good life, including time-intensive activities such as cultivating interpersonal relationships and orienting towards activities that provide existential meaning (Felice, 2020; Schwartz, 2004; Schor, 2011). An alternative culture is needed, and although it can only succeed as a result of numerous changes and transitions in various social subsystems, politics is called, as in the past, to play a role in promoting it to avoid the dangerous dissociation between economic change and the good life that has occurred at other times in the history of capitalism.

It is much less revolutionary than it seems. The idea that not only the production and distribution of wealth matter but also its use was part of economists' common sense for a long time (Collantes, 2022). In the mid-nineteenth century, when the gloomy world of satanic mills was just beginning to give way to the embryo of a consumer society, it was not necessary to read a radical like Karl Marx but simply a liberal like John Stuart Mill to view with favour the possibility that, once a certain degree of basic comfort was achieved, people would have more room to redirect towards non-economic purposes. At the turn of the century, it was not necessary to listen to an iconoclast like Thorstein Veblen (with his notion of conspicuous consumption) but simply to the prudent neoclassical Alfred Marshall to find certain patterns of consumption, both among the upper and lower classes, being questioned. And, of course, in the interwar period John Maynard Keynes (1930) believed that, fortunately, developed societies were a couple of generations away from that threshold where, once absolute needs were sufficiently satisfied, it would be possible to redirect towards less materialistic goals. These perspectives, however, were left out of the focus by later generations of economists. Especially after the Second World War, just as mass consumer societies were taking shape, the idea of a neutral state that does not interfere in the realm of the sovereign consumer became conventional wisdom (Olsen, 2019).

We need to reopen this academic conversation. So far, historians have done little for it: while economic historians have taken consumption as 'the latest form of the "idea of progress"' (Offer, 2012), cultural historians have been hostile to any attempt to evaluate consumption patterns and have claimed the need to respect the underlying cultures of consumption (Trentmann, 2012). Reopening the academic conversation about how we use our wealth is, however, essential to accompany the public debate on this matter so that our democracies are better prepared to face the challenges of affluence, including how to promote good diets.

Conclusion: '… or it will never exist'

Eighty years after Keynes (1930: 329) asserted that the issue would ultimately be 'how to use [our] freedom from pressing economic cares … to live wisely and agreeably and well', a reflection by Eric Hobsbawm (2009) illustrated how much this perspective had disappeared from public debate. For Hobsbawm, writing during the Great Recession in the final stretch of his life, 'a progressive policy needs more than just a bigger break with the economic and moral assumptions of the past 30 years', referring to the orientation of governments of different countries and political persuasions towards the neoliberal notion of unregulated capitalism. A progressive policy, Hobsbawm continued, 'needs a return to the conviction that economic growth and the affluence it brings is a means and not an end'. If there is something we have sought to emphasize in this chapter, beyond the reform proposal contained in it, it is the need for our democracies to reclaim this conversation. The fall of good diets is an early warning that, once we have escaped from the world of basic deprivations in which we have lived for most of our history as a species, we must reconsider priorities. Something is rotten in the state of our diet, and vigorous public policies are needed to remedy it. Identifying these policies can only be a long, never entirely closed process, repeatedly connected to successive waves of democratic deliberation. But for this, we need the challenge of affluence to return to public debate.

If we do not take the challenge of affluence seriously, we will have failed before even starting. The words of the great economic historian Paul Bairoch (1971: 316) resonate today with the same force, perhaps even more so, than when they were written half a century ago: 'Abundance exists already or it will never exist.' It is time to wake up.

References

Frequently referenced journals

DyC: Distribución y Consumo
ILE: Industrias Lácteas Españolas
REL: Revista Española de Lechería

References

Alonso, L. E., and Conde, F. 1994. *Historia del consumo en España: una aproximación a sus orígenes y primer desarrollo*. Madrid: Debate.

Altares, S. 1994. 'Quienes compran queso manchego tienen una cultura básica del mundo de los quesos', *ILE* 184: 26–7.

Angulo, A. M., Gil, J. M., and Gracia, A. 1996. 'Desarrollo económico e ingestión de calorías en España', *Revista Española de Economía Agraria* 175: 41–62.

ANSOAP. 2010. 'Consumo de leche y hábitos de desayuno. 50 aniversario de Tetra Pak en España', www.tetrapak.com, accessed April 2013.

Aranceta, J. 2005. 'La leche y los lácteos en la alimentación de los españoles', in J. Aranceta and Ll. Serra (eds), *Leche, lácteos y salud*, 31–41. Madrid: Médica Panamericana.

Aranceta-Bartrina, J., Partearroyo, T., López-Sobaler, A. M., Ortega, R. M., Varela-Moreiras, G., Serra-Majem, L., Pérez-Rodrigo, C., and Collaborative Group for the Dietary Guidelines for the Spanish Population (SENC). 2019. 'Updating the food-based dietary guidelines for the Spanish population: The Spanish Society of Community Nutrition (SENC) proposal', *Nutrients* 11 (11): 2675.

Arias, M. 2001. 'Este salón refleja la apuesta por calidad', *ILE* 268: 83.

Arrighi, G. 2009. 'The winding paths of capital', *New Left Review* 56: 61–94.

Arroyo, M. 1984. 'La gastronomía del queso', *ILE* 63: 45–7.

Arteaga, J. 1982. 'Ni aperitivo, ni postre: el español consume solo 4 kilos de queso al año', *ILE* 35–6: 43.

Astarloa, J. R. 1986. 'Las compensaciones de la Administración por renunciar a las concesiones administrativas de las Centrales Lecheras no son lo esperado por las industrias', *ILE* 86: 9–13.

Atkins, P. J. 2010. *Liquid materialities: A history of milk, science and the law*. Farnham: Ashgate.

Atkins, P. J. 2017. 'The long genealogy of quality in British milk-drinking sector', *Historia Agraria* 73: 35–58.

Bairoch, P. 1971. *El Tercer Mundo en la encrucijada: el despegue económico desde el siglo XVIII al XX*. Madrid: Alianza, 1973.

Bairoch, P. 1999. *L'agriculture dans les pays développés: Production, productivité, rendements*. Paris: Economica.

Bandrés, A. 2020. 'La pandemia está despertando una nueva conciencia en salud', *ILE* 487: 7–12.

Barili, D. 1988. 'Marketing y publicidad en la industria láctea', *REL* 2: 19–25.

Barreiro, J. M., Losada, F., and Ruzo, E. 2001. 'Valor de marca, calidad percibida y calidad real: un análisis comparativo del mercado de la leche', *Revista Española de Estudios Agrosociales y Pesqueros* 190: 195–221.

Bentley, A. 2013. 'Introduction', in A. Bentley (ed.), *A cultural history of food in the modern age*, 1–25. London: Bloomsbury.

Bernabeu, J. M., and Barona, J. L. (coords.). 2011. *Nutrición, salud y sociedad: España y Europa en los siglos XIX y XX*. Valencia: Universitat de València.

Bernardo, A. 1989. 'Bases científicas para la industrialización de quesos autóctonos', *REL* 12: 47–50.

Biltekoff, C. 2012. 'Critical nutrition studies', in J. M. Pilcher (ed.), *The Oxford handbook of food history*, 172–90. New York: Oxford University Press.

Boltanski, L., and Chiapello, È. 1999. *Le nouvel esprit du capitalisme*. Paris: Gallimard.

Bonmatí, A. M. 1990. 'En menos de diez años se ha duplicado el consumo de helados en España', *ILE* 137–8: 18–19.

Bonmatí, A. M. 1992. 'La venta de helados sigue estando muy ligada a la climatología', *ILE* 161–2: 15.

Brassley, P. 2009. 'Food production and food processing in Western Europe, 1850–1990: Some conclusions', in Y. Segers, J. Bieleman and E. Buyst (eds), *Exploring the food chain: Food production and food processing in Western Europe, 1850–1990*, 281–9. Turnhout: Brepols.

Braudel, F. 1958. 'Histoire et sciences sociales: la longue durée', *Annales: Économies, Sociétés, Civilisations* 13 (4): 725–53.

Braudel, F. 1977. *Afterthoughts on material civilization and capitalism*. Madrid: Alianza, 1985.

Braudel, F. 1979. *Civilización material, economía y capitalismo: siglos XV-XVIII*. Madrid: Alianza, 1984.

Burnett, J. 1999. *Liquid pleasures: A social history of drinks in modern Britain*. London: Routledge.

Buss, D. H. 1993. 'The British diet since the end of food rationing', in C. Geissler and D. J. Oddy (eds), *Food, diet and economic change past and present*, 121–32. Leicester: Leicester University Press.

Calatayud, S., and Media-Albaladejo, F. J. 2017. 'Leche sin prados: los factores ambientales e institucionales en el consumo lácteo (Valencia, 1870–1936)', *Ayer* 105: 157–85.

Calcedo, V. 1996. 'Crisis, evolución y cambio en la ganadería de vacuno de leche de la España húmeda (1950–2000)', in R. Domínguez (coord.), *La vocación ganadera del norte de España: del modelo tradicional a los desafíos del mercado mundial*, 207–86. Madrid: Ministerio de Agricultura, Pesca y Alimentación.

Calcedo, V. 2004. 'El ganado bovino en España', in F. Molinero, R. Majoral, J. M. García Bartolomé, and G. García (coords.), *Atlas de la España rural*, 258–65. Madrid: Ministerio de Agricultura, Pesca y Alimentación.

Calvo-González, Ó. 2021. *Unexpected prosperity: How Spain escaped the middle income trap*. New York: Oxford University Press.

Candela-Martínez, B., Cámara, A. D., López-Falcón, D., and Martínez-Carrión, J. M. 2022. 'Growing taller inequally? Adult height and socioeconomic status in Spain (cohorts 1940–1994)', *SSM – Population Health* 18: 101126.

Cano, M. 1993. 'Consumo de helados: imaginación y marketing para aumentar la demanda', *DyC* 10: 104–8.

Canut, E. 1991. 'En el plazo de cinco años, habrá diez denominaciones de origen más de los quesos españoles', *ILE* 152: 26–7.

Carreras, A., Prados de la Escosura, L., and Rosés, J. R. 2005. 'Renta y riqueza', in A. Carreras and X. Tafunell (coords.), *Estadísticas históricas de España: siglos XIX–XX*, 1297–376. Bilbao: Fundación BBVA.

Carreras, A., and Tafunell, X. 2020. *Between empire and globalization: An economic history of modern Spain*. Cham: Springer.

Casado, P. 2005. 'La fábrica de La Penilla y su contribución al desarrollo del sector lácteo de Cantabria', in *Nestlé en España. 1905–2005. Reflexiones sobre su contribución al desarrollo económico y social*, 30–45. Esplugues de Llobregat: Nestlé.

Casares, R. 1958. 'La alimentación española', *REL* 29: 137–8.

Castro, R. 2008. 'Danone', in F. Ribera (ed.), *Los números uno en España*, 131–43. Barcelona: Dobleerre.

Castro, R. 2010. '"Máquinas de vender". Una historia de la gran distribución francesa en España desde los años sesenta', *Revista de Historia Industrial* 44: 97–137.

Castro-Valdivia, M., and de-Prado-Herrera, M. L. 2023. 'La economía española entre dos siglos (1996–2023)', in L. Garrido-González and M. Castro-Valdivia (eds), *España (1923–2023): un siglo de economía*, 201–39. Madrid: Marcial Pons.

Central Lechera Asturiana. 1992. 'Productos lácteos de máxima confianza', *ILE* 160: 1.

Cerrillo, I., Saralegui-Díez, P., Morilla-Romero-de-la-Osa, R., González de Molina, M., and Guzmán, G. I. 2023. 'Nutritional analysis of the Spanish population: A new approach using public data on consumption', *International Journal of Environmental Research and Public Health* 20 (2): 1642.

Chai, A. 2017. 'Rethinking the economic possibilities of our grandchildren: What is the future of consumption?', *Journal of Evolutionary Economics* 27 (2): 215–19.

Chiapparino, F. 1995. 'Industrialization and food consumption in united Italy', in A. P. den Hartog (ed.), *Food technology, science and marketing: European diet in the twentieth century*, 66–78. East Linton: Tuckwell Press.

Cipolla, C. M. 1977. *Historia económica de la Europa preindustrial.* Barcelona: Crítica, 2003.

Clar, E. 2006. 'La soberanía del industrial. Industrias del complejo pienso-ganadero e implantación del modelo de consumo fordista en España: 1960–1975', *Revista de Historia Industrial* 36: 133–65.

Clark Burnett, S., and Ray, K. 2012. 'Sociology of food', in J. M. Pilcher (ed.), *The Oxford handbook of food history*, 135–53. New York: Oxford University Press.

Coclanis, P. 2019. 'Field notes: Agricultural history's new plot', *Journal of Interdisciplinary History* 50 (2): 187–212.

Collantes, F. 2014. 'La evolución del consumo de productos lácteos en España, 1952–2006', *Revista de Historia Industrial* 55: 103–34.

Collantes, F. 2015. 'Dairy products and shifts in Western models of food consumption: A Spanish perspective since 1950', *Rural History* 26 (2): 249–68.

Collantes, F. 2016. 'Food chains and the retailing revolution: Supermarkets, dairy processors and consumers in Spain, 1960 to the present', *Business History* 58 (7): 1055–76.

Collantes, F. 2017a. 'Nutritional transitions and the food system: Expensive milk, selective lactophiles and diet change in Spain, 1950–1965', *Historia Agraria* 73: 119–47.

Collantes, F. 2017b. *La economía española en 3D: oferta, demanda y largo plazo.* Madrid: Pirámide.

Collantes, F. 2017c. '"Because they just don't want to": Dairy consumers, food quality, and Spain's nutritional transition in the 1950s and early 1960s', *Agricultural History* 91 (4): 536–53.

Collantes, F. 2019a. 'Why did the industrial diet triumph? The massification of dairy consumption in Spain, 1965–90', *Economic History Review* 72 (3): 953–78.

Collantes, F. 2019b. 'From organized to disorganized capitalism? Market versus nonmarket coordination in Spain's dairy chain', *Journal of Agrarian Change* 19 (2): 295–318.

Collantes, F. 2020. 'Calidad alimentaria, transición nutricional y capitalismo lácteo en España (1965–1990)', *Ayer* 118: 283–315.

Collantes, F. 2022. 'Wealth and how to use it: Economists and the affluent society in the decades after the Second World War', paper presented at the 25th Annual Conference of the European Society for the History of Economic Thought (Padua).

Collantes, F., and Pinilla, V. 2011. *Peaceful surrender: The depopulation of rural Spain in the twentieth century.* Newcastle upon Tyne: Cambridge Scholars Publishing.

Comité Científico AESAN. 2020. 'Informe del Comité Científico de la Agencia Española de Seguridad Alimentaria y Nutrición (AESAN) de revisión y actualización de las Recomendaciones Dietéticas para la población española', *Revista del Comité Científico de la AESAN* 32: 11–58.

Compairé, C. 1966. 'Estudio del queso de Ulloa', *REL* 59: 3–23.

Comunidad de Madrid. 2001. 'Hábitos de salud en adultos, 2000', *Boletín Epidemiológico de la Comunidad de Madrid* 7 (8): 3–34.

Comunidad de Madrid. 2008. 'Hábitos de salud en la población adulta de la Comunidad de Madrid. Año 2007', *Boletín Epidemiológico de la Comunidad de Madrid* 14 (7): 3–39.

Contreras, J. 1997. 'Alimentación y sociedad. Sociología del consumo alimentario en España', in C. Gómez Benito and J. J. González (eds), *Agricultura y sociedad en la España contemporánea*, 417–51. Madrid: Centro de Investigaciones Sociológicas and Ministerio de Agricultura, Pesca y Alimentación.

Contreras, J., and Gracia, M. 2008. 'Preferencias y consumos alimentarios: entre el placer, la conveniencia y la salud', in C. Díaz Méndez y C. Gómez Benito (eds), *Alimentación, consumo y salud*, 153–91. Barcelona: Fundación 'la Caixa'.

Craig, L. A. 2016. 'Nutrition, the biological standard of living, and cliometrics', in C. Diebolt and M. Haupert (eds), *Handbook of cliometrics*, 113–30. Berlin: Springer.

Crawford, E. M. 1995. 'Food retailing, nutrition and health in Ireland, 1839–1989: One hundred and fifty years of eating', in A. P. den Hartog (ed.), *Food technology, science and marketing: European diet in the twentieth century*, 221–38. East Linton: Tuckwell Press.

Cussó, X. 2001. 'Alimentació, mortalitat i desenvolupament. Evolució i disparitats regionals a Espanya des de 1860', PhD thesis, Autonomous University of Barcelona.

Cussó, X. 2005. 'El estado nutritivo de la población española 1900–1970. Análisis de las necesidades y disponibilidades de nutrientes', *Historia Agraria* 36: 329–58.

Cussó, X., Gamboa, G., and Pujol, J. 2018. 'El estado nutritivo de la población española, 1860–2010: una aproximación a las diferencias de género y generacionales', *Nutrición Hospitalaria* 35 (extra 5): 11–18.

Cussó, X., Gamboa, G., and Pujol, J. 2023. 'The nutritional status of the Spanish population, 1860–2020: An approach to consider differences by sex and generations', in F. J. Medina-Albaladejo, J. M. Martínez Carrión and S. Calatayud (eds), *Inequality and the nutritional transition in economic history: Spain in the 19th-21st centuries*, 76–94. Abingdon: Routledge.

Cussó, X., and Garrabou, R. 2007. 'La transición nutricional en la España contemporánea: las variaciones en el consumo de pan, patatas y legumbres', *Investigaciones de Historia Económica* 7: 69–100.

Cussó, X., and Garrabou, R. 2009. 'Dieta mediterránea y transición nutricional moderna en España', in L. Germán, R. Hernández and J. Moreno (coords.),

Economía alimentaria en España durante el siglo XX, 25–63. Madrid: Ministerio de Medio Ambiente y Medio Rural y Marino.

Danone. 2006. 'Vitalínea', 'Maxifruit', 'Daníssimo', 'Frusion', www.anuncios.com, accessed November 2022.

de la Calle, A. L. 1969. 'Consumo de leche en Madrid', *Ganadería* 315: 479–80.

de la Torre, J., and Rubio-Varas, M. 2022. 'Democracia y mercado: un balance de la larga Transición española', in J. de la Torre and M. Rubio-Varas (eds), *Economía en transición: del tardofranquismo a la democracia*, 11–39. Madrid: Marcial Pons.

de Schutter, O. 2017. 'The political economy of food systems reform', *European Review of Agricultural Economics* 44 (4): 705–31.

de Vries, J. 2008. *The industrious revolution: Consumer behavior and the household economy, 1650 to the present*. Cambridge: Cambridge University Press.

de Vries, J. 2018. 'Changing the narrative: The New History that was and is to come', *Journal of Interdisciplinary History* 48 (3): 313–34.

del Arco, M. Á. 2021. 'Famine in Spain during Franco's dictatorship (1939–52)', *Journal of Contemporary History* 56 (1): 3–27.

del Río, A., and Matallana, S. 1966. 'Producción e industrialización de la leche en España', *REL* 61: 161–8.

Delgado, P. 2023a. 'From affluence to processed food: Meat consumption in Spain from 1950 to the present', *Historia Agraria* 91: 223–53.

Delgado, P. 2023b. 'Meat consumption and trade in historical perspective', PhD thesis, University of Zaragoza.

den Hartog, A. P. 1992. 'Dietary change and industrialization: The making of the modern Dutch diet (1850–1985)', *Ecology of Food and Nutrition* 27: 307–18.

den Hartog, A. P. (ed.). 1995. *Food technology, science and marketing: European diet in the twentieth century*. East Linton: Tuckwell Press.

Díaz, Á. 2011. 'Grandes diferencias de calidad en la leche entera', *El Mundo*, 21 June. <elmundo.es>, accessed June 2011.

Díaz Méndez, C., and Cardon, P. (eds). 2022. *La transformación de la alimentación en el Sur de Europa*. Valencia: Tirant Humanidades.

Díaz Méndez, C., García Espejo, I., Gutiérrez, R., and Novo, A. 2013. 'Conclusiones', in C. Díaz Méndez (coord.), *Hábitos alimentarios de los españoles*, 117–22. Madrid: Ministerio de Agricultura, Alimentación y Medio Ambiente.

Díaz Méndez, C., and Gómez Benito, C. 2004. 'El consumo alimentario en España', in F. Molinero, R. Majoral, J. M. García Bartolomé, and G. Garcia (coords.), *Atlas de la España rural*, 408–14. Madrid: Ministerio de Agricultura, Pesca y Alimentación.

Díaz Méndez, C., and Gómez Benito, C. (eds). 2008. *Alimentación, consumo y salud*. Barcelona: Fundación 'la Caixa'.

Díaz Méndez, C., and Gómez Benito, C. 2010. 'Nutrition and the Mediterranean diet. A historical and sociological analysis of the concept of a "healthy diet" in Spanish society', *Food Policy* 35: 437–47.

Díaz Méndez, C., and Gómez Benito, C. 2021. 'El malestar con la alimentación contemporánea', in C. Díaz Méndez and I. García Espejo (coords.), *El malestar con la alimentación*, 19–39. Gijón: Trea.

Díaz Méndez, C., and González, M. 2008. 'Industria y alimentación: de la publicidad referencial a los alimentos funcionales', in C. Díaz Méndez and C. Gómez Benito (eds), *Alimentación, consumo y salud*, 105–29. Barcelona: Fundación 'la Caixa'.

Díaz Yubero, I. 1984. 'El sector lácteo español', *REL* 133: 235–52.

Dixon, J. 2009. 'From the imperial to the empty calorie: How nutrition relations underpin food regime transitions', *Agriculture and Human Values* 26 (4): 321–33.

Domínguez, R. 2001. 'Las transformaciones del sector ganadero en España (1940–1985)', *Ager* 1: 47–83.

Domínguez, R. 2003. 'La industria láctea en España, 1830–1985', in C. Barciela and A. di Vittorio (eds), *Las industrias agroalimentarias en Italia y España durante los siglos XIX y XX*, 457–95. Alicante: Universidad de Alicante.

Domínguez, R., and Puente, L. de la. 2009. 'Ganadería e industrialización láctea. El complejo ganadero-industrial en Cantabria en el siglo XX', in L. Germán, R. Hernández, and J. Moreno (coords.), *Economía alimentaria en España durante el siglo XX*, 143–79. Madrid: Ministerio de Medio Ambiente y Medio Rural y Marino.

Dosi, G. 1982. 'Technological paradigms and technological trajectories', *Research Policy* 11 (3): 147–62.

Duelo, G. 1987. 'Marketing y publicidad en el sector quesero', *ILE* 106: 75–8.

Dun & Bradstreet. 1989. *Duns 15000: principales empresas españolas*. Madrid: Dun & Bradstreet.

DuPuis, E. M. 2002. *Nature's perfect food: How milk became America's drink*. New York: New York University Press.

Durá, T. 2008. 'Ingesta de leche y derivados lácteos en la población universitaria', *Nutrición Hospitalaria* 23 (2): 89–94.

Eichengreen, B. 2007. *The European economy since 1945: Coordinated capitalism and beyond*. Princeton, NJ: Princeton University Press.

Etilé, F. 2011. 'Food consumption and health', in J. L. Lusk, J. Roosen, and J. F. Shogren (eds), *The Oxford handbook of food consumption and policy*, 716–46. Oxford: Oxford University Press.

Extremo, R. J., García, M. J., Olavarría, M. S., Peláez, M. T., and Casado, P. 1992. 'Leches líquidas modificadas: 1. Modificaciones del contenido en grasa', *ILE* 158: 17–21.

Fabiosa, J. F. 2011. 'Globalization and trends in world food consumption', in J. L. Lusk, J. Roosen, and J. F. Shogren (eds), *The Oxford handbook of food consumption and policy*, 591–611. Oxford: Oxford University Press.

FAO. 2023. *Faostat* ('Suite of food security indicators', 'Food balances'). www.fao.org, accessed February 2023.

Farré, R. 1995. 'Interés de la leche y otros derivados lácteos en la alimentación humana', *DyC* 23: 117–19.

Felice, E. 2004. 'Il settore lattiero-caseario in Italia dal dopoguerra al Duemila', in G. Bertagnoni (ed.), *Una storia di qualità: il Grupo Granarolo fra valori etici e logiche di mercato*, 35–92. Bologna: Il Mulino.

Felice, E. 2020. *Historia económica de la felicidad: una nueva visión de la historia del mundo*. Barcelona: Crítica.

Fernández Prieto, L. 2001. 'Caminos del cambio tecnológico en las agriculturas españolas contemporáneas', in J. Pujol, M. González de Molina, L. Fernández Prieto, D. Gallego, and R. Garrabou, *El pozo de todos los males: sobre el atraso en la agricultura española contemporánea*, 95–146. Barcelona: Crítica.

Fernández Prieto, L., and Lanero, D. (coords.) 2019. *Leche y lecheras en el siglo XX: de la fusión innovadora orgánica a la Revolución Verde*. Zaragoza: Prensas Universitarias de Zaragoza.

Fernández-Albalat, M. P., and Méndez, J. F. 2004. 'Análisis sensorial de un yogur natural frente a dos competidores', *ILE* 308: 76–80.

Fine, B., Heasman, M., and Wright, J. 1996. *Consumption in the age of affluence: The world of food*. Abingdon: Routledge.

Flandrin, J.-L. 2004. 'Los siglos XIX y XX', in J.-L. Flandrin and M. Montanari (dirs.), *Historia de la alimentación*, 881–9. Gijón: Trea.

Flores de Lemus, A. 1914. 'Algunos datos estadísticos sobre el estado actual de la economía española', reprinted in *Hacienda Pública Española* 42–3: 421–65 (1976).

Flores de Lemus, A. 1926. *Sobre una dirección fundamental de la producción rural española*. Madrid: Sucesores de Rivadeneyra.

Floud, R., Fogel, R. W., Harris, B., and Hong, S. C. 2011. *The changing body: Health, nutrition, and human development in the Western world since 1700*. Cambridge: Cambridge University Press.

Fogel, R. W. 2004. *The escape from hunger and premature death, 1700–2100: Europe, America and the Third World*. Cambridge: Cambridge University Press.

Francks, P. 2009. *The Japanese consumer: An alternative economic history of Japan*. Cambridge: Cambridge University Press.

Francks, P. 2019. 'Diet and the comparison of living standards across the Great Divergence: Japanese food history in an English mirror', *Journal of Global History* 14 (1): 3–21.

Freeman, C. 2019. 'History, co-evolution and economic growth', *Industrial and Corporate Change* 28 (1): 1–44.

Freeman, C., and Louçã, F. 2001. *As time goes by: From the industrial revolutions to the information revolution*. Oxford: Oxford University Press.

Friedmann, H., and McMichael, P. 1989. 'Agriculture and the state system: The rise and decline of national agricultures, 1870 to the present', *Sociologia Ruralis* 29 (2): 93–117.

Frohlich, X. 2022. 'What is the Mediterranean diet? The reinvention of a traditional diet as bio-cultural capital', paper presented at the 25th Annual Congress of the European Business History Association (Madrid).

Frohlich, X. 2023. *From label to table: Regulating food in America in the information age*. Oakland: University of California Press.

Galbraith, J. K. 1973. *The affluent society*. Barcelona: Ariel, 1992.

Gallego, D. 2001. 'Sociedad, naturaleza y mercado: un análisis regional de los condicionantes de la producción agraria española (1800–1936)', *Historia Agraria* 24: 11–58.

Gallego, D. 2016. 'Obstáculos comerciales y salariales a la transición nutricional en la España de comienzos del siglo XX', *Investigaciones de Historia Económica* 12 (3): 154–64.

García Arroyo, L. 1992. 'Las exportaciones de queso manchego a la CEE se han duplicado en el último año', *ILE* 155–6: 37–9.

García Trabadelo, T. 1980. 'Las importaciones de quesos', *ILE* 21: 9–12.

García Trabadelo, T. 2002. 'Ha aumentado la cultura del queso porque se consumen quesos más diferenciados', *ILE* 277: 93–4.

Garrido, I. C. 1959. '¿Por qué bebo leche?', *Revista Española de Lechería* 32: 56.

Gavrilova, R. 2005. 'Changing tastes. The role of scientific and medical discoveries in changing the modern diet', in C. Sarasúa, P. Scholliers, and L. Van Molle (eds), *Land, shops and kitchens: Technology and the food chain in twentieth-century Europe*, 170–87. Turnhout: Brepols.

Germán, L. 2009. 'Introducción. De la Historia Agraria a la Historia de la Economía Alimentaria', in L. Germán, R. Hernández, and J. Moreno (coords.), *Economía alimentaria en España durante el siglo XX*, 7–23. Madrid: Ministerio de Medio Ambiente y Medio Rural y Marino.

Gil, Á. 1992. 'La leche y los productos lácteos en la nutrición humana', *REL* 39: 19–30.

Glickman, L. B. 2012. 'Consumer activism, consumer regimes, and the consumer movement: Rethinking the history of consumer politics in the United States', in F. Trentmann (ed.), *The Oxford handbook of the history of consumption*, 399–418. Oxford: Oxford University Press.

González de los Reyes-Gavilán, C. 2015. 'Innovación en el sector', *ILE* 431: 22–7.

González de Molina, M., Soto, D., Guzmán, G., Infante-Amate, J., Aguilera, E., Vila, J., and García, R. 2020. *The social metabolism of Spanish agriculture, 1900–2008: The Mediterranean way towards industrialization*. Cham: Springer.

Goodman, D., DuPuis, E. M., and Goodman, M. K. 2012. *Alternative food networks: Knowledge, practice, and politics*. London: Routledge.

Goodman, D., and Redclift, M. 2005. 'Modernisation and the international food system: Re-articulation or resistance', in C. Sarasúa, P. Scholliers, and L. Van Molle (eds), *Land, shops and kitchens: Technology and the food chain in twentieth-century Europe*, 120–38. Turnhout: Brepols.

Gozzer, S. 2015. 'Los pioneros de la leche de soja', *El País*, 22 December.

Gracia-Arnaiz, M. 2017. 'Taking measures in times of crisis: The political economy of obesity prevention in Spain', *Food Policy* 68: 65–76.

Granovetter, M. 1985. 'Economic action and social structure: The problem of embeddedness', *American Journal of Sociology* 91 (3): 481–510.

Grigg, D. 1995. 'The nutritional transition in Western Europe', *Journal of Historical Geography* 22 (1): 247–61.

Grigg, D. 1999. 'The changing geography of world food consumption in the second half of the twentieth century', *Geographical Journal* 165 (1): 1–11.

Haile, B., and Headey, D. 2023. 'Growth in milk consumption and reductions in child stunting: Historical evidence from cross-country panel data', *Food Policy* 118: 102485.

Hamilton, S. 2023. 'New directions in the history of food systems: Making space for heterodox economic theory', paper presented at the *Rural History 2023* conference (Cluj).

Harris, B., Floud, R., and Hong, S. C. 2014. 'Food for thought: Comparing estimates of food availability in England and Wales, 1700–1014', National Bureau of Economic Research, working paper no. 20177.

Hernández Adell, I. 2012. 'La difusión de un nuevo alimento: producción y consumo de leche en España, 1865–1936', PhD thesis, Autonomous University of Barcelona.

Hernández Adell, I.,Muñoz, F., and Pujol, J. 2019. 'A new statistical methodology for evaluating the diffusion of milk in the Spanish population: Consumer groups and milk consumption, 1865–1981', *Investigaciones de Historia Económica* 15 (1): 23–37.

Hernández Adell, I., and Pujol, J. 2017. 'Cities and milk consumption in Europe, 1890–1936: The emergence of a new market in Spain', *Historia Agraria* 73: 59–90.

Hirschman, A. O. 1985. 'Against parsimony: Three easy ways of complicating some categories of economic discourse', in A. O. Hirschman, *Enfoques alternativos sobre la sociedad de mercado y otros ensayos recientes*, 142–59. Mexico D.F.: Fondo de Cultura Económica, 1989.

Hobsbawm, E. 2009. 'Socialism has failed. Now capitalism is bankrupt. So what comes next?', *The Guardian*, 10 April.

INE [Instituto Nacional de Estadística]. 1959. *Encuesta sobre cuentas familiares, marzo 1958*. Madrid: INE.

INE. 1965–95. *Encuesta de presupuestos familiares* (1964/5–1990/1). Madrid: INE.

INE. 2023a. *Encuesta de presupuestos familiares* (1997–2021), www.ine.es, accessed March 2023.

INE. 2023b. *Censo de población*, 1950–2021, www.ine.es, accessed March 2023.

INE. 2023c. *Índice de precios al consumo*, 1958–2021, www.ine.es, accessed March 2023.

INE. 2023d. *Anuario estadístico de España*, 1960–1993, www.ine.es, accessed March 2023.

INE. 2023e. *Contabilidad nacional de España*, 1985–2007, www.ine.es, accessed March 2023.

INE. 2023f. *Estadística estructural de empresas*, 2015–2019, www.ine.es, accessed March 2023.

INE. 2023g. *Encuesta de condiciones de vida*, 2009–2020, www.ine.es, accessed March 2023.

INE. 2023h. *Encuesta sobre la estructura de las explotaciones agrarias*, 1987–2016, www.ine.es, accessed March 2023.

Just, D. R. 2011. 'Behavioral economics and the food consumer', in J. L. Lusk, J. Roosen, and J. F. Shogren (eds), *The Oxford handbook of food consumption and policy*, 99–118. Oxford: Oxford University Press.

Keynes, J. M. 1926. 'The end of *laissez-faire*', in J. M. Keynes, *Ensayos de persuasión*, 275–97. Barcelona: Crítica, 1988.

Keynes, J. M. 1930. 'Economic possibilities for our grandchildren', in J. M. Keynes, *Ensayos de persuasión*, 323–33. Barcelona: Crítica, 1988.

Kjaernes, U. 1995. 'Milk: Nutritional science and agricultural development in Norway, 1890–1990', in A. P. den Hartog (ed.), *Food technology, science and marketing: European diet in the twentieth century*, 103–16. East Linton: Tuckwell Press.

Kjaernes, U., and Doving, R. 2009. 'Controlling fat and sugar in the Norwegian welfare state', in D. J. Oddy, P. J. Atkins, and V. Amilien (eds), *The rise of obesity in Europe: A twentieth century food history*, 131–44. Aldershot: Ashgate.

Knittel, F. 2023. *La fabrique du lait: Europa occidentale, Moyen Âge – XXe siècle*. Paris: CNRS Éditions.

Kuznets, S. 1951. 'Comment', in National Bureau of Economic Research, *Conference on business cycles*, 155–62. New York: National Bureau of Economic Research.

Lacasa, A. 1968. 'La leche en polvo, alimento excepcional', *REL* 68: 83–116.

Lacasa, A. 1981. 'Evolución del consumo de leche y productos lácteos en España: hábitos, actitudes y tendencias', *REL* 121: 182–92.

Lacasa, A. 1990. 'La publicidad y su importancia en el conjunto de productos lácteos', *REL* 14: 17–26.

Lanero, D., Martiin, C., Fernández Prieto, L., and Herment, L. (eds). 2023. *From breeding & feeding to medicalization: Animal farming, veterinarization and consumers in twentieth-century Western Europe*. Turnhout: Brepols.

Langreo, A. 1995. *Historia de la industria láctea en España: una aplicación a Asturias*. Madrid: Ministerio de Agricultura, Pesca y Alimentación.

Langreo, A. 1996. 'Las relaciones contractuales entre ganaderos e industrias dentro del sistema lácteo', in R. Domínguez (ed.), *La vocación ganadera del norte de España: del modelo tradicional a los desafíos del mercado mundial*, 359–94. Madrid: Ministerio de Agricultura, Pesca y Alimentación.

Langreo, A. 2003. 'Cambios de fondo en el sistema lácteo español', *DyC* 67: 93–104.

Langreo, A. 2004. '¿Qué está pasando en el sector lácteo? Reflexiones sobre los grandes procesos de cambio', *DyC* 77: 93–100.

Langreo, A. 2005. 'El sistema alimentario español desde la perspectiva de los sectores productivos (I)', *DyC* 81: 5–57.

Langreo, A., and García-Azcárate, T. 2021. 'El papel de la estrategia de la industria y la distribución alimentaria en el consumo. La experiencia española', in C. Díaz-Méndez and I. García-Espejo (coords.), *El malestar con la alimentación*, 55–70. Gijón: Trea.

Langreo, A., and Germán, L. 2018. 'Transformaciones en el sistema alimentario y cambios de dieta en España durante el siglo XX', *Historia Agraria* 74: 167–200.

Langthaler, E. 2018. 'The soy paradox: The Western nutrition transition revisited, 1950–2010', *Global Environment* 11 (1): 79–104.

Levenstein, H. 2003. *Paradox of plenty: A social history of eating in modern America*. Berkeley: University of California Press.

Llona, J. 1962. 'La leche concentrada estéril', *REL* 45: 161–6.

Logan, T. D. 2009. 'The transformation of hunger: The demand for calories past and present', *Journal of Economic History* 69 (2): 388–408.

López Plaza, E. 1995. 'Los derivados lácteos compiten con las frutas en el postre. Continúa aumentando el consumo de leche y productos lácteos', *DyC* 23: 110–15.

López, S., and Cebrián, M. 2005. 'La innovación a la luz de la demanda', in *Nestlé en España. 1905–2005. Reflexiones sobre su contribución al desarrollo económico y social*, 68–83. Esplugues de Llobregat: Nestlé.

López, A. L., Pedregosa, A., Ruz, J. M., Ruiz, F. A., and Ureña, L. P. 2020. 'Yogur natural de cabra: aspectos tecnológicos y valoración sensorial', *ILE* 479: 30–5.

Lozano, J. 1959. '¿Por qué bebo leche?', *REL* 32: 55–6.

McMichael, P. 2013. *Food regimes and agrarian questions*. Halifax: Fernwood.

Maddison, A. 2001. *The world economy: A millennial perspective*. Paris: OECD.

Madrid, A. 1979. 'Principales riesgos y puntos críticos en los procesos de elaboración y envasado de leches líquidas', *ILE* 7: 8–22.

Magnan, A. 2012. 'Food regimes', in J. M. Pilcher (ed.), *The Oxford handbook of food history*, 370–88. New York: Oxford University Press.

Maixé, J. C. 2009. 'La modernización de la distribución alimentaria en España, 1947–1995', *Revista de Historia Industrial* 41: 125–60.

Malassis, L. 1997. *Les trois âges de l'alimentaire: essai sur une historie sociale de l'alimentation et de l'agriculture*. Paris: Cujas.

Malassis, L., and Padilla, M. 1986. *Économie agro-alimentaire, III: L'économie mondiale*. Paris: Cujas.

Maluquer de Motes, J. 2005. 'Consumo y precios', in A. Carreras and X. Tafunell (coords.), *Estadísticas históricas de España: siglos XIX-XX*, 1247–96. Bilbao: Fundación BBVA.

Maluquer de Motes, J. 2014. *La economía española en perspectiva histórica*. Barcelona: Pasado y Presente.

MAPA [Ministerio de Agricultura, Pesca y Alimentación]. 1988–91. *Consumo alimentario en España*. Madrid: Ministerio de Agricultura, Pesca y Alimentación.

MAPA. 1992–2006. *La alimentación en España*. Madrid: Ministerio de Agricultura, Pesca y Alimentación.

MAPA. 2018. *Caracterización del mercado de productos de calidad diferenciada protegidos por denominaciones de origen e indicaciones de calidad protegida.* Madrid: Ministerio de Agricultura, Pesca y Alimentación.

MAPA. 2023a. *Panel de consumo alimentario*, 1999–2021, www.mapa.gob.es, accessed March 2023.

MAPA. 2023b. *Anuario de estadística agraria*, 1990–2021, www.mapa.gob.es, accessed March 2023.

Martiin, C. 2010. 'Swedish milk, a Swedish duty: dairy marketing in the 1920s and 1930s', *Rural History* 21 (2): 213–32.

Martín Villa, M. A. 1986. 'El queso de Cantabria tiene futuro', *ILE* 83–4: 106–7.

Martínez, E. 2001. 'Sector exterior y crecimiento en la España autárquica', *Revista de Historia Económica* 19 (special issue): 229–52.

Martínez-Carrión, J. M. 2016. 'Living standards, nutrition and inequality in the Spanish industrialization. An anthropometric view', *Revista de Historia Industrial* 25: 11–50.

Martins, N. O. 2014. *The Cambridge revival of political economy*. Abingdon: Routledge.

Mataix, J. 2005. 'Reflexiones "lácteas"', in J. Aranceta and Ll. Serra (eds), *Leche, lácteos y salud*, IX–XI. Madrid: Médica Panamericana.

Matallana, S. 1963. 'Algunos comentarios sobre la Asamblea Nacional Ganadera', *REL* 49: 133–7.

Matallana, S. 1973. 'Situación y problemas de las Industrias lácteas en el presente momento', *REL* 87: 15–23.

Mateos, J. A. 1991. 'Nutrición, legislación e innovación en los productos lácteos frescos', *REL* 32: 36–7.

Mazzucato, M. 2013. *The entrepreneurial state: Debunking public vs. private sector myths.* London: Anthem Press.

Mazzucato, M. 2018. *The value of everything: Making and taking in the global economy.* London: Allen Lane.

Mazzucato, M. 2021. *Mission economy: A moonshot guide to changing capitalism.* London: Allen Lane.

Medina, F. X. 2022. 'La transformación del concepto de Dieta Mediterránea. De la salud a la sostenibilidad, pasando por la cultura y el patrimonio', in C. Díaz-Méndez and P. Cardon (coords.), *La transformación de la alimentación en el Sur de Europa*, 215–31. Valencia: Tirant Humanidades.

Medina, M. Á. 2023. 'Agricultura es partidaria de no regular la publicidad de alimentos insanos para niños, en contra de lo anunciado por Pedro Sánchez', *El País*, 9 February.

Medina-Albaladejo, F. J., and Calatayud, S. 2020. 'Unequal access to food during the nutritional transition: Evidence from Mediterranean Spain', *Economic History Review* 73 (4): 1023–49.

Medina-Albaladejo, F. J., Martínez-Carrión, J. M., and Catalayud, S. (eds). 2023. *Inequality and nutritional transition in economic history: Spain in the 19th-21st centuries.* Abingdon: Routledge.

Mendelson, A. 2008. *Milk: The surprising story of milk through the ages.* New York: Knopf.

Mendelson, A. 2023. *Spoiled: The myth of milk as a superfood.* New York: Columbia University Press.

Mercasa. 2003. *Alimentación en España.* Madrid: Mercasa.

Mercasa. 2010. *Alimentación en España.* Madrid: Mercasa.

Mesonero-Romanos, G. 1998. 'Bases para el crecimiento económico de la empresa láctea', *ILE* 230: 66–70.

Mill, J. S. (1848): *Principles of political economy.* London: John W. Parker. [The Spanish edition was used: *Principios de economía política, con algunas de sus aplicaciones a la filosofía social,* México D.F.: Fondo de Cultura Económica, 1985.]

Mintz, S. W. 1985. *Sweetness and power: The place of sugar in modern history.* New York: Viking Penguin.

Montanari, M. 1993. *El hambre y la abundancia: historia y cultura de la alimentación en Europa.* Barcelona: Crítica.

Monteiro, C. A., Cannon, G., Lawrence, M., Costa Louzada, M. L., and Pereira Machado, P. 2019. *Ultra-processed foods, diet quality, and health using the NOVA classification system.* Rome: Food and Agriculture Organization.

Moré, R. 2006. 'Probablemente necesitemos una Federación Nacional de Productores de Leche al igual que existe en Francia', *ILE* 328: 61–3.

Moreno, J. M. 1984. 'La calidad: razón de ser de Leche Pascual', *ILE* 61: 9–12.

Moscoso, A. 1997. 'Más de la mitad de los españoles están dispuestos a pagar más por un producto con Denominación de Origen', *ILE* 218: 23–4.

Moser, P., and Brodbeck, B. 2007. *Du lait pour tous: portrait en images, documents et analyses de l'économie et de la politique laitières en Suisse au 20ᵉ siècle.* Baden: Hier+Jetzt.

Naredo, J. M. 1971. *La evolución de la agricultura en España: desarrollo capitalista y crisis de las formas de producción tradicionales.* Barcelona: Laia.

Nelson, M. 1993. 'Social-class trends in British diet, 1860–1980', in C. Geissler and D. J. Oddy (eds), *Food, diet and economic change past and present,* 101–20. Leicester: Leicester University Press.

Nestle, M. 2000. 'Food lobbies and U.S. dietary guidance policy', in K. F. Kiple y K. C. Ornelas (eds), *The Cambridge world history of food,* 1628–43. Cambridge: Cambridge University Press.

Nicolau, R., and Pujol, J. 2005. 'El consumo de proteínas animales en Barcelona entre las décadas de 1830 y 1930: evolución y factores condicionantes', *Investigaciones de Historia Económica* 3: 101–34.

Nicolau, R., and Pujol, J. 2007. 'Urbanization and dietary change in Mediterranean Europe: Barcelona, 1870–1935', in P. J. Atkins, P. Lummel, and D. J. Oddy (eds), *Food and the city in Europe since 1800,* 39–49. Aldershot: Ashgate.

Nombela, J. 1984. 'La leche, producto básico de alimentación', *ILE* 62: 9–10.

Oddy, D. J. 2003. *From plain fare to fusion food: British diet from the 1890s to the 1990s*. Woodbridge: Boydell Press.

Oddy, D. J., and Atkins, P. J. 2009. 'Introduction', in D. J. Oddy, P. J. Atkins, and V. Amilien (eds), *The rise of obesity in Europe: A twentieth century food history*, 1–11. Aldershot: Ashgate.

Oddy, D. J., and Drouard, A. (eds). 2013. *The food industries of Europe in the nineteenth and twentieth centuries*. Burlington: Ashgate.

Offer, A. 2007. *The challenge of affluence: Self-control and well-being in the United States and Britain since 1950*. Oxford: Oxford University Press.

Offer, A. 2012. 'Consumption and well-being', in F. Trentmann (ed.), *The Oxford handbook of the history of consumption*, 653–71. Oxford: Oxford University Press.

Offer, A. 2017. 'The market turn: From social democracy to market liberalism', *Economic History Review* 70 (4): 1051–71.

Offer, A., and Söderberg, G. 2016. *The Nobel factor: the prize in economics, social democracy, and the market turn*. Princeton, NJ: Princeton University Press.

Olsen, N. 2019. *The sovereign consumer: A new intellectual history of neoliberalism*. Cham: Palgrave.

Ortega, R. M. 2020. 'Circulan muchos mitos y errores sobre el consumo de lácteo', *ILE* 482: 9–13.

Ortí, A. 2019. 'Verdades y mentiras sobre los probióticos, los microbios vivos que todos quieren tomar', *El País*, 12 September.

Otero, G. 2018. *The neoliberal diet: Healthy profits, unhealthy people*. Austin: University of Texas Press.

Otero, G. 2024. 'Blaming the victim or structural conditioning? COVID-19, obesity and the neoliberal diet', *Journal of Agrarian Change* 24 (1): e12564.

Otero, T. 2022. 'A transformación da agricultura galega no camino cara a especialización leiteira: ruptura coa innovación labrega, industria láctea e modernización (1900–1980)', PhD thesis, University of Santiago de Compostela.

Otter, C. 2020. *Diet for a large planet: Industrial Britain, food systems, and world ecology*. Chicago: University of Chicago Press.

Paarlberg, R. 2021. *Resetting the table: Straight talk about the food we grow and eat*. New York: Knopf.

Palacios, J. M. 1968. 'Importancia de la leche en la alimentación', *REL* 68: 75–7.

Palacios, R. 1996. 'Se ha potenciado más la copia de quesos ajenos que nuestros quesos artesanos', *ILE* 201: 78–81.

Pascual, T. 2018. 'El consumidor demanda respuestas cada vez más complejas', *ILE* 467: 16–22.

Patterson, K. D. 2000. 'Lactose intolerance', in K. F. Kiple and K. C. Ornelas (eds), *The Cambridge world history of food*, 1057–62. Cambridge: Cambridge University Press.

Peinado, M. L. 1985. *El consumo y la industria alimentaria en España*. Madrid: Instituto de Estudios Agrarios, Pesqueros y Alimentarios.

Pérez de Lema, M. 2020. 'Incertidumbre: el sector lácteo ante el covid-19', *ILE* 479: 16–22.

Pérez de Lema, P. 2018. 'Productos lácteos a debate', *ILE* 466: 6–10.

Petrick, G. 2012. 'Industrial food', in J. M. Pilcher (ed.), *The Oxford handbook of food history*, 258–78. New York: Oxford University Press.

Piketty, T. 2013. *Capital in the twenty-first century*. Mexico D.F.: Fondo de Cultura Económica, 2014.

Pilcher, J. M. 2012. 'Introduction', in J. M. Pilcher (ed.), *The Oxford handbook of food history*, xvii–xxviii. New York: Oxford University Press.

Plaja, B. 1965. 'Estudio sobre la industrialización de la leche en España', *REL* 56: 62–72.

Pollan, M. 2008. *In defense of food: An eater's manifesto*. New York: Penguin.

Popkin, B. M. 1993. 'Nutritional patterns and transitions', *Population and Development Review* 19 (1): 138–57.

Popkin, B. 2009. *The world is fat: The fads, trends, policies, and products that are fattening the human race*. New York: Avery.

Prados de la Escosura, L. 2008. 'Inequality, poverty, and the Kuznets curve in Spain, 1850–2000', *European Review of Economic History* 12 (3): 287–324.

Prados de la Escosura, L. 2017. *Spanish economic growth, 1850–2015*. Cham: Palgrave Macmillan.

Prados de la Escosura, L. 2022. *Human development and the path to freedom: 1870 to the present*. Cambridge: Cambridge University Press.

Presa, M., and Román, C. 2023. 'Changes in food consumption from an agricultural-based economy to industrialization: Uruguay (1900–70)', *Rural History* 34 (2): 220–42.

Pujol, J., and Cussó, X. 2014. 'La transición nutricional en Europa occidental, 1865–2000: una nueva aproximación', *Historia Social* 80: 133–57.

Pujol, J., Nicolau, R., and Hernández Adell, I. 2007. 'El consumo de leche fresca en Cataluña: entre mediados del siglo XIX y 1935: la difusión de un nuevo alimento', *Historia Agraria* 42: 303–25.

Rama, R. 1997. 'Evolución y características de la alimentación fuera del hogar y del consumo de alimentos procesados en España', *Agricultura y Sociedad* 84: 107–40.

Ramírez, M. Á. 2013. 'Apuntes comunitarios. Un breve recorrido por el planeta alimentario: ¿la utopía funcional continúa?', *ILE* 420: 10–11.

Ramos, M. 1955. 'Producción y consumo de la leche', *REL* 15: 29–55.

Ramos, M. 1991. 'Panorama del sector lácteo español', *REL* 27: 28–33.

Rivas, M., and Cussó, X. 2023. 'La soberanía alimentaria como indicador de la transformación integral de los sistemas agroalimentarios', *Historia Agraria* 90: 7–38.

Robles, J. 2002. 'El sector lácteo español ha demostrado ser de los más punteros en innovación', *ILE* 278: 14–15.

Rodríguez, F. 2008. 'El Ministerio de Agricultura', *ILE* 351: 15.

Rodríguez, F. 2017. 'Siempre apoyando al sector', *ILE* 452: 40–4.

Roig, D. 2005. 'Nuestra industria heladera está preparada para alcanzar el nivel de Europa', *ILE* 317–18: 32–3.
Roncaglia, A. 2005. *The wealth of ideas: A history of economic thought.* Cambridge: Cambridge University Press.
Roncaglia, A. 2019. *The age of fragmentation: A history of contemporary economic thought.* Cambridge: Cambridge University Press.
Rosado, A. G. 2015. 'El lácteo en los lineales', *ILE* 430: 34–8.
Sánchez Perona, J. 2022. *Los alimentos ultraprocesados.* Madrid: CSIC and Catarata.
Sanz, M. 1992. 'El circuito del queso', *DyC* 6: 98–101.
Sanz, M. 2002. 'En el mercado exterior, hemos dejado atrás el calvario y estamos en una época absolutamente de gloria', *ILE* 277: 103–4.
Schmelzer, M. 2016. *The hegemony of growth: The OECD and the making of the economic growth paradigm.* Cambridge: Cambridge University Press.
Scholliers, P. 2014. 'Post-1945 global food developments', in P. Freedman, J. E. Chaplin and K. Albala (eds), *Food in time and place: The American Historical Association companion to food history*, 340–64. Oakland: University of California Press.
Schor, J. 2011. *Plenitude: The new economics of true wealth.* New York: Penguin.
Schumpeter, J. A. 1939. *Business cycles: A theoretical, historical, and statistical análisis of the capitalist process.* Zaragoza: Prensas Universitarias de Zaragoza, 2002.
Schumpeter, J. A. 1942. *Capitalism, socialism, and democracy.* Barcelona: Orbis, 1988.
Schumpeter, J. A. 1951. 'Historical approach to the analysis of business cycles', in National Bureau of Economic Research, *Conference on business cycles*, 149–55. New York: National Bureau of Economic Research.
Schumpeter, J. A. 1954. *History of economic analysis.* Barcelona: Ariel, 1994.
Schwartz, B. 2004. *The paradox of choice: Why more is less.* New York: Harper Collins.
Sen, A. 1999. *Development as freedom.* New York: Oxford University Press.
Sheingate, A. 2000. *The rise of the agricultural welfare state: Institutions and interest group power in the United States, France, and Japan.* Princeton, NJ: Princeton University Press.
Simpson, J. 1989. 'La producción agraria y el consumo español en el siglo XIX', *Revista de Historia Económica* 7 (2): 355–88.
Skidelsky, E. 2012. 'We need the good life, not pre-washed salad leaves', *The Guardian*, 23 July.
Skidelsky, R., and Skidelsky, E. 2012. *How much is enough? Money and the good life.* London: Other Press.
Smil, V. 2001. *Feeding the world: A challenge for the twenty-first century.* Cambridge: MIT Press.
Smil, V. 2016. '*Addio* to the Mediterranean diet', *Spectrum*, September.
Smith, A. 1776. *An inquiry into the nature and causes of the wealth of nations.* Madrid: Alianza, 2001.

Smith-Howard, K. 2014. *Pure and modern milk: An environmental history since 1900.* New York: Oxford University Press.

Spiekermann, U. 2009. 'Twentieth-century product innovations in the German food industry', *Business History Review* 83 (2): 291–315.

Stanziani, A. 2005. *Histoire de la qualité alimentaire (XIXe-XXe siècle).* Paris: Seuil.

Stewart, H., Dong, D. and Carlson, A. 2013. 'Why are Americans consuming less fluid milk? A look at generational differences in intake frequency', ERR-149, U.S. Departament of Agriculture (Economic Research Service).

Stigler, G. J. 1945. 'The cost of subsistence', *Journal of Farm Economics* 27 (2): 303–14.

Stiglitz, J. E. 2008. 'Toward a general theory of consumerism: Reflections on Keynes's *Economic possibilities for our grandchildren*', in L. Pecchi and G. Piga (eds), *Revisiting Keynes: Economic possibilities for our grandchildren*, 41–85. Cambridge: MIT Press.

Stilwell, F. 2019. 'From economics to political economy: Contradictions, challenge, and change', *American Journal of Economics and Sociology* 78 (1): 35–62.

Teisl, M. F. 2011. 'Environment and food consumption', in J. L. Lusk, J. Roosen, and J. F. Shogren (eds), *The Oxford handbook of food consumption and policy*, 843–68. Oxford: Oxford University Press.

Tetra Pak. 1981. 'Investigación y desarrollo del envase', *ILE* 23–4: 15–18.

Tetra Pak 1982. 'Los consumidores opinan sobre la leche', *ILE* 38: 13.

Teuteberg, H. J. 1982. 'Food consumption in Germany since the beginning of industrialisation: A quantitative longitudinal approach', in H. Baudet and H. van der Meulen (eds), *Consumer behaviour and economic growth in the modern economy*, 231–77. London: Croom Helm.

Teuteberg, H. J. (ed.) 1992. *European food history: A research overview.* Leicester: Leicester University Press.

Teuteberg, H. J., and Flandrin, J.-L. 2004. 'Transformaciones del consumo alimentario', in J.-L. Flandrin and M. Montanari (dirs.), *Historia de la alimentación*, 891–914. Gijón: Trea.

Tilly, C. 1984. *Big structures, large processes, huge comparisons.* New York: Russell Sage Foundation.

Torregrosa, S. 2021. *The Spanish fiscal transition: Tax reform and inequality in the late twentieth century.* Cham: Palgrave Macmillan.

Toutain, J.-C. 1971. *La consummation alimentaire en France de 1789 à 1964.* Geneva: Droz.

Trentmann, F. 2012. 'Introduction', in F. Trentmann (ed.), *The Oxford handbook of the history of consumption*, 1–19. Oxford: Oxford University Press.

Trescastro-López, E. M., Galiana, M. E., Pereyra, P., Moncho, J., Nolasco, A., and Bernabeu, J. 2014. 'Malnutrición y desigualdades en la España del franquismo: el impacto del complemento alimenticio lácteo en el crecimiento de los escolares españoles (1954–1978)', *Nutrición Hospitalaria* 29 (2): 227–36.

Trescastro-López, E. M., Galiana-Sánchez, M. E., and Bernabeu-Mestre, J. 2016. 'Transición epidemiológica-nutricional y cambios demográficos en la España contemporánea', *Panorama Social* 23: 63–71.

Trillo, J. 1988. 'El consumidor atiende más a la calidad que al precio', *ILE* 113–14: 28.

Trueba, D. 1968. 'La higienización obligatoria de la leche en las ciudades', *REL* 68: 69–73.

Tutusaus, M. 2004. 'Se come más queso que antes y se utiliza más en la cocina', *ILE* 305–6: 71–2.

Valenze, D. 2011. *Milk: A local and global history*. New Haven, CT: Yale University Press.

Valero, T., Ibarra, J., Rodríguez, P., Ávila, J. M., and Varela, G. 2020. *Informe sobre el consumo de leche, yogur y queso como indicador de calidad de la dieta y estilos de vida en la población española*. Madrid: Fundación Española de la Nutrición.

Varela, G. 1992. 'No existen alimentos buenos o malos, sino dietas', *ILE* 166: 35–6.

Vatin, F. 1990. *L'industrie du lait*. Paris: L'Harmattan.

Vázquez de Prada, M. Á. 1991. 'La demanda de leche y productos lácteos. Evolución del consumo en España', *REL* 23: 24–34.

Vázquez de Prada, M. Á. 1992. 'Evolución del consumo de leche y productos lácteos en España', *REL* 41: 15–25.

Vázquez de Prada, M. Á. 2004. 'El queso ibérico aumentará la oferta exportable de los quesos españoles', *ILE* 303: 29–30.

Veblen, T. 1899. *The theory of the leisure class*. New York: Macmillan.

Vecchi, G. and Coppola, M. 2006. 'Nutrition and growth in Italy, 1861–1911: What macroeconomic data hide', *Explorations in Economic History* 43 (3): 438–64.

Velarde, J. 2005. 'Introducción', in *Nestlé en España. 1905–2005. Reflexiones sobre su contribución al desarrollo económico y social*, 8–17. Esplugues de Llobregat: Nestlé.

Velten, H. 2010. *Milk: A global history*. London: Reaktion Books.

Viñas, J. 1993. 'El consumidor español asocia los quesos franceses con tradición y calidad', *ILE* 177: 23–6.

Vivanco, F., Palacios, J. M., García, A., and López, C. 1976. *Alimentación y nutrición*. Madrid: Dirección General de Sanidad.

von Braun, J. 2011. 'Increasing and more volatile food prices and the consumer', in J. L. Lusk, J. Roosen, and J. F. Shogren (eds), *The Oxford handbook of food consumption and policy*, 612–28. Oxford: Oxford University Press.

Warde, A. 2016. *The practice of eating*. Cambridge: Polity Press.

Watts, S. 2012. 'Food and the Annales school', in J. M. Pilcher (ed.), *The Oxford handbook of food history*, 3–22. New York: Oxford University Press.

Wiley, A. 2011. *Re-imagining milk: Cultural and biological perspectives*. New York: Routledge.

Willet, W., Rockström, J., Loken, B., Springmann, M., Lang, T., Vermeulen, S., Garnett, T., Tilman, D., DeClerck, F., Wood, A., Jonell, M., Clark, M., Gordon, L. J., Fanzo, J., Hawkes, C., Zurayk, R., Rivera, J. A., de Vries, W., Sibanda, L. M., Afshin, A., Chaudhary, A., Herrero, M., Agustina, R., Branca, F., Lartey, A., Fan, S., Crona,

B., Fox, E., Bignet, V., Troell, M., Lindahl, T., Singh, S., Cornell, S. E., Reddy, K. S., Narain, S., Nishtar, S., and Murray, C. L. 2019. 'Food in the Anthropocene: The EAT-Lancet Commission on healthy diets from sustainable food systems', *The Lancet* 393: 447–92.

Wood, B., Williams, O., Baker, P., and Sacks, G. 2023. 'Behind the "creative destruction" of human diets: An analysis of the structure and market dynamics of the ultra-processed food manufacturing industry and implications for public health', *Journal of Agrarian Change* 23 (4): 811–43.

Yubero, Á. 1972. 'Queso manchego', *REL* 86: 231–5.

Anonymous sources

'Actualidad' (2000), *ILE* 260: 13–21.

'Actualidad' (2006), *ILE* 331: 25–31.

'Análisis sectoriales: la cadena de producción del sector lácteo' (2006), *DyC* 90: 115–25.

'Ángulo editorial y de comentarios' (1979), *ILE* 3: 3.

'Ángulo editorial y de comentarios' (1980), *ILE* 14: 3.

'Barcelona, capital mundial de la alimentación, gracias a Alimentaria y BTA' (2002), *ILE* 277: 73–83.

'Boletín: noticias del sector lácteo' (2010a), *ILE* 381: 41–8.

'Boletín: noticias del sector lácteo' (2010b), *ILE* 371–2: 59–67.

'Boletín: noticias del sector lácteo' (2011a), *ILE* 393: 45–8.

'Boletín: noticias del sector lácteo' (2011b), *ILE* 387: 33–40.

'Boletín: noticias del sector lácteo' (2011c), *ILE* 385: 33–40.

'Campaña promocional de Puleva' (1995), *ILE* 195: 39.

'Consumo alimentario 2019' (2020), *ILE* 484: 8–12.

'Crece el consumo' (2018), *ILE* 463: 6–12.

'Crónica de asuntos del sector lácteo' (2012a), *ILE* 400: 39–41.

'Crónica de asuntos del sector lácteo' (2012b), *ILE* 398: 27–30.

'Danone recomienda Danacol para reducir el nivel de colesterol' (2005), *ILE* 313: 37.

'Decimocuartas Jornadas Lactológicas: alto nivel temático, destacados coloquios y mucha actualidad' (1996), *REL* 81: 8–14.

'Dentro del laberinto' (2014), *ILE* 422: 6–7.

'Desmontados los mitos contra el consumo de leche' (2010), *ILE* 375: 6–7.

'Día Internacional Lácteo: los lácteos contribuyen a prevenir deficiencias nutricionales' (2016), *ILE* 442: 20–2.

'Día Internacional Lácteo: Fenil avala el papel de los lácteos como parte esencial de la dieta' (2018), *ILE* 462: 10–13.

'Dimensión y categoría empresarial' (1982), *ILE* 40: 9.

'Diversificar la oferta, alternativa en productos lácteos' (1988), *ILE* 111: 7.

'El 81% de los españoles ha cambiado sus hábitos de consumo en el último año' (2012), *ILE* 401: 23–4.
'El aumento del consumo de queso en España se lo llevan las importaciones' (1994), *ILE* 184: 9–10.
'El Caserío: el queso fundido de siempre' (1996), *ILE* 211: 57–62.
'El consumidor está cada día más interesado en conocer cómo y dónde se producen los alimentos' (2004), *ILE* 308: 88–90.
'El consumo de productos lácteos' (2012), *ILE* 403: 7.
'El consumo de yogur en España tiene un crecimiento superior al 10%' (2004), *ILE* 308: 37–8.
'El problema del abastecimiento de leche sigue sin resolver' (1964), *La Vanguardia Española*, 18 August.
'El protocolo con el sector lácteo es el más ambicioso que se ha firmado nunca en España' (2012), *ILE* 404: 10–11.
'El sector lácteo, codo con codo' (1983), *ILE* 51: 17–35.
'El sector lácteo en la nueva Política Agrícola Común' (1991), *REL* 31: 14–19.
'El Senado propondrá al Gobierno que impulse la dieta mediterránea' (2002), *ILE* 277: 119.
'El tirón de la marca blanca' (2008), *ILE* 356: 16.
'El XVII Congreso Internacional de Lechería de Munich' (1966), *REL* 61: 175–80.
'Empresas: nuevos productos' (1997), *ILE* 217: 44–5.
'Empresas' (2010), *ILE* 377–8: 51–2.
'En 8 de cada 10 hogares el yogur consolida su rol esencial en la alimentación' (2020), *ILE* 485: 18.
'En Huelva se consumen a diario 9.000 litros de leche sin higienizar' (1981), *ILE* 31: 56.
'Esfuerzo recompensado' (2016), *ILE* 447: 4.
'España va bien, los españoles no tanto' (1997), *El País*, 4 May.
'Exagerada sanción' (2015), *ILE* 429: 4–5.
'Fenil vuelve al 'cole' para acercar los productos lácteos a los niños' (2009), *ILE* 368: 22–3.
'I Edición de los Premios 'Quesos de Francia', una apuesta por la gastronomía' (2006), *ILE* 334: 70–1.
'II encuentro anual AEFY' (2019), *ILE* 477: 6–8.
'Información' (1956a), *REL* 19: 59–67.
'Información' (1956b), *REL* 21: 199–207.
'Información' (1958a), *REL* 28: 105–9.
'Información' (1958b), *REL* 27: 49–53.
'Información' (1960), *REL* 38: 205–11.
'Información' (1962), *REL* 44: 119–125.
'Información' (1968a), *REL* 67: 59–63.
'Información' (1968b), *REL* 70: 275–84.
'Información' (1974), *REL* 91: 61–74.

'Información federativa' (1993), *REL* 48: 35–6.
'Intolerancia a la lactosa' (2019), *ILE* 474: 32.
'IV Encuentro AEFY: el yogur, esencial para una buena alimentación infantil' (2022), *ILE* 502: 10–16.
'Jornada ACES: 2015 puede ser el año de la recuperación del consumo' (2015), *ILE* 430: 30–3.
'Jornada platónica' (1958), *La Vanguardia Española*, 7 June.
'La Comisión Europea aprueba ayudas para la promoción de productos lácteos' (1997), *ILE* 219: 37.
'La cuota láctea y la supertasa centran la preocupación de los ganaderos del Valle de los Pedroches' (1993), *ILE* 176: 54–6.
'La decisión del señor Roig' (2009), *ILE* 359–60: 18.
'La importancia de la comercialización' (2010), *ILE* 379: 29–30.
'La innovación tira del consumo de lácteos' (2004), *ILE* 308: 6–7.
'La jornada del sector lácteo cada vez más profesional' (1991), *REL* 28: 17–18.
'La realidad del azúcar en los yogures' (2018), *ILE* 467: 5.
'La salud, la nutrición y los productos lácteos en la sociedad actual' (1993), *REL* 46: 13–15.
'*Lactobacillus casei:* un lactobacilo para reforzar las defensas del organismo' (1998), *ILE* 231: 44–6.
'Lactonoticias' (1990), *REL* 14: 4–10.
'Lactonoticias' (1991a), *REL* 28: 4–7.
'Lactonoticias' (1991b), *REL* 23: 4–8.
'Lactonoticias' (1991c), *REL* 30: 4–13.
'Lactonoticias' (1996), *REL* 79: 4–9.
'Leche es salud' (1958), *REL* 30: 195–201.
'Los consumidores asocian los quesos con denominación de origen a una excelente calidad' (2003), *ILE* 286: 40.
'Mirar atrás' (2015), *ILE* 436: 4–5.
'Multa histórica: ¿quién paga la rebaja y la sanción de la leche?' (2015), *ILE* 429: 20–4.
'Noticias del sector' (1987), *ILE* 105: 72–4.
'Nuevas innovaciones en yoghourt de sabores destinadas a niños' (1995), *ILE* 196: 55–6.
'Nuevas tendencias en alimentación' (2002), *ILE* 284: 33–8.
'Nuevos frentes para el sector lácteo en otoño' (2002), *ILE* 283: 7.
'Panel de consumo: el consumo de helados crece un cuatro por ciento en un año' (2021), *ILE* 493: 34–5.
'Panorama de la alimentación: sector lácteo' (1988), *ILE* 110: 73–80.
'Panorama de la alimentación' (1992a), *ILE* 163: 65–72.
'Panorama de la alimentación' (1992b), *ILE* 155–6: 73–80.
'Panorama de la alimentación' (1998a), *ILE* 237: 49–56.
'Panorama de la alimentación' (1998b), *ILE* 229: 65–7.
'Panorama de la alimentación' (1999a), *ILE* 241: 49–56.

'Panorama de la alimentación' (1999b), *ILE* 243: 57–64.
'Panorama de la alimentación' (1999c), *ILE* 239–240: 73–80.
'Panorama de la alimentación' (2000), *ILE* 254: 65–72.
'Panorama de la alimentación' (2001a), *ILE* 267: 65–72.
'Panorama de la alimentación' (2001b), *ILE* 266: 65–72.
'Panorama de la alimentación' (2003a), *ILE* 286: 49–56.
'Panorama de la alimentación' (2003b), *ILE* 298: 65–72.
'Panorama de la alimentación' (2004), *ILE* 303: 73–80.
'Panorama de la alimentación' (2005a), *ILE* 315: 57–64.
'Panorama de la alimentación' (2005b), *ILE* 320: 65–72.
'Panorama de la alimentación' (2005c), *ILE* 311–12: 105–12.
'Panorama de la alimentación' (2005d), *ILE* 313: 41–8.
'Panorama de la alimentación' (2008a), *ILE* 357–8: 198–210.
'Panorama de la alimentación' (2008b), *ILE* 355: 57–64.
'Panorama de la alimentación' (2009), *ILE* 362: 57–64.
'Pascual: la imagen de una marca' (1996), *ILE* 213: 49–54.
'Postura y argumentos de Leche Pascual para ampliar la norma del yogur a los pasteurizados' (1999), *ILE* 243: 33–7.
'Potenciar el queso nacional' (2021), *ILE* 491: 22–3.
'Precios de la leche de vaca: baja, baja y baja' (2014), *ILE* 424: 14–16.
'Precios y márgenes comerciales en las Centrales Lecheras' (1965), *REL* 58: 203.
'Probióticos y leches enriquecidas: un mercado en alza' (2001), *ILE* 273: 31–5.
'Puleva Biotech cuadriplica su producción de Omega 3 y duplica su facturación' (2008), *ILE* 349: 75–6.
'Quesos Boffard: una marca centenaria para un queso único' (1998), *ILE* 230: 35–40.
'Reordenación y concentración' (1992), *ILE* 163: 20–3.
'¿Se podrá soportar?' (2010), *ILE* 371–2: 3–4.
'Serpientes de verano' (2017), *ILE* 453: 6.
'Sólo el 40% de los españoles entrevistados conoce la Denominación de Origen Queso Manchego' (1997), *ILE* 226: 26–31.
'Tiempos que no volverán' (1999), *ILE* 239–40: 9.
'Tomás Pascual, un vendedor nato' (2006), *ILE* 325: 11–12.
'Un mapa de los quesos de España' (1983), *ILE* 52: 11.
'Un segmento que crece: esperanzador repunte del consumo de helados' (2016), *ILE* 442: 36–40.
'Una apuesta por el queso del país' (1983), *ILE* 51: 89–90.
'Variedad y calidad, aspectos sobresalientes de los quesos españoles' (2004), *ILE* 303: 27–8.
'Zapatero afirma que España juega en la 'Champions League' económica' (2007), *El Mundo*, 11 September.

Statistical appendix

Table A1 Apparent Dietary Energy Supply in Four Western European Countries (Kilocalories Per Person and Day)

	France	Italy	UK	Spain
1850	2480		2505	
1860	2854			
1861		2466		
1870	2875			
1871		2400		
1880	3085			
1881		2508		
1890	3220			
1891		2582		
1900	3192	2682		2404
1909	3323			
1910		2752	2977	2674
1921			2905	
1922	3133			
1926			3020	
1930	3127	2520		2672
1931			3115	
1936			3080	
1950				2222
1961	3194	2958	3231	2659
1962	3258	3021	3196	2788
1963	3233	3092	3225	2696
1964	3220	3086	3208	2593
1965	3233	3131	3240	2657
1966	3219	3157	3243	2713
1967	3278	3234	3224	2744

(*Continued*)

Table A1 (*Continued*)

	France	Italy	UK	Spain
1968	3279	3298	3223	2752
1969	3284	3340	3239	2642
1970	3306	3463	3279	2731
1971	3288	3445	3245	2760
1972	3255	3487	3170	2834
1973	3269	3572	3237	2844
1974	3272	3482	3119	3076
1975	3242	3393	3126	3084
1976	3276	3388	3169	3049
1977	3337	3326	3160	3005
1978	3382	3504	3095	3003
1979	3379	3610	3164	3049
1980	3375	3603	3116	3116
1981	3417	3512	3091	2982
1982	3419	3393	3120	3070
1983	3456	3359	3114	3045
1984	3444	3407	3129	3036
1985	3486	3414	3192	3110
1986	3462	3495	3212	3098
1987	3531	3524	3227	3150
1988	3560	3537	3248	3208
1989	3556	3555	3217	3240
1990	3506	3587	3241	3260
1991	3541	3648	3208	3410
1992	3549	3543	3271	3405
1993	3543	3473	3218	3308
1994	3512	3489	3235	3304
1995	3534	3508	3185	3217
1996	3519	3567	3268	3357
1997	3547	3582	3328	3302
1998	3593	3674	3352	3337
1999	3604	3695	3400	3331
2000	3605	3668	3362	3360
2001	3640	3671	3400	3332
2002	3656	3661	3416	3359
2003	3587	3621	3400	3297

Table A1 (*Continued*)

	France	**Italy**	**UK**	**Spain**
2004	3555	3626	3445	3246
2005	3538	3567	3438	3220
2006	3513	3625	3438	3227
2007	3466	3618	3417	3223
2008	3551	3595	3422	3208
2009	3530	3599	3412	3205
2010	3527	3583	3416	3177
2011	3504	3575	3428	3188
2012	3451	3575	3417	3168
2013	3473	3579	3437	3170
2014	3411	3487	3376	3163
2015	3488	3483	3393	3195
2016	3532	3472	3374	3274
2017	3510	3477	3393	3303
2018	3479	3463	3351	3342
2019	3519	3520	3377	3349
2020	3538	3563	3381	3354

Sources: 1850–1960: Cussó and Garrabou (2007: 75), Harris et al. (2014: 49), Oddy (2003: 114), Toutain (1971: 1977), Vecchi and Coppola (2006), Cussó et al. (2023: 82); 1960–2020: FAO (2023).

Table A2 Share of Dietary Energy Derived from Foods Other Than Cereals, Roots, and Tubers (%)

	1900	**1930**	**1961**	**1990**	**2018**
France	30	44	64	73	67
Italy			52	66	66
Spain	36	39	51	71	74
UK			71	72	67

Sources: 1900–1990: Cussó and Garrabou (2007: 79, 85, 93–4); 2018: FAO (2023).

Table A3 Consumption of Milk and Dairy Products in Spain (Kilograms Per Person and Year)

	Milk only		All dairy products	
	Balance sheets	Household budgets	Household budgets	Including outside the home
1865	23.7			
1906	23.7			
1917	31.9			
1933	57.7			
1946	47.4			
1952	55.4			
1953	53.2			
1954	61.0			
1955	58.4			
1956	62.5			
1957	64.0			
1958	61.0	80.2	83.4	
1959	56.6			
1960	59.6			
1961	63.5			
1962	63.8			
1963	65.0			
1964	63.5	81.1	85.7	
1965	59.4			
1966	67.0			
1967	75.0	97.1		
1968	78.8	101.7		
1969	84.1			
1970	80.9			
1971	84.2			
1972	82.9			
1973	93.1	119.4		
1974	102.9			
1975	95.3			
1976	94.1			
1977	97.3			
1978	95.7			

Table A3 (*Continued*)

	Milk only		All dairy products	
	Balance sheets	**Household budgets**	**Household budgets**	**Including outside the home**
1979	101.1			
1980	104.4	128.9	143.0	
1981	95.8			
1982	102.6			
1990		121.1	138.1	150.7
1998		106.8	129.4	
1999		105.9	131.0	
2000		105.2	131.6	155.7
2001		102.5	131.1	
2002		99.8	129.2	
2003		96.9	127.3	
2004		96.2	124.1	
2005		92.2	124.7	
2006		84.0	116.1	140.0
2007		85.3	119.8	
2008		82.9	117.8	
2009		81.5	117.2	
2010		78.5	113.7	
2011		78.6	113.2	
2012		79.2	113.3	128.8
2013		78.1	112.0	
2014		76.0	109.5	
2015		74.6	109.5	
2016		69.7	101.1	
2017		68.0	99.4	
2018		65.7	95.7	
2019		65.2	94.6	
2020		70.1	100.1	
2021		72.6	104.1	

Sources: 1865–1935: Hernández Adell (2012: 190); 1950–2000: Collantes (2015), updated with INE (2023a) and MAPA (2023a).

Table A4 Three Waves of Expansion in Dairy Consumption (Kilograms Per Person and Year)

	Raw milk	Processed milk	Other dairy products
1865	23.7		
1906	23.7		
1917	31.9		
1933	57.7		
1952	53.2	2.2	
1958			3.2
1964	68.9	12.2	4.6
1973	64.2	55.2	
1980	50.3	78.6	14.2
1990	26.6	94.5	16.9
1998	6.6	100.2	22.6
1999	6.0	99.9	25.1
2000	3.7	101.5	26.4
2001	3.0	99.5	28.6
2002	2.3	97.5	29.4
2003	2.3	94.6	30.4
2004	2.7	93.6	27.9
2005	2.5	89.7	32.5
2006	1.4	82.6	32.1
2007	1.3	84.0	34.5
2008	1.1	81.9	34.9
2009	1.1	80.4	35.7
2010	0.8	77.7	35.2
2011	1.0	77.6	34.6
2012	1.0	78.2	34.1
2013	0.9	77.2	33.9
2014	0.7	75.3	33.5
2015	0.5	74.0	34.9
2016	0.3	69.4	31.4
2017	0.4	67.6	31.4
2018	0.3	65.4	30.0
2019	0.3	64.9	29.4
2020	0.2	69.9	30.0
2021	0.5	72.2	31.5

Sources: 1865–1935: Hernández Adell (2012: 190); 1950–2000: Collantes (2015), updated with INE (2023a).

Table A5 Differences in Dairy Consumption between Consumer Profiles

	Highest/lowest status group	North region/ Mediterranean region	65 years old or more/less than 30–35 years old
1964	1.68	2.37	
1980	1.01	1.61	
1988	1.00		
1989	1.00		1.29
1990	0.94	1.48	1.30
1992	0.96		1.23
1993	0.92		1.30
1994	0.88		1.37
1995	0.80		1.14
1997	0.84		1.26
1998	0.85		1.21
1999	0.85	1.20	1.34
2000	0.77	1.24	1.65
2001	0.95	1.22	1.24
2002	1.05	1.22	1.39
2003	1.29	1.24	1.35
2004	1.37	1.21	1.40
2005	1.33	1.20	1.48
2006	1.27	1.20	1.48
2007		1.18	
2008	1.38	1.09	1.49
2009	1.35	1.21	1.58
2010	1.28	1.19	1.48
2011	1.26	1.18	1.55
2012	1.30	1.19	1.59
2013	1.31	1.19	1.57
2014	1.42	1.17	1.62
2015	1.33	1.20	1.71
2016	1.28	1.26	1.61
2017	1.30	1.22	1.57
2018	1.24	1.22	1.66
2019	1.26	1.25	1.70
2020	1.26	1.26	1.64
2021	1.31	1.26	1.75

Sources: Collantes (2015), updated with MAPA (2023a). The highest and lowest status group are the highest and lowest quartiles, respectively. North region: Asturias, Basque Country, Cantabria, and Galicia; Mediterranean region: Balearic Islands, Catalonia, Murcia, and Valencian Community. Age refers to the household member in charge of purchasing food and drink.

Table A6 Apparent Consumption of Milk and Dairy Products (Equivalent Kilograms Per Person and Year)

	United States	Europe	Spain	China	India
1961	226.2	137.8	76.1	2.0	23.1
1962	218.6	138.7	76.2	2.0	22.4
1963	219.7	143.2	86.7	2.0	21.7
1964	220.0	141.5	85.4	2.0	20.7
1965	216.4	138.0	83.7	2.0	19.7
1966	215.9	142.2	93.1	2.0	19.8
1967	209.1	149.7	99.4	1.9	19.6
1968	209.1	153.0	102.5	1.8	20.7
1969	209.2	155.0	110.8	1.8	20.8
1970	206.7	157.0	110.8	1.8	19.4
1971	208.0	156.0	118.0	1.8	20.8
1972	209.5	156.6	117.2	1.8	20.7
1973	209.9	153.5	118.1	1.9	20.5
1974	202.3	160.6	129.5	2.0	21.3
1975	197.2	162.9	126.8	2.0	21.1
1976	204.3	163.9	132.0	2.1	22.0
1977	203.9	162.0	131.6	2.2	22.5
1978	204.1	165.5	138.8	2.5	22.2
1979	206.0	167.8	143.3	2.4	22.7
1980	203.0	165.6	145.7	2.4	23.0
1981	203.7	164.7	144.3	2.6	24.8
1982	207.4	163.1	151.9	2.9	26.0
1983	211.2	165.5	157.8	3.1	27.2
1984	210.1	168.6	161.7	3.3	29.0
1985	217.8	172.5	155.8	3.6	30.1
1986	219.0	172.6	146.4	4.0	30.7
1987	223.6	171.5	142.7	4.3	30.5
1988	216.4	171.2	139.1	4.6	30.6
1989	213.8	172.4	138.1	4.4	31.7
1990	218.6	169.4	138.5	4.7	31.8
1991	218.6	162.7	147.1	5.1	31.2
1992	221.8	156.5	143.6	5.3	32.2
1993	217.5	157.7	150.9	5.2	32.9
1994	220.5	161.6	151.5	5.7	33.4

Table A6 (*Continued*)

	United States	Europe	Spain	China	India
1995	221.3	163.3	147.9	6.1	34.9
1996	217.1	165.6	151.8	6.4	35.6
1997	215.2	164.5	143.7	6.4	36.2
1998	214.4	168.6	151.7	6.5	37.0
1999	216.5	169.4	151.0	7.1	38.2
2000	218.7	166.5	153.4	7.7	37.3
2001	221.3	168.2	151.8	8.9	37.7
2002	223.9	172.7	151.1	10.7	37.3
2003	222.2	172.1	148.4	13.3	37.6
2004	219.0	172.8	149.7	16.8	38.6
2005	219.6	175.7	145.7	18.9	39.6
2006	215.9	175.9	147.6	21.5	41.4
2007	219.6	177.1	150.6	23.0	44.3
2008	215.7	175.8	147.6	23.2	45.8
2009	218.6	176.5	154.9	24.2	47.1
2010	218.3	175.6	157.4	26.3	47.7
2011	213.4	176.6	155.8	26.6	50.5
2012	216.7	173.9	153.3	26.8	51.6
2013	213.8	174.0	153.0	25.5	52.5
2014	220.5	167.1	144.8	26.7	55.5
2015	221.6	168.9	151.3	23.2	60.5
2016	226.7	169.9	160.3	22.6	63.2
2017	227.2	172.0	157.9	22.3	66.7
2018	229.9	177.1	155.3	22.5	71.0
2019	231.6	180.6	165.1	23.3	75.6
2020	229.5	181.6	156.6	24.8	67.0

Source: FAO (2023). The current methodology, starting in 2010, has been retained. Data taken from the old methodology have been corrected according to the average of the deviations observed for the period 2010–13, in which data from both methodologies are available.

Table A7 Dairy Servings Per Person and Day

	Actual consumption		Dietary references	
	Domestic	**Total**	**Reference A**	**Reference B**
1958	1.22			
1960			2.21	1.65
1964	1.46			
1970			2.21	1.65
1980	2.35			
1981			2.21	1.66
1990	2.06	2.25		
1991			2.18	1.64
1999	1.73			
2000	1.73	2.05		
2001	1.76		2.13	1.60
2002	1.73			
2003	1.66			
2004	1.63			
2005	1.59			
2006	1.46	1.76		
2007	1.50			
2008	1.48		2.13	1.60
2009	1.47			
2010	1.44			
2011	1.45			
2012	1.44	1.64		
2013	1.46		2.13	1.60
2014	1.41			
2015	1.42			
2016	1.31			
2017	1.30			
2018	1.26			
2019	1.25	1.47	2.13	1.60

Source: Consumption: INE (1959, 1965–95, 2023a). MAPA (1988–91, 1992–2006, 2023a); references A and B: Valero et al. (2020) and Willet et al. (2019), adapted to age structures with INE (2023b).

Table A8 Dietary Calcium Intake: Recommended, Observed, and Disaggregated by Quartiles of Dairy Consumption

	1950	1960	1970	1980	1990	2000	2010
Dietary reference	1056	1055	1059		1082		1069
Consumer intake	533	619	773		945	872	865
Quartile 4							1245
Quartile 3							927
Quartile 2							751
Quartile 1							537

Sources: Dietary reference and consumer intake: Cussó et al. (2018: 14–15); quartiles of dairy consumption: Valero et al. (2020: 51), scaled to the average level reported by Cussó et al.

Table A9 Composition of the Dairy Basket According to NOVA Categories (Energy Intake Shares)

	NOVA 1	NOVA 2	NOVA 3	NOVA 4
1958	86.9	5.3	7.8	0.0
1964	88.7	3.7	7.3	0.2
1980	81.8	2.8	12.4	2.9
1990	74.1	2.2	16.9	6.8
2000	55.6	2.5	18.0	23.9
2006	47.6	3.0	21.6	27.8
2012	41.0	3.5	25.6	29.9
2019	39.6	2.6	26.2	31.7

Source: INE (1959, 1965–95, 2023a).

Table A10 Consumer Domestic Spending on Dairy Products: Actual and 'Basic' (Constant 2019 Euros Per Person and Year)

	Actual spending		Basic spending	
	INE	MAPA	1990 basket	Dietary reference
1958	136.0			188.4
1964	146.0			202.9
1967				201.1
1968				214.3
1973				218.7
1980	255.3			178.8
1990	233.4	197.1	201.0	162.9
1998	194.4			122.9
1999	193.8	183.1	153.3	119.5
2000	200.5	175.0	149.7	119.3
2001	213.1	192.6	160.6	127.6
2002	217.1	195.0	160.6	130.0
2003	215.4	191.5	155.4	127.2
2004	213.9	201.7	150.7	127.9
2005	211.4	196.4	147.5	128.3
2006	220.6	193.6	147.7	140.7
2007	220.3	197.0	152.7	136.4
2008	235.9	228.7	168.1	154.5
2009	215.7	209.4	150.2	135.0
2010	201.7	198.9	141.7	123.5
2011	199.8	194.8	137.9	119.5
2012	192.2	187.9	135.1	114.9
2013	190.7	188.4	136.7	117.8
2014	189.3	191.1	141.9	120.6
2015	192.1	192.0	146.8	121.2
2016	186.7	190.4	139.1	120.8
2017	177.6	178.9	135.1	115.8
2018	174.9	179.4	134.5	114.5
2019	172.5	177.4	134.4	112.6
2020	189.4	194.5	135.6	114.3
2021	192.8	177.0		109.6

Sources: Nominal spending: INE (1959, 1965–95, 2023a), MAPA (1988–91, 1992–2006, 2023a); deflator: INE (2023c). Dietary reference is the average of references A and B in Table A7.

Table A11 Surplus Spending as a Percentage of Total Dairy Spending: Alternative Methods of Calculation

	Method 1	Method 2	Method 3	Method 4
1990	–2.0	17.3	10.7	27.6
1999	16.3	34.8	18.0	36.1
2000	14.4	31.8	22.6	38.3
2001	16.6	33.7	21.9	37.9
2002	17.6	33.4	23.3	37.9
2003	18.8	33.6	25.2	38.8
2004	25.3	36.6	27.0	38.0
2005	24.9	34.7	27.7	37.1
2006	23.7	27.4	30.6	33.9
2007	22.5	30.7	28.2	35.8
2008	26.5	32.5	26.2	32.1
2009	28.2	35.5	27.8	35.1
2010	28.8	37.9	27.2	36.5
2011	29.2	38.7	28.4	38.0
2012	28.1	38.8	27.1	38.0
2013	27.5	37.5	25.7	36.0
2014	25.7	36.9	22.3	33.9
2015	23.5	36.9	20.8	34.6
2016	26.9	36.6	22.8	32.9
2017	24.5	35.3	21.2	32.4
2018	25.0	36.2	20.2	32.1
2019	24.3	36.5	19.2	32.3
2020	30.3	41.2	25.8	37.4
2021	24.3	38.1	28.0	41.1

Method 1: Total spending: MAPA; basic spending: 1990 basket.

Method 2: Total spending: MAPA; basic spending: dietary reference.

Method 3: Total spending: INE; basic spending: 1990 basket.

Method 4: Total spending: INE; basic spending: dietary reference.

Source: Table A10.

Table A12 Surplus Spending on Milk and Dairy Products (Method 1) by Social Class (%)

	Upper class	Middle-upper class	Middle-lower class	Lower class
1990	2.9	−3.9	−1.4	−2.7
2000	30.7	19.9	8.9	−11.1
2008	42.5	29.9	24.8	4.9
2013	39.5	30.4	26.2	12.4
2019	37.3	26.5	23.5	10.5

Source: MAPA (1988–91, 2023a).

Table A13 Percentage of Households That Purchase Milk and Dairy Products (%)

	1990	2000	2008	2019
Liquid milk	91.5	86.1	85.5	83.7
Cheese	80.7	83.6	86.3	88.1
Yoghurt	67.6	70.4	83.3	81.1
"Other"	37.5	58.1		
Ice cream		20.8	29.3	34.0

Source: MAPA (1988–91, 2023a).

Table A14 Milk Prices (Constant 2013 Euros Per Litre)

	Consumer price (corrected)	Consumer price (observed)	Processor price (observed)	Farmer price (observed)
1958		1.15		1.06
1964	1.42	1.24	1.12	0.95
1967		1.22	1.16	0.93
1968		1.30	1.15	0.91
1973	1.43	1.33	1.12	0.83
1980	1.10	1.09	0.94	0.61
1990	1.03	1.00	0.93	0.46

Source: Collantes (2017a: 135, 2019a: 964, 969). The 'corrected' consumer price is an average of province-level prices weighted by the population of each province, whereas 'observed' prices are unweighted national-level prices.

Table A15 Relative Contributions of Income and Price to Increases in the Purchasing Power for Milk (%), 1964–80

	Income	Price
Total (corrected)	70.2	29.8
Upper class	80.4	19.6
Middle-upper class	86.2	13.8
Middle-lower class	83.6	16.4
Lower class	85.0	15.0
North	100.1	-0.1
Interior	90.2	9.8
Mediterranean	48.9	51.1
Andalusia	69.5	30.5

Source: INE (1965–95, 2023c).

Table A16 Response Factors of Milk Consumption

	1917–33	1958–64	1964–80	1980–90
Milk (total)	2.31	0.12	0.56	-0.20
Raw milk			-0.34	-1.73
Processed milk			2.15	0.55

Source: Collantes (2019a: 967–8).

Table A17 Consumption of Fermented Milks (Kilograms Per Person and Year)

	'Classic' yoghurts	New fermented milks
1980	5.3	
1990	7.1	
1999	9.3	2.6
2000	8.9	3.1
2001	8.2	3.3
2002	7.6	3.7
2003	6.8	3.8
2004	6.1	4.1
2005	5.5	8.5

(Continued)

Table A17 (*Continued*)

	'Classic' yoghurts	New fermented milks
2006	5.3	9.2
2007	5.1	9.8
2008	5.0	10.2
2009	5.0	10.2
2010	5.0	10.6
2011	4.9	11.2
2012	4.9	10.9
2013	4.2	11.4
2014	4.2	11.1
2015	4.1	11.2
2016	4.3	11.1
2017	4.1	10.3
2018	4.3	10.3
2019	4.4	10.1
2020	5.1	9.9
2021	4.6	9.7

Source: MAPA (1988–91, 2023a). The 1980 figure is re-scaled back from INE (1965–95).

Table A18 Retailer Shares of the Dairy Market (%)

	Small retailers	Large retailers	Self-consumption and other
1963	73.0	8.0	19.0
1988	26.3	50.6	23.1
2000	9.4	85.7	4.9
2008	6.1	88.4	5.5
2013	5.1	89.8	5.1
2019	3.0	92.0	5.0

Sources: Collantes (2016: 5), updated with MAPA (2023a).

Table A19 Added Value[a] and Profitability[b] in Dairy Processing

	Gross added value (million 2010 euros)	Gross profit rate (%)
1961	53.5	
1962	145.7	12.5
1963	155.3	14.9
1964	184.6	14.2
1965	309.8	13.8
1966	272.5	15.0
1967	349.5	13.2
1968	352.6	15.7
1969	506.7	15.6
1970	466.7	16.2
1971	521.1	13.7
1972	573.0	13.4
1973	722.5	12.8
1974	696.6	14.2
1975	994.9	13.6
1976	908.4	14.7
1977	1044.0	14.5
1978	1322.1	15.0
1979	1313.8	15.9
1980	1616.4	16.0
1981	1732.5	16.3
1982	1702.5	15.1
1983	1739.8	15.3
1984	1725.9	16.1
1985	1852.1	17.4
1986	1896.6	18.5
1987	1880.4	19.0
1988	1866.6	18.9
1989	1983.2	18.6
1990	1946.0	19.4
1991	2173.8	20.0
1992	2009.0	19.8
1993	1848.4	18.5
1994	1788.7	15.0
1995	1712.8	12.4

(Continued)

Table A19 (*Continued*)

	Gross added value (million 2010 euros)	Gross profit rate (%)
1996	1741.2	10.2
1997	1792.8	10.0
1998	1715.1	9.6
1999	1762.4	9.3
2000	1797.5	9.3
2001	1782.9	9.9
2002	1932.9	10.7
2003	1936.8	11.8
2004	2069.4	11.8
2005	1989.7	11.4
2006	1918.2	10.9
2007	1852.9	
2015	1598.6	
2016	1570.0	9.0
2017	1647.0	8.8
2018	1707.5	8.4

Notes: [a] ($V - C$), where V is output value and C is intermediate consumption (in 1961, when electricity costs are not available, we assume that the ratio of electricity to fuel costs was similar to the one that we can observe for 1962).

[b] Three-year moving average of [$S/(C + P)$], where S is the gross operating surplus, C is intermediate consumption, and P is personnel costs. For 1961–80. S is calculated as output value minus all costs (personnel, electricity, fuel, and raw materials) and C includes electricity, fuel, and raw materials.

Sources: 1961–80: INE (2023d), old series; 1978–92: INE (2023d), new series; 1985–94: INE (2023e), 1986 baseline; 1995–2000: INE (2023e), 1995 baseline; 2000–7: INE (2023e), 2000 baseline; 2015–18: INE (2023f), 'legal units' series; 2018–19: INE (2023f), 'statistical units' series; deflator: Prados de la Escosura (2017), updated series, htpps://frdelpino.es. When two different sources overlap at any given year, it is their average that is retained.

Table A20 Farmer and Consumer Prices (Constant 2013 Euros)

	Consumer price		Farmer price (raw milk)
	All milk-based products	Processed milk	
1990	1.63	1.00	0.46
1998	1.45	0.77	0.44
1999	1.43	0.75	0.41
2000	1.47	0.75	0.39
2001	1.57	0.80	0.43
2002	1.62	0.82	0.39
2003	1.63	0.80	0.40
2004	1.66	0.81	0.39
2005	1.64	0.81	0.37
2006	1.83	0.89	0.35
2007	1.77	0.86	0.41
2008	1.93	0.97	0.43
2009	1.78	0.85	0.33
2010	1.71	0.78	0.32
2011	1.70	0.75	0.33
2012	1.64	0.72	0.31
2013	1.64	0.74	0.35
2014	1.67	0.76	0.36
2015	1.69	0.76	0.31
2016	1.78	0.76	0.30
2017	1.72	0.73	0.32
2018	1.76	0.72	0.31
2019	1.76	0.71	0.32
2020	1.82	0.72	0.32
2021	1.79	0.69	0.32

Sources: Consumer price: INE (1965–95, 2023a); farmer price: MAPA (2023b).

Table A21 Per Capita Consumer Spending in Milk and Dairy Products (Constant 2019 Euros)

	Actual	Basic (conventional milk)	Basic (organic milk)
1990	197.1	201.0	
1999	183.1	153.3	
2000	175.0	149.7	
2001	192.6	160.6	
2002	195.0	160.6	241.9
2003	191.5	155.4	
2004	201.7	150.7	
2005	196.4	147.5	
2006	193.6	147.7	
2007	197.0	152.7	
2008	228.7	168.1	
2009	209.4	150.2	
2010	198.9	141.7	
2011	194.8	137.9	
2012	187.9	135.1	
2013	188.4	136.7	
2014	191.1	141.9	
2015	192.0	146.8	
2016	190.4	139.1	
2017	178.9	135.1	
2018	179.4	134.5	
2019	177.4	134.4	
2020	194.5	135.6	181.3
2021	177.0	133.9	177.2

Sources: MAPA (1988–91, 2023a), 'Barcelona' (2002: 76), INE (2023c). 'Basic (organic milk)': modified 1990 dairy basket, with organic instead of conventional milk; the figure for 2002 is approximate.

Table A22 Share of Consumer Income Required to Purchase Three Alternative Dairy Baskets (%)

	Actual	**Basic (conventional milk)**	**Basic (organic milk)**
1990	2.38	2.43	
1999	1.78	1.49	
2000	1.64	1.40	
2001	1.73	1.44	
2002	1.73	1.42	2.15
2003	1.66	1.35	
2004	1.72	1.28	
2005	1.66	1.24	
2006	1.59	1.21	
2007	1.59	1.23	
2008	1.78	1.31	
2009	1.64	1.18	
2010	1.67	1.19	
2011	1.69	1.19	
2012	1.72	1.23	
2013	1.75	1.27	
2014	1.75	1.30	
2015	1.71	1.31	
2016	1.67	1.22	
2017	1.54	1.16	
2018	1.52	1.14	
2019	1.44	1.09	
2020	1.58	1.10	1.47

Sources: Spending on dairy: Table A21; income: INE (2023e, 2023g).

Index

www.ingramcontent.com/pod-product-compliance
Ingram Content Group UK Ltd.
Pitfield, Milton Keynes, MK11 3LW, UK
UKHW020247290926
15470UKWH00002B/792

9 781350 401549